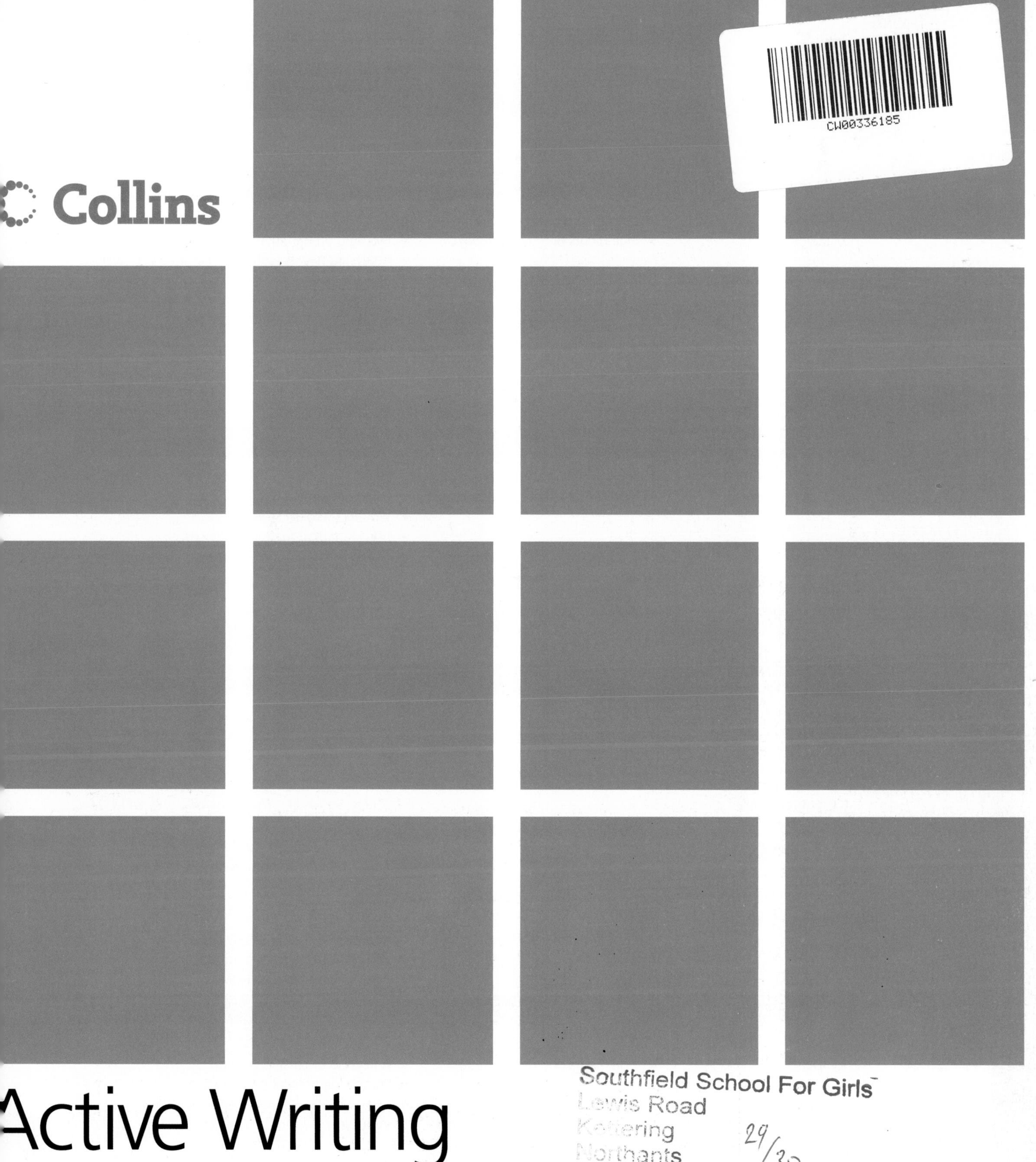

Collins

Active Writing

Understand, practise, succeed

ULIA STRONG & KIM RICHARDSON

KEY STAGE 3 / YEAR 9

Contents Grid

Contents

Section 3 – Text structure/organisation	Section 4 – Sentence structure/organisation	Section 5 – Composing own text
S5, W8, S6, Wr5 • Shaping ideas into cohesive paragraphs • Exploring and using paragraphs • Experimenting with narrative perspective	S1, S2, R11 • Using complex and simple sentences • Examining punctuation and how writers sustain Standard English	Wr5, S3 • Writing a story, maintaining a clear writer's voice throughout
S5, S6 • Evaluating cohesive paragraphs • Using note-making to sum up an article	S4, S3 • Integrating reference and quotation • Using the past tense and modal verbs	S3, R2, S9, S4, Wr11, Wr1 • Writing a lively news article • Inform, explain, describe
S5, W8, R3 • Analysing cohesive paragraphs • Using text skeletons	S1, S2 • Using a full range of punctuation • Developing compex sentences	Wr9, Wr11, Wr7, S5, W8 • Writing an entertaining and informative account about wildlife
Wr9, Wr10, W7, W8, S5 • Explaining connections between ideas • Analysing cohesive paragraphs that use signposting and connectives	S1, S2 • Using complex sentences • Using a full range of puncuation	Wr9, Wr10, Wr11 • Writing a text explaining complex ideas
S6, S7 • Comparing and using paragraphs • Analysing stylistic conventions of text types	S1, S2, W8 • Using sentences of different lengths and structures • Using commas and sentence signposts	S9, Wr13 • Writing a speech, using techniques of persuasive writing
W7, W8, S5 • Analysing cohesive paragraphs that use signposting and connectives	S1, S2 • Reviewing and punctuating relative clauses	S9, Wr14, Wr13 • Writing an argument for or against a topic
S6, Wr9 • Comparing opening paragraphs • Integrating information coherently	S1, S2 • Using modal verbs • Using punctuation effectively	S9, Wr15 • Writing advice in a formal style
S6, S7, W7, S5 • Developing paragraphs • Analysing style of discursive texts • Analysing cohesive paragraphs that use signposting and connectives	S1, S2, S4, Wr6 • Developing use of reported speech • Using quotations and punctuation effectively	S9, S4, R7, Wr16, Wr17 • Writing a compare and contrast essay

Section 2 – The shorter writing task	Section 3 – The longer writing task
Wr3, Wr1 • Completing a shorter task in exam conditions • Understanding the marking system and setting targets	Wr3, Wr1 • Completing a longer writing task in exam conditions • Understanding the marking system and improving writing

Contents

Introduction

Collins Active Writing 3 is a practical guide to writing in different text types for students in Year 9. It will help students increase and apply their knowledge of language, grammar and the craft of writing. *Active Writing* puts the emphasis firmly on practice through a step-by-step approach to learning the features of each text type, with every unit building towards the writing of a complete piece. This approach should enable students to tackle any type of writing task confidently, as well as preparing them for their end of Key Stage writing test.

How the book is organised

The units

The book has nine units. Eight of these each focus on one of the main text types that together cover all the different forms and purposes of writing. These are: Narrative, Recount, Information, Explanation, Persuasion, Argument, Advice and Discussion. The units are grouped together under the triplet headings from the National Curriculum for English.

A unit has five sections based on the QCA's assessment focuses.

Section 1 – How the text type works This gives an overview of the range of a particular text type, e.g. Narrative, and highlights its typical language and structural features.

Section 2 – Composition and effect This introduces a longer text of the type focused on in the unit and forms the basis of the work in Sections 2, 3, and 4. This time the focus is on the way the writer has used different language features to create specific effects. Students will practise using these effects.

Section 3 – Text structure and organisation The emphasis is on the structure of the main text and how the writer has linked sections and ideas within paragraphs. Using a text skeleton (a note-making tool) and sentence signposts, students will analyse the structure of the main text and plan a text of their own.

Section 4 – Sentence structure and punctuation The focus is firmly on the sentence grammar and punctuation that underpins the text type. Students will practise changing and developing sentences to add more variety to their writing.

Section 5 – Composing your own text This delivers the main task of the unit and offers the chance to write a longer piece in the text type. As students brainstorm ideas, plan, draft and revise their own writing, they will draw on all the work they have done in Sections 1–4. To help them further, this section also provides plenty of reminders and support for the writing task.

The final unit focuses on how to succeed in English Writing Tests. It helps students analyse test questions, produces test practice and offers 'clinics' to strengthen areas of weakness.

The Exemplar section

The X icon indicates an exemplar at the back of the book for selected tasks in Sections 1 to 4. These are not intended as the 'only answer', but as a guide to how someone might respond to the task.

The TR icon indicates that there is a worksheet to support the task (see Teacher's Resource).

Tasks as building blocks

The tasks in each unit provide practice in the following vital skills for writing.

- **Learning from example –** understanding the writer's voice (see page 14)
- **Planning practice** - using text skeletons to help structure writing (see page 17), achieving coherence and cohesion (see pages 31-32)
- **Spinning sentences** - understanding how to structure sentences to suit a range of purposes (see pages 18–19)
- **Targeted activities** - throughout, mini-writing tasks, supported by discussion, allow practice in the language features explored (see page 15) building towards the main writing task at the end of each unit (see pages 20–22).

Part of a model answer is often provided to help students tackle a task.

The class organisation for each task is shown by the following icons:

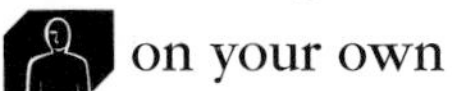 on your own  in pairs 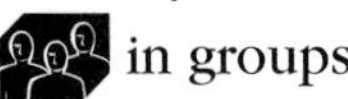 in groups

The emphasis is on interactive tasks to maximise student understanding through focused paired and group work. This builds up to support independent writing. Only the teacher introductions and class feedback and presentations are whole-class activities.

Clear explanations

Explanations of vocabulary, grammar, structure and style features are outlined through the following.

- Annotations of model text types showing the key form and language features.
- Grammar panel - explaining a grammar point clearly and providing examples.
- Glossary panel - defining tricky words in texts and explanations.
- Highlighted text - emphasising each language feature consistently for instant recognition. For example, students will always know that text highlighted in orange is a topic sentence (see page 10).

How *Collins Active Writing* increases confidence for the test

Students' ability to write well for a wide range of audiences and purposes is all-important in gaining a high mark in the Year 9 English writing tests. *Collins Active Writing* helps students prepare in several ways.

- The main task in Section 5 acts as full-scale practice for the type of task students will meet in the test
- On-going formative assessment is provided by the pair evaluation task and the setting of own writing targets task at the end of Section 5. These are supported by copymasters in the Teacher's Resource
- A test unit (see pages 130–153), supported by resources is devoted to building up experience of responding to test questions and analysing student responses.

By using *Collins Active Writing 3*, students will not only improve their writing skills and chances of success in the end of Key Stage tests, but will increase their confidence as writers.

Introduction

A The Art of Narrative Writing

1 Revisiting how narrative text works

AIMS

- Analyse the stylistic conventions of narrative text.
- Compare the presentation of ideas in related stories.

In this section you will analyse how different storywriters have chosen to begin their stories and decide what, if any, stylistic features they share.

Different ways of telling a story

'Once upon a time' is just one way of telling a story.

There are many different ways to **structure** a story.

- The classic story structure is chronological.[1] That is, the story begins at the beginning, develops the plot, includes a complication, which reaches a crisis, and ends with a resolution. It can be planned like this (see below and page 16).

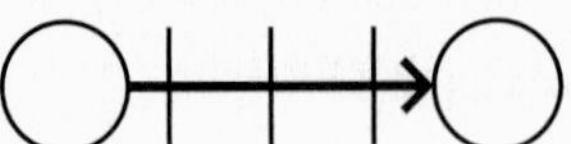

- Or you can begin at the end or the middle and then tell the story of what happened.
- Or you can include a range of flashbacks.

Then there is the question of **narrative perspective** – that is, the viewpoint from which the story is told. For example, the story could be told:

- in the third person, telling the story that has happened to other people. This is known as the omniscient[2] narrator (the person who writes as if they were God), who knows everything that happens and how everyone feels. The Harry Potter stories are written in this way.
- in the first person, telling the story as if it happened to you
- in the first person, but with more than one narrator so the story is told by two or more characters. This gives the reader insight from different perspectives.

Then there's the **writer's voice** – that is, the voice that will be telling the story, and the tone and style of that voice which develops the narrative perspective.

- The narrator can be very involved (being very sympathetic – almost as if the events were happening to them) or very distant (seeming to be standing a long way back and commenting on events).
- Or he/she can use very descriptive language full of fancy imagery.
- Or he/she can use very plain, bare language.

1 **chronological** – arranged in the order in which things happened

2 **omniscient** – all-seeing and all-knowing

Below and on page 8 are the opening paragraphs from six different stories, together with summaries of their narrative and stylistic features.

Task 1 Analysing

Match openings 1–6 with the key features A–F on page 9. Be prepared to present your findings.

1 The opening of *Metamorphosis* by Franz Kafka

As Gregor Samsa awoke one morning from uneasy dreams he found himself transformed in his bed into a gigantic insect. He was lying on his hard, as it were armour-plated, back and when he lifted his head a little he could see his dome-like brown belly divided into stiff arched segments on top of which the bed-quilt could hardly keep in position and was about to slide off completely. His numerous legs, which were pitifully thin compared to the rest of his bulk, waved helplessly before his eyes.

What has happened to me? he thought. It was no dream. His room, a regular human bedroom, only rather too small, lay quiet between the four familiar walls.

2 The opening of *Brighton Rock* by Graham Greene

Hale knew, before he had been in Brighton three hours, that they meant to murder him. With his inky fingers and his bitten nails, his manner cynical and nervous, anybody could tell he didn't belong – belong to the early summer sun, the cool Whitsun wind off the sea, the holiday crowd.

They came in by train from Victoria every five minutes, rocked down Queen's Road standing on the tops of the little local trams, stepped off in bewildered multitudes into the fresh glittering air: the new silver paint sparkled on the piers, the cream houses ran away into the west like a pale Victorian water-colour; a race in miniature motors, a band playing, flower gardens in bloom below the front, an aeroplane advertising something for the health in pale vanishing clouds across the sky.

3 The opening of *David Copperfield* by Charles Dickens

I Am Born

Whether I shall turn out to be the hero of my own life, or whether that station will be held by anybody else, these pages must show. To begin my life with the beginning of my life, I record that I was born (as I have been informed and believe) on a Friday at twelve o'clock at night. It was remarked that the clock began to strike, and I began to cry, simultaneously.

4 The opening of *Anita and Me* by Meera Syal

I do not have many memories of my very early childhood, apart from the obvious ones, of course. You know, my windswept bewildered parents in their dusty Indian village garb standing in the open doorway of a 747, blinking back tears of gratitude and heartbreak as the fog cleared to reveal the sign they had been waiting for, dreaming of, the sign planted in the tarmac and emblazoned in triumphant hues of red, blue and white, the sign that said simply, WELCOME TO BRITAIN.

5 The first two pages of *Stone Cold* by Robert Swindells

You can call me Link. It's not my name, but it's what I say when anybody asks, which isn't often. I'm invisible, see? One of the invisible people. Right now I'm sitting in a doorway watching the passers-by. They avoid looking at me. They're afraid I want something they've got, and they're right. Also, they don't want to think about me. They don't like reminding I exist. Me, and those like me. We're living proof that everything's not all right and we make the place untidy.

Hang about and I'll tell you the story of my fascinating life.

Daily Routine Orders 1

Shelter. Yes. I like it. It's got a ring to it as I'm sure you'll agree. Shelter, as in shelter from the stormy blast. It's what they're all seeking. The street people. What they crave. If they can only find shelter everything will be fine. Well – get fell in, my lucky lads. I'm ready for you.

6 The opening of *Love That Dog* by Sharon Creech

ROOM 105 – MISS STRETCHBERRY

SEPTEMBER 13
I don't want to
because boys
don't write poetry.

Girls do.

SEPTEMBER 21
I tried.
Can't do it.
Brain's empty.

Key Features

A **Narrative perspective:** first-person narrative (autobiographical style)

Writer's voice: – informal casual everyday language, as if chatting to reader
– long descriptive sentences, as if listening to someone recounting an event.

B **Narrative perspective:** third-person omniscient narrator

Writer's voice: – fairly formal, distant but noticing everything
– detailed descriptive language.

C **Narrative perspective:** first-person narrative (autobiographical style)

Writer's voice: – formal but friendly
– flowery use of language
– long complex sentences.

D **Narrative perspective:** first-person dual narrative (dual autobiographical style)

Writer's voice: – both informal and casual, as if chatting to reader
– casual everyday language
– short sharp sentences.

E **Narrative perspective:** third-person omniscient narrator

Writer's voice: – distanced and formal
– precise, unemotive[1] use of language
– straightforward, plain sentence structure.

F **Narrative perspective:** first-person narrative (autobiographical style)

Structure: – layout a cross between a diary and a poem

Writer's voice: – very personal, reveals inner thoughts
– short sharp sentences.

[1] **unemotive** – calm and straightforward, lacking in emotion or feeling

Task 2 Comparing openings

Openings 2 and 5 are both rather menacing. Fill in the grid below with evidence to show what language features they have in common and what differences there are.

Features	Brighton Rock	Stone Cold
Narrative perspective – first person or third person		
Writer's voice: – formal or informal		
– personal or distanced		
– plain or descriptive		
Language features – short sharp sentences – longer complex sentences		

Hooking your reader

The opening paragraphs of any story are the most important. If you don't hook your reader from the beginning, they may not continue reading.

Task 3 Discussing

Select the two openings that you find the most effective and decide what features appealed to you. You may want to consider some of the following features.

- An effective hook that grabs your interest.
- A mystery that makes you want to read on and find out more.
- An excellent description that helps you picture what is being described.
- Interesting characters that make you want to find out more about them.
- The writer's voice appeals – it makes you want to read more.
- It is entertaining – it makes you think the story may be funny.

2 Composition and effect

Learning from example

AIMS

- Analyse ways of opening, and ending a narrative, focusing on narrative perspective.
- Analyse how a sustained narrative voice can affect meaning.
- Analyse how writers can relate formality, vocabulary and grammar to context.

In this section you will focus on the difference narrative perspective and purpose makes to the style of a story.

Narrative perspective

The narrative perspective a writer chooses can make a big difference to the story told (see page 6 for more on different narrative perspectives).

Task 4 Reading

As you read *The Room* by David Karp, consider the narrative perspective and writer's voice he has used. Be prepared to support your conclusions with evidence.

Time signposts – help reader follow chronology of story

Opening hook – grabs attention of reader

Third-person narrative – story told by omniscient (all-knowing) narrator

Topic sentence – starting with this directs reader

Formal English used throughout

Past tense

Short sharp sentences build up tension

The Room

Burden's first awareness was that he was naked and the room was cold. He opened his eyes and saw only the grey light. He thought for an instant that he was lying naked on the floor of the corridor. It was not the corridor, nor his room in the hospital section. It was a bare, enormous room, perhaps two stories tall, and it was so huge that it curved almost out of sight. There were no windows in it, not a stick of furniture, nothing but the soaring monotony of rough concrete. The floor was smooth and cold to his bare feet. Burden rose and walked slowly. There was enough light for him to see the room in its entirety. It was perhaps twenty feet in width and fifty feet in height and it curved with the building. Cautiously Burden followed the wall, looking for a door, a window, a break in the concrete. But there was none. He followed the curving wall for what seemed two hundred feet and came up against another wall, twenty feet wide and stretching fifty feet towards the ceiling.

Straightforward description of features of room

Unemotional description – focuses on physical surroundings rather than feelings

Objective – calling man by his surname only distances reader from victim

The light appeared to come from the ceiling. Burden's first thought was that the room was once an immense storage place. High up along the curving walls there seemed to be ventilators but they were far too high for Burden to reach or to see clearly. The light of the room was unvarying and strange. It didn't seem like daylight and yet it did not resemble artificial light. It was a uniform, flat grey. Burden crossed to the opposing wall and, brushing his hand lightly against it, walked back the curving length of the room. It brought him back to the opposite wall. The room was so long and so curved that he could not see from one end to the other. How had he been put in the room? Lowered perhaps from somewhere on the ceiling? There seemed to be no breaks in the ceiling and yet he felt that his eyes probably deceived him.

Burden sat down on the floor, his back against the wall. The room was cold, so cold that goose-flesh began to rise along his arms and legs, prickling his buttocks. The cold was not intense, but it would not be easy to bear. What sort of room was it? Why had he been put in it? He began to long for his pyjamas, thin and dirty as they were, for the slippers, cold and sleazy as they were. Nakedness was an awful feeling. A terrible sense of vulnerability began to seep into him. He drew his knees up and clasped his hands across his shins, looking up at the ceiling. They would not leave him there to starve. They had to give him food. He would see then where the food came from, perhaps find out from the person who brought it how long he would have to stay in the room. Or would it be lowered from the ceiling? If it came down on a rope he could seize hold of it and refuse to let go. They would either have to haul him up or cut the rope. In any case he would have something in the room with him – even if it was only a rope. Burden shuddered at the thought of being left so utterly alone. He had read of dungeons, of prisoners left in the darkness without the sound of a human voice, without the sight of a human face. But this was not a dungeon. It was a large room, it was not at all dark, and its shape was more interesting than a box. It suddenly occurred to Burden that someone could enter the other end of the room that curved out of his sight and he would not see him. He rose and walked to a spot he judged to be the exact centre of the arc and sat down again on the floor, able now to see both opposing walls. But he discovered that in that position there were at least two corners of the room he could not see. A sobering thought struck him then. No matter where he sat in the room, there would always be some part of it he could not see. Was that how they intended to get his food to him? To watch him from the ceiling, determine his position, and then allow someone to slip in, leave the food in the blind spot, and then slip out again? Burden rose to his feet. It was a devilishly planned room if that was the plan. It meant that he had to keep walking to be certain he missed no one who entered. But how could entry be made? He saw no signs of doors. Perhaps there were ordinary doors behind the concrete, with knobs and locks and wood panelling. Perhaps the walls were not so thick as they seemed. Burden struck the wall with his fist hard enough to hurt himself. The wall seemed solid, at least several inches thick. The question, he realized suddenly, was whether the inner curved wall faced a corridor or the other wall. Burden looked at the two walls and felt foolish. One was inner and the other outer, but he did not know which. The walls were of equal length and it was the trick of perspective that made one seem longer than the other. The question was, did the room follow the inside curve of the building or the outside curve? If he knew that he would know which curved wall opened on a corridor and which formed part of the building's limit.

Burden sighed at his own foolishness and sat down. It was a pointless question. Why did it matter at all? Except, he thought, rising again, the wall which faced the corridor would be the wall in which he would find the door – if there were such a door. Burden crossed to the opposing wall and struck it with his fist. It felt as solid as the first. He leaned his face against the rough concrete to see if he could hear through the wall. There was no sound but the steady throbbing of his own blood. The hollow roaring one could hear when cupping a hand over an ear. Burden sighed again – a sick, small, helpless sigh. He sank down to the floor and crossed his legs. It was then that he noticed what seemed to be a stain on the sole of his foot. He took hold of his ankle and turned the sole of his foot towards him. The hair on the nape of his neck rose with terror. Someone had carefully, with ink or iodine, printed in small but clear letters across the sole of his foot:

'You will be alone until you can no longer bear it.'

Task 5 Annotating

The first part of the story has been annotated to bring out some of its language features. Annotate the second half of the opening paragraph to illustrate another example of as many of these features as possible.

Making the opening effective

The Room is a very short story. The writer has the challenge of involving the reader quickly in its central idea.

Task 6 Annotating

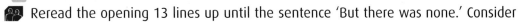

Reread the opening 13 lines up until the sentence 'But there was none.' Consider how it hooks the reader's attention and introduces the main idea of the story. Annotate this section to bring out the features that make it effective as an opening. Think about the following questions:

- Why are the opening lines striking?
- Do they jump straight into the story rather than setting the scene?
- What mysterious information do these lines include to make the reader want to find out more?

Changing the narrative perspective

The writer has chosen to write this story in the third person. In addition, rather than focusing on Burden's emotions and how he feels, he has employed an unemotional description of Burden's physical surroundings.

Task 7 Discussing

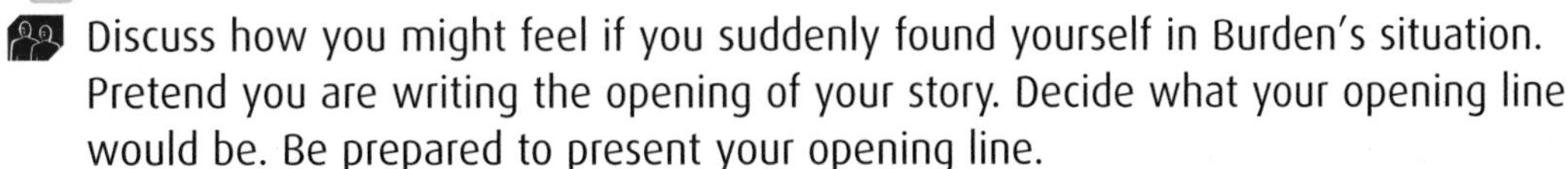

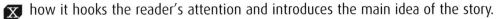

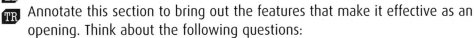

Discuss how you might feel if you suddenly found yourself in Burden's situation. Pretend you are writing the opening of your story. Decide what your opening line would be. Be prepared to present your opening line.

Below are two alternative openings for the story written in the first person.

My first awareness was that I was naked and the room was cold...

What has happened to me? I gasped. What is this room? I'm naked and so, so cold.

What difference does the first-person perspective make to how you might want to develop the language and content of the opening?

Building mystery and tension

This story relies on the reader knowing enough to be intrigued but not so much as to make the story lose its mystery. To achieve this, the writer has built in several interesting clues in the first half of the narrative.

Task 8 Analysing

Reread lines 1–47, up to 'But this was not a dungeon.' Comment on the effectiveness of the following clues and the questions they raise in the reader's mind. Be prepared to present your findings.

Clues	Questions this raises and effectiveness
He thought for an instant that he was lying naked on the floor of the corridor. It was not the corridor, nor his room in the hospital section.	
He began to long for his pyjamas, thin and dirty as they were, for the slippers, cold and sleazy as they were.	
They would not leave him there to starve. They had to give him food.	

The importance of the writer's voice

Whenever you write anything you have to decide what role you are taking as you write, just as in a role play you have to know what your character is and to act in role. This role is known as the 'writer's voice'. The voice may range from very friendly and informal (often first person) to very distant and formal (often third person). The voice always depends on the audience and purpose of the writing.

Range of writer's voice

very friendly and informal ←→ very distant and formal

The writer of *The Room* has chosen a very distanced voice that focuses on the kind of room Burden has found himself in and his sense of being watched, rather than on how he actually feels. As the narrator describes Burden's attempts to understand the room, it is almost as if the reader were watching Burden, too.

Task 9 Analysing

The annotations below explain exactly how the writer has achieved this effect. Match the annotations to the extract on page 15, selecting the sentences that best illustrate the effect that is described. Be prepared to present your conclusions.

1. Unemotional, simple description helps reader picture room in a clinical manner.
2. Blow-by-blow account of Burden's movements makes us feel as if we are watching him as he tries to establish if he is being watched.
3. Focus is on Burden analysing his situation logically rather than becoming emotional.
4. Blow-by-blow stark[1] account of Burden's attempt to understand nature of room means that reader comes to understand things exactly at the moment he does.

[1] **stark** – bare and striking

But this was not a dungeon. It was a large room, it was not at all dark, and its shape was more interesting than a box. It suddenly occurred to Burden that someone could enter the other end of the room that curved out of his sight and he would not see him. He rose and walked to a spot he judged to be the exact centre of the arc and sat down again on the floor, able now to see both opposing walls. But he discovered that in that position there were at least two corners of the room he could not see. A sobering thought struck him then. No matter where he sat in the room, there would always be some part of it he could not see. Was that how they intended to get his food to him? To watch him from the ceiling, determine his position, and then allow someone to slip in, leave the food in the blind spot, and then slip out again? Burden rose to his feet. It was a devilishly planned room if that was the plan. It meant that he had to keep walking to be certain he missed no one who entered.

Task 10 Discussing

Discuss why you think the writer chose to focus on Burden's physical surroundings rather than his mental state. Draw on the work you have done so far on the following and be prepared to present your ideas. Consider:

- third- versus first-person narrative in the story
- clues that build suspense
- the use of stark unemotional description.

Task 11 Changing voice and perspective

Rewrite the opening lines of *The Room* up until the sentence 'Burden rose and walked slowly' (lines 8–9). Your version should be in the first person and the writer's voice should reflect Burden's emotions. It will help to:

- include some of the emotions that would race through your head, such as fear, confusion, shock and disbelief
- include some images (metaphors or similes) to describe the emotions
- emphasise your reaction to what has happened, perhaps asking *why* it has happened to you.

You may want to begin like this:

Naked. My mind was screaming like a siren as I tried to come to terms with what had happened to me.

Text structure and organisation

Getting the structure right

AIMS

- Analyse how a writer has shaped ideas into cohesive paragraphs using topic sentences, sentence signposts, connectives and repetition of words or sentence structure to link paragraphs.
- Compare and use different ways of opening, developing, linking and completing paragraphs.
- Explore different ways of opening, structuring and ending narratives and experiment with narrative perspective.

In this section you will consider how a story has been structured and composed to make it cohesive, as well as a range of ways it could have been structured.

Structuring the story 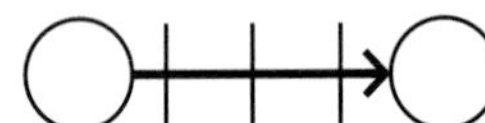

The Room follows the classic structure of the five stages of narrative fairly closely, but ends more at the height of the crisis than with a sense of resolution, as expressed by the diagram below.

Introduction – sets scene
Tension rises as story develops
Tension increases again as complication arises
Tension reaches height at crisis point
Ends at crisis point – no resolution

Task 12 Discussing

 Discuss whether this was a good point at which to end the story. Why do you think the writer chose to make the final paragraph so short, in contrast with all the other paragraphs in the story? Consider the alternatives below and decide which one offers the best reason:

- The writer wanted ending to contrast with the rest of the story.
- The writer wanted to leave the detail of Burden's reaction to the reader's imagination.
- It ends with a quotation so it should have a paragraph to itself.

Crafting cohesive paragraphs

Cohesive[1] **paragraphs** hang together effectively. To achieve this, a writer can guide the reader by:

- using topic sentences so the reader understands the focus of the paragraph
- organising the points logically, often using a main point supported in a range of ways
- using sentence signposts, connectives and repetition of ideas or sentence structure to show links between the points, and between the paragraphs.

[1] **cohesive** – with effective links and well organised. (See page 92 for a fuller explanation of this term.)

Task 13 Annotating

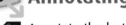

 Annotate the last two paragraphs (see page 17) of the story to show how the writer has used all these techniques to make them cohesive. A few examples have been completed for you. Find another example of each technique and be prepared to present your findings.

Sentence signpost – here signalling beginning of a new idea

Topic sentence – here indicating resignation and helplessness

Repetition of key words – 'wall' repeated to help maintain focus

Repetition of sentence structure – several sentences begin with 'He', emphasising Burden's repeated attempts to find a solution

Burden sighed at his own foolishness and sat down. It was a pointless question. Why did it matter at all? Except, he thought, rising again, the wall which faced the corridor would be the wall in which he would find the door – if there were such a door. Burden crossed to the opposing wall and struck it with his fist. It felt as solid as the first. He leaned his face against the rough concrete to see if he could hear through the wall. There was no sound but the steady throbbing of his own blood. The hollow roaring one could hear when cupping a hand over an ear. Burden sighed again – a sick, small helpless sigh. He sank down to the floor and crossed his legs: It was then that he noticed what seemed to be a stain on the sole of his foot. He took hold of his ankle and turned the sole of his foot towards him. The hair on the nape of his neck rose with terror. Someone had carefully, with ink or iodine, printed in small but clear letters across the sole of his foot.

'You will be alone until you can no longer bear it.'

Varying narrative structure

This story has been carefully structured and composed to build up to the bombshell of the last line.

Task 14 Planning practice

Discuss whether it would be possible to make an equally effective story if the story was structured in the following ways:

- It began with the last line.
- It included a flashback.
- It began at the midpoint (beginning of second paragraph).

Below is a completed text skeleton representing the structure and key content of *The Room*.

Intro sets context: A man (Burden) finds himself naked in cold room. He had been in hospital. Bare, windowless, doorless and enormous (200ft x 20ft x 50ft) but some light – curves out of sight.

Developing plot: story focuses on how Burden tries to make sense of room, wondering how he had been put in room. Is very cold. Wonders how will be fed.

Complication: Burden realises that curve means someone could enter and he wouldn't see them. Has to keep walking to make certain sees anyone who enters. But how would they get in? Can't tell whether room follows outside or inside curve of building – to know would help him know which wall opens onto a corridor.

Crisis: Burden rallies from moment of despair. Thinks he might be able to find a door. Strikes wall with fist but senses nothing but throbbing of own blood. Despairs again. Then sees writing on foot telling him he will be alone until he can't bear it.

Choose one of the three starting points above and plan how the story could be restructured while maintaining the same key content.

Sentence structure and punctuation

Making the sentences work

AIMS

- Use the appropriate balance of complex and simple sentences when writing to achieve just the impact you require.
- Examine how punctuation can emphasise meaning for a reader.
- Examine how writers achieve sustained Standard English with the formality suited to reader and purpose.

In this section you will develop your ability to improve your writing by using varied sentence structures to suit your purpose, while punctuating them effectively.

Selecting sentence structure to suit purpose

- **Sentence types:** Although there are technically many complex sentences throughout *The Room*, the overall impression is of short simple sentences, many of which are in question form as Burden thinks through the immediate options that face him. (Look at the grammar panel below to remind yourself of the main sentence types.)
- **Vocabulary:** The vocabulary selected in the story is also generally simple so that the overall effect is matter of fact and stark, which makes the situation confronting Burden all the more alarming.
- **Punctuation:** This simplicity is also reflected in the punctuation since there is little need for commas to separate off embedded clauses, and no need for brackets to separate off information.

GRAMMAR

A **main clause** is a single idea or event – it has a **subject** and one **verb** and makes complete sense on its own, e.g. Burden sighed at his own foolishness.
Subject – Verb

A **simple sentence** has one main clause, e.g. He sat down.

A **compound sentence** is two or more simple sentences (main clauses) joined together with coordinating conjunctions ('and', 'but', 'so', 'or'), e.g.
Burden sighed at his own foolishness and sat down.
Main clause – Coordinating conjunction – Main clause

A **complex sentence** is one main clause plus at least one subordinate clause. A subordinate clause doesn't make complete sense on its own – it relies on the main clause to make sense. The **subordinate clause** can be placed at the beginning of the sentence, at the end of the sentence or be embedded inside a main clause, e.g.
Burden sighed at his own foolishness as he sat down.
As he sat down, Burden sighed at his own foolishness.
Burden, as he sat down, sighed at his own foolishness.
Subordinate clause

A **minor sentence** isn't, technically, a sentence because it doesn't have a complete verb. However, it makes sense because of its context, e.g.
Seated. Burden sighed at his own foolishness.
Minor sentence

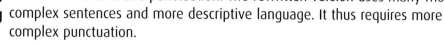

Task 15

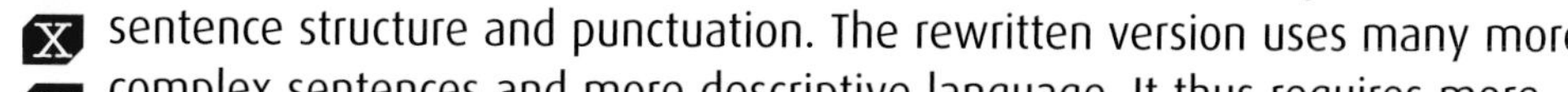

The original extract below illustrates the writer's use of straightforward sentence structure and punctuation. The rewritten version uses many more complex sentences and more descriptive language. It thus requires more complex punctuation.

Annotate the two passages to bring out the differences in sentence structure, level of description and punctuation.

Original extract

But how could entry be made? He saw no signs of doors. Perhaps there were ordinary doors behind the concrete, with knobs and locks and wood panelling. Perhaps the walls were not so thick as they seemed. Burden struck the wall with his fist hard enough to hurt himself.

Rewritten version

Burden frowned repeatedly: he was asking himself how entry could be made. Regardless of how hard he examined the room, with eagle-like intensity, he was unable to see any sign of any sort of door. Perhaps, behind the endless pall of grey concrete, there were ordinary doors with intricate iron locks, decorative knobs and exquisitely carved wooden panelling. Perhaps, he thought, the very walls were not so alarmingly thick as they seemed to his frightened eyes. Burden suddenly struck the mocking wall with his tightly clenched fist hard – hard enough to cause himself considerable hurt.

Task 16 **Writing**

Look again at the opening of Kafka's *Metamorphosis*, page 7. Write your own third-person opening paragraph about someone waking up and finding that either they or the room that they are in has changed totally. Try to keep your sentences straightforward, bare and simple in David Karp's style.

5 Composing your own story

AIMS

- Select your narrative perspective, deciding whether you want to write a story in the first or third person.
- Write a story with a clear sustained writer's voice to achieve a particular effect relating formality, vocabulary and grammar to context.
- Write a well-structured story.

Write your own story about suddenly being in totally inexplicable[1] circumstances, maintaining a clear writer's voice throughout.

[1] **inexplicable** – with no explanation

1 Improvising your ideas

Improvise a range of possibilities about someone suddenly finding they, or their surroundings, have totally and inexplicably changed. Be prepared to select one improvisation to present to the class. You may want to use some of the following ideas:

- waking up in an unknown room
- waking up to find you have become an insect or animal
- waking up to find you have become an object in the room (e.g. alarm clock, teddy bear)
- waking up in a different time, e.g. medieval London or Roman Rome.

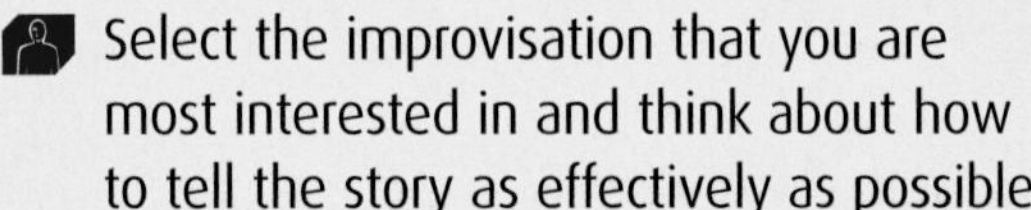

2 Deciding on narrative perspective, writer's voice and structure

Select the improvisation that you are most interested in and think about how to tell the story as effectively as possible.

First decide on the **narrative perspective** – the viewpoint from which your story is going to be told. Choose between:

- the third person – telling a story about what has happened to other people. The narrator is omniscient, knowing everything that happens and how everyone feels. *The Room* is written like this.
- the first person – telling the story as if it happened to you or creating a persona (a character) and writing as if you were them. Sharon Creek has done the latter in *Love That Dog*.

Next decide on your **writer's voice** – whose voice will be telling the story in what tone and style? Choose between the storyteller:

- being very involved (*Love That Dog*)
- being very distant (*The Room*)
- using very descriptive imaginative imagery (*Brighton Rock*)
- using very plain bare language (*The Room* or *Love That Dog*).

Finally, decide on the general **structure**. The classic story structure is chronological – the story begins at the beginning, develops the plot, includes a complication which reaches a crisis and ends with a resolution, as shown by the text skeleton below.

Alternatively, you can:

- begin at the end and then tell the story of how it happened
- start at the middle and move backwards and forwards
- include a range of flashbacks.

Planning the story in detail

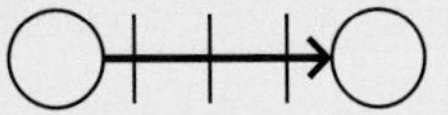

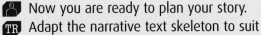

Now you are ready to plan your story. Adapt the narrative text skeleton to suit your ideas. Jot down the key things that will happen at each stage. Then decide whether you are going to end with the crisis or try to have some sort of resolution to the mystery. Finally, remembering the narrative perspective and writer's voice that you have selected, work out five topic sentences or sentence signposts that will guide the reader through the key stages of the story.

Discussing what you are going to write

Tell your partner the opening of your story using the narrative perspective and writer's voice that you have chosen. Help each other to get a sense of the writer's voice you have each selected.

Composing your piece

Now you are ready to write.

Points to remember

- Make the opening grab your reader's interest. Try to picture someone reading your story as you write (see pages 9 and 13).
- Keep to your chosen narrative perspective and sustain the writer's voice you have selected to achieve the effect you want (see pages 14–15).
- Select the appropriate level of formality, vocabulary and grammar to achieve the required effect (see pages 14–15).
- Include mystery and tension to keep the reader hooked (see page 14).
- Use the appropriate balance of complex and simple sentences to achieve the impact you require and include questions, if appropriate (see pages 18–19).
- Shape ideas into cohesive paragraphs using a variety of devices such as topic sentences, sentence signposts, connectives and repetition of key words or sentence structure (see pages 16–17).
- Create an effective ending (see page 16).

You may want to use some of the sentence signposts below to help you.

Sentence signposts

- What happened to me? she thought
- X first became aware of
- Where am I? he wondered
- As X awoke one morning
- She stared fixedly at the window high above
- Perhaps it would be possible
- He resigned himself
- How can this have
- Whichever way she thought about it

Top tip You will probably want to adjust your plan when you start drafting the paragraphs.

6 Peer comment

Swap your draft with your partner's and agree how to improve your work. Discuss what really works well and highlight this on your draft. Then discuss what needs to be done to improve your story and jot down up to three suggestions on the draft. Redraft the selected sections of the draft using the comments to guide you.

7 Pulling it all together

Listen to extracts from stories written by members of your class. Decide on the key features that make these extracts effective. Be prepared to share your ideas. Note down up to three targets for yourself for the next time you write a story.

B The Art of Recount Writing

Revisiting how recount text works

AIMS

- Analyse and exploit the stylistic conventions of recount text.
- Compare the presentation of ideas in related texts.

In this section you will build on your existing knowledge of how a recount text works, thinking about how its language features and structure may change depending on its audience and purpose.

Different kinds of recount

Recount texts retell a series of events that have actually happened. Some typical examples are:

- **diary entries**, in which someone records what happened to them on that day
- **autobiographies** that tell a person's own life story (in the first person)
- **biographies** that tell someone else's life story (in the third person)
- **newspaper articles** that recount an incident
- sections of a **history textbook**.

The main feature that distinguishes a recount text from a narrative (see page 6) is that the events described are real. The audience and purpose will determine the appropriate style and tone.

Task 1 Reading and annotating

Read the opening paragraphs from two books about famous footballers on pages 24–25. The first is from Tony Adams' autobiography, which tells how the ex-England football captain overcame his addiction to alcohol and regained both his club captaincy and the captaincy of the England team. The second is a recount of Paul Gascoigne's rollercoaster footballing career by sports journalist Ian Hamilton.

The first opening has been annotated to bring out its key features. Annotate the second opening to illustrate its features, adapting the annotations from the first text as appropriate.

Opening 'I' suggests recount is autobiographical – rest of passage confirms this

Topic sentence – introduces focus of paragraph and introduction

Topic sentence – starting with this orientates reader

Formal but friendly style – as if talking to reader

Descriptive language – brings events alive

Interesting use of sentence signposts to increase immediacy of memory

Reference to specifics – names, games, places to add detail/signpost events

Opening hook – dives straight into middle of key event – builds tension – hooks reader

Use of simple past and past perfect ('had' + past tense) – helps reader follow earlier events

Effective sentence structure, including repetition for effect

Repetition for effect

Time connective – helps reader understand event happened earlier

Addicted by Tony Adams

I just knew what would happen. Not that Gareth Southgate would fail to score with his penalty, but that if he did miss, and if the Germans then scored with their next one, I was going to get drunk. I had not had a drink all the way through Euro '96, which, for a man coming to realise he was an alcoholic, took some doing. But then, I had been consumed by my first addiction – football. And as soon as that was taken away from me, I just knew what would happen. It was as if I had no choice.

It had been the pattern of both my career and my life: get drunk to deal with the deep disappointments, get drunk to deal with the joyous moments of achievement – and there had been many of both. Booze acted for me as an anaesthetic to avoid intense feelings, bad or good, and right now on this balmy summer night of Wednesday 26 June 1996, with the England team I was captaining just having lost 6–5 on penalties to Germany in the semi-final of the European Championships at Wembley, was as bad as it got. I needed to numb the pain. And so I would drink. For the next seven weeks. I would drink until the pain would be numbed no more.

We had not actually planned for this. For penalties, yes, but not going beyond the first five that had failed to separate the teams after the 1–1 draw in 120 minutes of play. I was standing in the centre circle congratulating those who had already scored – Alan Shearer, David Platt, Stuart Pearce, Paul Gascoigne and Teddy Sheringham. I have never been a great penalty-taker myself, and although I would have taken one if others had declined, as had happened with Arsenal in a European Cup Winners' Cup semi-final against Sampdoria the previous year, I was in no rush to volunteer. Gareth, bravely, fatefully, was.

Gazza Antagonistes[1]

My first sighting of Paul Gascoigne was in 1987, when he was playing for Newcastle. I didn't exactly fall for him that day but I certainly looked twice. There was, as they say, 'something about him'. His giftedness was self-evident: he was a natural. You could tell that from his touch. However the ball came at him, fast, medium or slow, he welcomed it; he took it in his stride.

His appearance was unprepossessing.[2] He was plump, twitchy and pink-faced, and on the small side. And he was cheeky in a puerile[3] sort of way. He was always looking to nutmeg[4] defenders when it would have been easier to pass them by. He wanted the ball *all the time*: for throw-ins, free kicks, corners – goal-kicks, if they had let him. He seemed fragile but he wasn't: there was a mean streak underneath the puppy fat. He was always glancing behind him, or from side to side, even when the ball was nowhere near. He talked a lot, played to the crowd, or tried to. At nineteen, Gascoigne came across as a trainee star, a star whose moment was – well, any second now.

I was intrigued by the way he related to his centre forward, a Brazilian called Mirandinha. Mirandinha had not long before scored for Brazil against England at Wembley, and when Newcastle signed him there had been a small fuss in the press. Wags[5] said that the Newcastle board thought they were signing Maradona. For the most part, though, the appearance of a Brazilian in our English league was a matter for great celebration. We would learn from Mirandinha. He would bring sunshine to our drizzly field of play.

What he actually brought was a repertoire[6] of muttered curses and black looks, and in the game I watched most of them were directed at young Gascoigne.

[1] ***Antagonistes*** – a play on words. John Milton, a famous seventeenth-century poet, wrote a verse drama about the sufferings of biblical strongman Samson, called *Samson Agonistes*. Gazza's biographer has changed this to *Antagonistes* to suggest that Gazza's antagonistic personality may have led to some of his suffering

[2] **unprepossessing** – unattractive

[3] **puerile** – childish

[4] **nutmeg** – pass the ball between opponents' legs

[5] **wags** – jokers

[6] **repertoire** – stock, range

Task 2 Discussing and recording

Using the annotations to help you, establish the key stylistic similarities and differences between the two extracts by comparing the features in the grid below. Be prepared to feed back your findings.

Features	Text 1: Adams	Text 2: Gascoigne
Has the writer used a hook to grab the reader's interest?		
Is the first person or third person used?		Written in third person – biography
Writer's voice: is this a formal but friendly voice as if talking to the reader?		
Are topic sentences used to guide the reader through the account?		
Do time connectives guide the reader through the recount?	Yes: Uses the time connective 'previous year' to signal is referring to an even earlier memory	
Is the main tense used the past tense?	Yes: Large variety of past tenses used because reflecting on his thoughts at the time	
Is descriptive, powerful language used to bring the account alive?		

Composition and effect

Learning from example

AIMS

- Analyse how successful article writers sustain a coherent writer's voice while synthesising information from a range of sources.
- Analyse how telling use of descriptive detail helps make writing effective.
- Analyse how the degree of formality, vocabulary and grammar suits audience and purpose.

In this section you will consider how journalists sustain a coherent writer's voice and narrative perspective while recounting events.

Sustaining a coherent writer's voice

Whenever you write anything, you have to decide what role you are playing and write in role – just as in a role play you have to know what your character is and act in role. This is known as the 'writer's voice'. The voice may be friendly and informal or distant and formal. The voice should always depend on the audience and purpose of the writing and may include viewpoint, just as a character has a viewpoint. The style and tone of the writing is dependent on this voice.

Task 3 Reading

As you read award-winning football journalist Henry Winter's account of Chelsea's victory over Manchester United in November 2003 below,

- consider how his voice helps guide the reader
- find up to three pieces of evidence that Winter has a viewpoint on the match.

Topic sentences have been highlighted to help you follow the key points being made. Be prepared to present your evidence.

Third-person perspective on events maintained throughout

Past tense – helps reader follow earlier events

Chelsea United in Blue

Henry Winter at Stamford Bridge

Chelsea 1 Manchester United 0

1 **UNDER THE approving gaze of Roy Bentley,** the great centre forward whose goals shot Chelsea to their last title almost a half-century ago, the modern generation yesterday installed themselves as Premiership leaders and bookmakers' favourites with this convincing, thoroughly deserved victory over Manchester United. "They must have a wonderful chance of the title now," smiled Bentley after Frank Lampard's penalty had so embarrassed the champions.

Opening hook – links Chelsea's present success with past glory

Writer's voice – Winter clearly states in formal but friendly English that 'the better team won'

Powerful language – helps build up image of Chelsea's power

Topic sentence – introduces focus of paragraph

Interesting sentence signpost – compares present and past

Time connective – makes reader clear when match happened. (Note: written for daily newspaper.)

Descriptive language – brings events alive

Varied choice of words so doesn't have to keep repeating 'Chelsea'

2 **Past glories and present strengths** – rolled into one at the Bridge yesterday. Bentley and Stan Willemse, the left-back from that 1955 trophy-winning side of Ted Drake's, delighted in the marvellous defensive organisation built around the growing colossus[1] that is John Terry, thrilled to the clever forward moves of Lampard and Joe Cole, and warmed to the work ethic that united all the men in blue.

3 **The future looks brighter than ever**. Hours earlier, Chelsea's interim[2] chief executive, Paul Smith, had warned opponents that the club would not baulk[3] "at spending £50 million" on one player if required. The huge resources in Roman Abramovich's vaults and the human resources in Claudio Ranieri's dressing room signal why Chelsea must be feared in the chase for the championship.

4 **"Our confidence is flying now," observed Terry, echoing the self-belief flooding through Ranieri's players**. The view from the vanquished[4] dressing room was inevitably one of defiance. "It is a great result for them but it is too early to say," commented Sir Alex Ferguson on whether this was a decisive moment for Chelsea in the title race. "When you are top in April, you will feel the pressure then."

5 **Ferguson was unimpressed with the decision by Alan Wiley, a wholly correct one, to award the first-half penalty that settled this decent but unspectacular game**. Normally such a fine interceptor of the ball, Roy Keane misjudged his challenge on Cole and clearly brought down Chelsea's spinning-top of a No 10. "The players are disappointed with the penalty," Ferguson said. "He was going away from goal."

6 **Irrelevant**. Cole was caught by Keane and the angle simply saved Keane from a red card. Gary Neville and Ryan Giggs led the protests and Tim Howard did the St Vitus' Dance routine on the line, but amid the storm, one man remained calm. Lampard slotted the penalty smoothly to Howard's left before sprinting away and kissing the Chelsea crest on his shirt.

7 **All of his colleagues were imbued[5] with similar commitment to the cause.** The Blues were now really in the mood, raiding forward with real conviction. Mario Melchiot drew a great save from Howard and Cole shot over the bar before the half finished with the excellent Lampard firing wide.

1 **colossus** – giant
2 **interim** – temporary
3 **baulk** – hesitate
4 **vanquished** – defeated
5 **imbued** – inspired

8 **United are not champions by accident and they sought to impose their game on Chelsea.** Keane drove them forward and Giggs tried to slip his markers – but Chelsea's defence stood firm. Cristiano Ronaldo's arrival 19 minutes from time at last gave United a proper right-sided outlet, allowing Giggs to switch to his preferred left. Van Nistelrooy shot wide, Ronaldo had an effort deflected but still Chelsea refused to yield, their determination embodied[6] by Terry throwing himself into a flying block on a van Nistelrooy strike. And so, assisted by the midfield patrolling of Claude Makelele, a famous sixth consecutive clean sheet was assured for Terry and company.

9 **"The defence were excellent and John Terry is improving every day," Bentley, 79, said.** "I talked to him at the training ground last week and I always knew he had great potential. His performance was inspired today. "Bentley and Willemse were moved by the warmth of their reception. "The fans treat us like royalty when we come here," Willemse said, "and none of them could have seen us play. You would have to be 70 to remember us!"

10 But they have never forgotten around here, some of the more mature fans even arriving with battered copies of *Going for Goal*, Bentley's autobiography, for the great man to sign. Only a fool would write off resilient[7] rivals like United and Arsenal but the theme at the Bridge now is 'Going for the Title'.

[6] **embodied** – summed up
[7] **resilient** – tough

Task 4 Annotating

The first two paragraphs of the extract have been annotated to illustrate some of the language features of a recount text. Annotate the next two paragraphs to illustrate a second example of as many of these features as possible.

Using topic sentences to influence the reader

The purpose of topic sentences is to guide the reader through a text. They are also a way of stamping the writer's distinctive voice on a text and highlighting the key ideas so that the reader comes to understand the writer's viewpoint.

Task 5 Annotating

Reread all the topic sentences from the article. Which words and phrases particularly give you a sense of Winter's viewpoint?

Hooking the audience

Opening an article in an interesting way is vital to gaining the reader's interest. Writers use a **hook** (a piece of interesting information) to achieve this.

Task 6 Discussing

Reread the opening two paragraphs on pages 26–27 and decide what hook Winter has used to begin his article. Why do you think he chose to focus on this rather than on the final score? Be prepared to feed back your findings.

Using detail effectively

Winter is precise in his use of language, selecting just the right words and phrases to recreate the images and feelings he wants his audience to experience.

Task 7 Discussing

X TR Reread the extract from the article below and identify which words illustrate Winter's vivid choice of vocabulary. Discuss how these words help the reader picture the scene and note down your ideas. A few examples have been annotated for you.

Alliteration – helps strengthen effect of words

Vivid and appropriate selection of verb

Vividly recreates retired players' sense of joy

Unusual word selected to emphasise that John Terry will become a very significant player

Past glories and present strengths rolled into one at the Bridge yesterday. Bentley and Stan Willemse, the left-back from that 1955 trophy-winning side of Ted Drake's, delighted in the marvellous defensive organisation built around the growing colossus that is John Terry, thrilled to the clever forward moves of Lampard and Joe Cole, a warmed to the work ethic that united all the men in blue.

The future looks brighter than ever. Hours earlier, Chelsea's interim chief executive, Paul Smith, had warned opponents that the club would not baulk "at spending £50 million" on one player if required. The huge resources in Roman Abramovich's vaults and the human resources in Claudio Ranieri's dressing room signal why Chelsea must be feared in the chase for the championship.

"Our confidence is flying now," observed Terry, echoing the self-belief flooding through Ranieri's players. The view from the vanquished dressing room was inevitably one of defiance. "It is a great result for them but it is too early to say," commented Sir Alex Ferguson on whether this was a decisive moment for Chelsea in the title race. "When you are top in April, you will feel the pressure then."

Changing the writer's voice

As you have seen, Winter's use of language influences the reader's image of the game. His words reinforce the view that Chelsea were the rightful winners. If he had wanted to suggest that Chelsea did not deserve to win, he could have written the article using negative sentence signposts and descriptive words. This would leave the reader with a very different impression, as you can see by the way paragraph 3 has been rewritten below.

But does the future look brighter than ever? Hours earlier, Chelsea's interim chief executive, Paul Smith, had arrogantly warned opponents that the club would not baulk "at spending £50 million" on one player if required. The excessive resources in Roman Abramovich's vaults and the human resources in Claudio Ranieri's dressing room signal why Chelsea might be feared by the faint-of-heart in the chase for the championship.

Task 8 Writing

Rewrite paragraph 4 above to continue this negative effect. Underline the changed parts of your rewritten version. Be prepared to read it out.

Text structure and organisation

Getting the structure right

AIMS

- Evaluate a writer's ability to shape ideas rapidly into cohesive paragraphs.
- Consider how a writer has used different ways of opening, developing, linking and completing paragraphs.
- Use note-making skills to sum up structure of an article.

In this section you will analyse a typical news article planning frame, and investigate how Henry Winter's article is skilfully constructed so that the text is coherent and cohesive in a varied and interesting way.

Structuring a newspaper article

A typical newspaper article fits the following planning frame. It differs from the recount timeline because its order is based on the news impact of events rather than their chronological order.

News article planning frame

Introduction (could be two paragraphs): News hook[1] to grab reader's interest including vital Who? What? Where? Why? When? and How? questions.

↓

Main paragraph(s): Important news relating to main topic (include a quote about how a key character feels).

↓

Later paragraph/s: Less important news that relates to topic (may include quotes).

↓

Final para: should act as a pointer[2] or it may be an idea or image from earlier in the article.

[1] **news hook** – key news point in article to grab the reader's interest

[2] **pointer** – an ending that suggests how the story may develop

Task 9 **Discussing**

Annotate Henry Winter's article to show how it reflects all four stages of the planning frame above. Be prepared to present your conclusions.

TR X

Varying how you make writing coherent and cohesive

Uniform, repetitive writing tends to be dull and will lose the reader's interest. The more you can vary the structure of paragraphs with topic sentences, sentence signposts and connectives that hold them together, the more interesting the writing will be.

Part of the extract on page 32 has been annotated to show how Winter has achieved coherence[1] and cohesion[2] in a varied way.

[1] **coherence** – how the whole text is organised

[2] **cohesion** – how the individual sections of the text are organised

(See page 92 for a fuller explanation of these terms.)

Task 10 Annotating

Annotate the rest of the extract to show how this coherence and cohesion continues to be varied. Be prepared to present your conclusions.

Complex topic sentence introduces next section of article

Comment interrupts topic sentence to emphasise writer's viewpoint

Ferguson was unimpressed with the decision by Alan Wiley, a wholly correct one, to award the first-half penalty that settled this decent but unspectacular game. Normally such a fine interceptor of the ball, Roy Keane misjudged his challenge on Cole and clearly brought down Chelsea's spinning-top of a No 10. "The players are disappointed with the penalty," Ferguson said. "He was going away from goal."

Evidence supporting point introduced by sentence signpost assuring reader that Keane's error was out of character

Ferguson's comment closes paragraph

Irrelevant. Cole was caught by Keane and the angle simply saved Keane from a red card. Gary Neville and Ryan Giggs led the protests and Tim Howard did the St Vitus' Dance routine on the line, but amid the storm, one man remained calm. Lampard slotted the penalty smoothly to Howard's left before sprinting away and kissing the Chelsea crest on his shirt.

Task 11 Planning practice

Below is some information about Portsmouth's 2–1 victory over Blackpool in early 2004. Your task is to use the news article planning frame to combine all the information into a plan for three punchy paragraphs that support Portsmouth's French defender, Sebastien Schemmel.

Decide which group of information best suits which paragraph. Then work out the key topic sentences that will introduce each paragraph.

P's home ground is known as Fratton Park and the manager is Harry Redknapp

Redknapp refused S permission to train part-time so he could care for his sick mother-in-law in France

S blamed for Chelsea's first goal in a 3–0 defeat at Chelsea's ground, Stamford Bridge, the previous week

S given a second chance in New Year – scored 35th minute goal

S scored his first goal for P who are near bottom of Premiership

Schemmel transferred from West Ham to Portsmouth (sometimes known as Pompey) in August 2003

Has had troubles on and off the pitch in Nov and Dec 2003

Sentence structure and punctuation

Making the sentences work

AIMS

- Integrate reference and quotation effectively into text.
- Investigate how the ability to vary past tense forms and use modal verbs effectively can add to the quality of writing.

In this section you will learn more about different tenses and integrating quotation into a text, and then write a short article that practises these skills.

Manipulating tenses effectively

Writing usually has a dominant tense (one that appears more than any other). For example, a recount text is largely written in the past tense, but more sophisticated recount writing often includes a wide range of tenses for a variety of purposes.

GRAMMAR

Verbs are the only words that alter their form to indicate when the action takes place. The **tense** of verbs can be used to suggest a wide range of times in subtle ways:

He warned (*past*)
He warns (*simple present*)
He is warning (*present continuous*)
He will warn (*future*)
He has warned (*the present perfect*)
He had warned (*the past perfect*)
He will have warned (*the future perfect*)

Modal verbs help the writer modify the meaning of verbs. They range from possibility ('you could warn') to necessity ('you must warn').

'Can', 'could', 'may', 'might', 'shall', 'should', 'ought', 'must', 'need' and 'dare' are all modal verbs.

Paragraph 3 from the article on page 27 has been annotated to show the range of tenses Winter has used and the reason for the tense chosen.

Simple present tense because writer is generalising

Past perfect to indicate that this event had happened before the match had begun

The future looks brighter than ever. Hours earlier, Chelsea's interim chief executive, Paul Smith, had warned opponents that the club would not baulk "at spending £50 million" on one player if required. The huge resources in Roman Abramovich's vaults and the human resources in Claudio Ranieri's dressing room signal why Chelsea must be feared in the chase for the championship.

Indicating future possibility

Modal verb indicating necessity

Task 12 Analysing

Annotate the verbs in paragraph 4 to explain why each type and tense of verb has been chosen.

Integrating quotation and references

Newspaper articles usually contain at least one quotation to add human interest and reality. Integrating quotations and references[1] seamlessly into a text is part of the writer's skill. Henry Winter has introduced former Chelsea players, Bentley and Willemse, at the beginning of the article so he can now refer to them without having to explain who they are. His closing paragraphs begin with a quotation from Bentley on the game.

[1] **references** – a book or passage that is referred to

Task 13 Annotating

Annotate paragraphs 9 and 10 on page 28 to answer these questions:

- Why do you think Winter chose to return to Bentley and Willemse to close the article?
- How has Winter integrated quotations into the paragraphs?
- What does each quotation or reference add in terms of human interest or reality?

The annotations have been begun for you.
Be prepared to present your ideas.

Ending (pointer) echoes beginning (hook) – began with reference to Bentley and Willemse, heroes of Chelsea's past glories

Includes fact that old heroes are welcome as means of introducing pointer he has planned for closing paragraph

"The defence were excellent and John Terry is improving every day," Bentley, 79, said. "I talked to him at the training ground last week and I always knew he had great potential. His performance was inspired today." Bentley and Willemse were moved by the warmth of their reception. "The fans treat us like royalty when we come here," Willemse said, "and none of them could have seen us play. You would have to be 70 to remember us!"

But they have never forgotten around here, some of the more mature fans even arriving with battered copies of *Going for Goal*, Bentley's autobiography, for the great man to sign. Only a fool would write off resilient rivals like United and Arsenal but the theme at the Bridge now is 'Going for the Title'.

Punctuating quotations

Not only do the quotations need to flow naturally within the text, but they must be properly punctuated. Remind yourself of how to punctuate quotations by looking at the extract in Task 13. (See also pages 123–124 for explanations of how to include reported speech, or to quote from other texts.)

Task 14 Discussing

Decide on the key advice you would give to anyone about how to punctuate quotations. Be prepared to present your ideas.

The writing challenge

Integrating a range of information and quotation into a lively coherent text is a significant skill.

Task 15 Writing

You have already planned how to structure the paragraphs about Schemmel's New Year goal for Portsmouth (see Task 11, page 32). Use that planning to help you write three lively, well-expressed paragraphs that are supportive of the French defender. Integrate all the information on page 32 and the following quotations.

- Schemmel: This was a good start for us for 2004. I don't know how the ball went in. It's my first goal for the club. I'm very happy for the team and for my manager and I'm hoping this is a new start for the both of us.
- Redknapp: I was pleased for Sebastien. We asked him to get forward more and he was there to get on the end of a great cross from Matt Taylor.

Composing a news article

AIMS

- Sustain a coherent writer's voice in Standard English with the formality and grammatical forms suited to reader and purpose.
- Make telling use of descriptive detail and integrate reference and quotation effectively.
- Review your ability to write an effective article, recognising strengths and identifying skills for further development.

Write a lively magazine news article with a clear writer's voice.

1 Audience and purpose

You are on the editorial committee of your school magazine. Your job is to write the lead news article. The audience will be parents and students.

Discuss what effect the audience and purpose will have on the style of this article. Consider these questions:

- What writer's voice should you adopt – informal, formal and friendly or very formal?
- How will you hook your readers' interest?

Be prepared to feed back your ideas.

2 Brainstorming the focus

Brainstorm the issues that might become the focus of this article, e.g. the sporting, musical or other success of a present or past student; a report of a school performance or match; or an issue that is causing concern, e.g. the need to provide healthier, less fattening school meals or the state of the buildings.

Decide on the topic that you think would make the best news article. Be prepared to present your ideas.

3 Establishing the content

TR

Once the group has agreed on its focus, decide what information needs to be included in the article. Use the spider diagram below to help you gather the raw information suited to your article. Change any headings, if necessary.

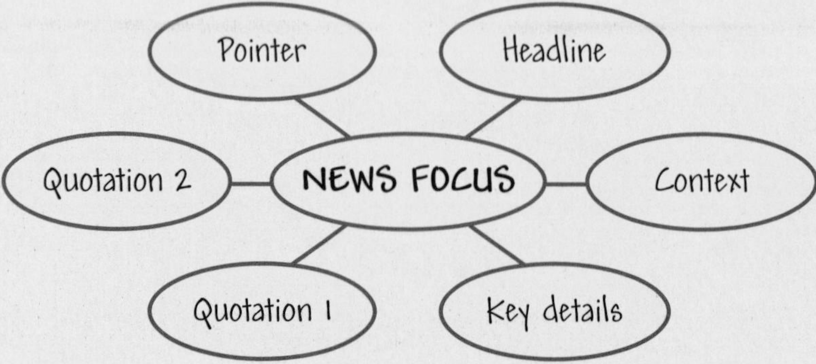

Planning your structure

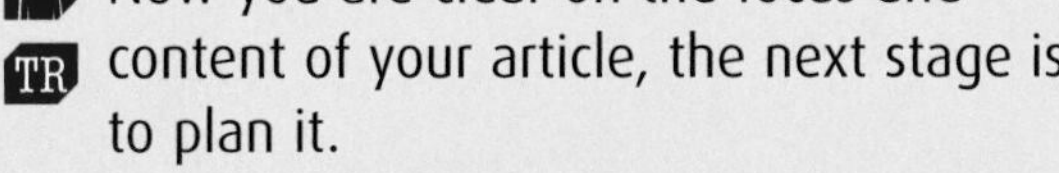

Now you are clear on the focus and content of your article, the next stage is to plan it.

Organise the information you have gathered above into a news article planning frame, like the one below. Decide on the topic sentences that will guide the reader through the key events and points. Jot these down on your plan. Decide on the writer's voice you will use in the article.

Top tip

You will probably have to adjust your plan when you start writing the paragraphs.

News article planning frame

Planning frame	Plan	Topic sentence
Introduction (up to two paragraphs): news hook to grab reader's interest answering vital Who? What? Where? Why? When? and How? questions		
Main paragraph(s): important news relating to main topic (include a quote about how a key character feels)		
Later paragraph/s: less important news that relates to topic (may include quotes)		
Final paragraph: should act as a pointer or it may be an idea or image from earlier in the article		

Discussing what you are going to write

Now you have established the writer's voice, attempt to present a coherent spoken version of the article, in role, using the topic sentences to get you going in the right direction. Help each other to develop the appropriate style. Practise until you can present a reasonable spoken version of your article.

Before you start writing remember to:

- Picture your audience
- Remember your purpose
- Establish writer's voice by rehearsing it in your head
- Stay in role and guide your reader

Composing your piece

 Now you are ready to write.

Points to remember

- Spin the news hook to make it as interesting as possible (see page 29).
- Remember to include who, what, where, why, how and when questions in the first one or two paragraphs (see page 31).
- Sustain your chosen writer's voice throughout guiding the reader through the text (see pages 21 and 28).
- Make your sentences interesting. Think about how to spin clauses to make your complex sentences interesting. Use short simple sentences to add variety and focus (see pages 18–19).
- Select just the right words and phrases and descriptive detail to engage the audience (see page 29).
- Vary how you make your article coherent and cohesive (see pages 31–32).
- Manipulate the tenses effectively (see page 33).
- Integrate quotations into your article (see pages 34–35).
- End with a pointer suggesting how the story may develop (see page 31).

You may want to use some of the sentence signposts and connectives below to help you.

Sentence signposts and connectives

- The issue that has got everyone talking
- Who would have thought that X's
- X School is proud to announce that
- When X decided to
- "I still can't believe my luck...
- Things went even better after
- We'll be keeping an eye on
- In only a few days

Peer comment

Read your draft through and check that you have maintained a clear consistent writer's voice throughout. Swap your draft with your partner's. Discuss and jot down up to three suggestions on the draft of how to improve particular sections. Decide together what really works well and highlight this on your draft. Redraft the selected sections of the draft using the comments to guide you.

Pulling it all together

Listen to some of the articles written by members of your class. With a partner, decide on the key features that make these articles effective. Be prepared to present your ideas. Set yourself three targets for the next time you write an article.

C The Art of Information Writing

Revisiting how information text works

AIMS

- Analyse and exploit the stylistic conventions of information text.
- Compare the presentation of ideas in related information texts.
- Consider the difference layout makes to how readers approach text.

In this section you will build on your existing knowledge of how an information text works, thinking about how its style and form varies to suit different audiences and purposes.

Different kinds of information text

Information text tells us about the key characteristics of places, people, concepts, animals or things. It comes in a wide variety of shapes and forms, depending on audience and purpose, ranging from **dictionaries**, **encyclopaedias** and **handbooks** to **telephone directories** and **leaflets** in the doctor's surgery.

It can also be included in a wide range of media from **books** and **leaflets** to **websites**, **CDs**, **text messages** and **Teletext**.

It can be written in technical language, Standard English, very simple English or note form.

Task 1 **Analysing**

TR

Read the three information texts on sharks on pages 39–40 and match each text with its audience. Choose from:

- children
- adults
- specialists.

Then match the text to the type of publication it is liable to have come from:

- dictionary
- children's encyclopaedia
- website.

Text 1

shark n. any of various usually ferocious selachian fishes, typically marine with a long body, two dorsal fins, rows of sharp teeth and between five and seven gill slits on each side of the head. (C16 of uncertain origin) – **shark + like** adj.

Annotations:

- **Heading**
- **Abbreviation**
- **Generalisation** – summing up key points
- **Technical language**
- **Detail** – illustrating typical features
- **Logical connective** – joining points
- **Information presented in logical order**
- **Note form** – entry not written in sentences; no verbs
- **Writer's voice** – formal, impersonal language throughout including third person

Text 2

WHITE DEATH

A great white shark's colouring makes it difficult to see in the water, so it is able to sneak up on its victims. When seen from below, this shark's white undersides blend in with a bright sky's reflection at the water's surface. This magnificent shark is sometimes called 'white pointer', referring to its pointed snout which makes it more streamlined. Great whites often have scratches and scars on their snouts, which may be the result of their prey fighting back. They may also be bitten by larger members of their own kind, which move in to take bait away from them.

Text 3

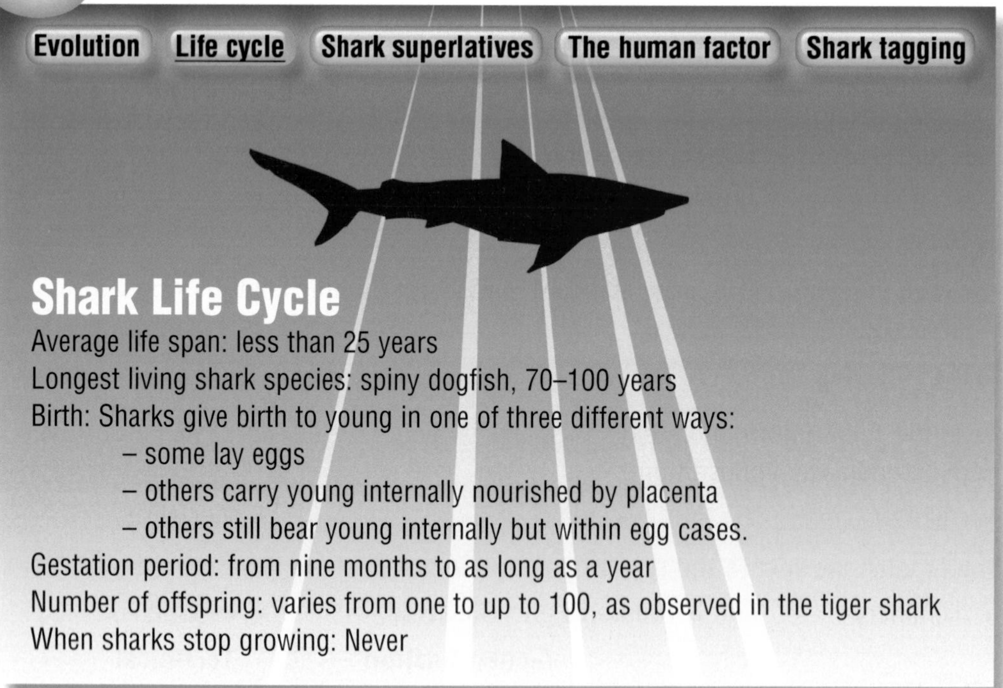

Evolution | Life cycle | Shark superlatives | The human factor | Shark tagging

Shark Life Cycle

Average life span: less than 25 years
Longest living shark species: spiny dogfish, 70–100 years
Birth: Sharks give birth to young in one of three different ways:

- some lay eggs
- others carry young internally nourished by placenta
- others still bear young internally but within egg cases.

Gestation period: from nine months to as long as a year
Number of offspring: varies from one to up to 100, as observed in the tiger shark
When sharks stop growing: Never

Typical features

Now look at how the first extract on page 39 has been annotated to bring out the key structural and language features of information text, as well as some features related to this particular type of information.

Task 2

Discussing and recording

Using the annotations on page 39 to help you, establish the key structural and stylistic similarities and differences between the three texts. Complete the table below, with evidence to back up your points. Be prepared to feed back your findings.

Features	Text 1	Text 2	Text 3
Writer's voice			
Is it first or third person?	Third person – 'fishes'		
Is it formal and distanced?	Yes – 'any of various...'		
Structure			
Is it in logical order?	Yes – moves from definition to features to origin		
Does it include logical connectives?	Yes – 'typically'		
Does it use headings?	Yes – 'shark'		
Language features			
Does it include any generalisations?	Yes – 'any of various usually ferocious selachian fishes'		
Is detail used to illustrate typical features?	Yes – 'long body, two dorsal fins...'		
Is it in the present tense?	Assumed as in note form – entry not written in sentences as has no verbs		
Does it include technical language?	Yes – 'selachian'		
Are there any other key language features?	Abbreviations, e.g. 'n.' for 'noun'		

Composition and effect

Learning from example

AIMS

- Explore how non-fiction texts can convey information from a range of sources in amusing or entertaining ways making telling use of descriptive detail.
- Analyse how an author's standpoint can affect meaning in a non-literary text and discuss the use made of rhetorical devices recognising layers of meaning in the writer's choice of words.
- Write sustained Standard English with the formality, vocabulary and grammar suited to reader and purpose, integrating speech, reference and quotation effectively.

In this section you will analyse how travel writer Bill Bryson has integrated information into his writing in an entertaining way, through the use of authorial comment (writer's viewpoint).

Mixing information with autobiography

Bill Bryson's *A Walk in the Woods* tells the story of his attempt to walk the 2,100-mile Appalachian Trail in America. Since this is autobiographical writing, much of the text recounts his experiences, but he also provides the reader with information about the trail and the plants, trees and animals that live there.

The extract on pages 42–44 gives his personal thoughts while reading an information text on bear attacks just before he set out on the trail.

Task 3 Reading and analysing

Read the extract and discuss what you learn about bears in this passage, and what you learn about Bill Bryson's response to this information.

TR The topic sentences in the first two paragraphs have been highlighted for you. Identify the topic sentences in the following four paragraphs. Then consider why there isn't a topic sentence in the final paragraph. Be prepared to share your conclusions.

Writer's voice – introduces Herrero's book and circumstances in which read

Bear Attacks

Now imagine reading a non-fiction book packed with stories of bear attacks – true tales soberly related – just before setting off alone on a camping trip of your own into the North American wilderness. The book to which I refer is *Bear Attacks: Their Causes and Avoidance* by a Canadian academic named Stephen Herrero…

Straightforward information about book

Straightforward information about bears, probably taken from book

Colourful additions – make information more lively

Author's comment – keeps reader aware of his perspective (viewpoint)

Straightforward information about bears, probably taken from book

Now it is important to establish right away that the possibility of a serious bear attack on the Appalachian Trail is remote. To begin with, the really terrifying American bear, the grizzly – *Ursus horribilis* as it is so vividly and correctly labelled – doesn't range east of the Mississippi, which is good news because grizzlies are large, powerful and ferociously bad-tempered. When Lewis and Clark went into the wilderness, they found that nothing unnerved the native Indians more than the grizzly, and not surprisingly since you could riddle a grizzly with arrows – positively porcupine it – and it would still keep coming. Even Lewis and Clerk with their big guns were astounded and unsettled by the ability of the grizzly to absorb volleys of lead with barely a wobble…

If I were to be pawed and chewed – and this seemed to me entirely possible, the more I read – it would be by a black bear, *Ursus americanus*. There are at least 500,000 black bears in North America, possibly as many as 700,000. They are notably common in the hills along the Appalachian Trail (indeed, they often *use* the trail, for convenience), and their numbers are growing. Grizzlies, by contrast, number no more than 35,000 in the whole of North America, and just 1,000 in the mainland United States principally in and around Yellowstone National Park. Of the two species, black bears are generally smaller (though this is a decidedly relative condition; a black bear can still weigh up to 650 pounds) and unquestionably more retiring.

Black bears rarely attack. But here's the thing. Sometimes they do. All bears are agile, cunning and immensely strong, and they are always hungry. If they want to kill you and eat you, they can, and pretty much whenever they want. That doesn't happen often, but – and here is the absolutely salient point – once would be enough. Herrero is at pains to stress that black bear attacks are infrequent, relative to their numbers. In the eight decades to 1980 he found just twenty-three confirmed black bear killings of humans (about half the number of killings by grizzlies), and most of these were out west or in Canada. In New Hampshire there has not been an unprovoked fatal attack on a human by a bear since 1794. In Vermont, there has never been one.

I wanted very much to be calmed by these assurances but could never quite manage the necessary leap of faith. After noting that just 500 people were attacked and hurt by black bears between 1960 and 1980 – and twenty-five attacks a year from a resident population of at least half a million bears – Herrero adds that most of these injuries were not severe. 'The typical black bear-inflicted injury,' he writes blandly, 'is minor and usually involves only a few scratches and light bites.'

> Pardon me, but what exactly is a light bite? Are we talking a playful wrestle and gummy nips? I think not. And is 500 certified attacks really such a modest number, considering how many people go into the North American woods? And how foolish must one be to be reassured by the information that no bear has killed a human in Vermont or New Hampshire in 200 years? That's not because the bears have signed a treaty, you know. There's nothing to say they won't start a modest rampage tomorrow.

Key features of information text

The grid you completed in Task 2 (page 41) provides you with the key features of information text.

Task 4 Annotating

Use the Task 2 grid to help you annotate the opening two paragraphs of the extract to illustrate these features.

Integrating information and comments

Task 5 Analysing

Skim read the extract to identify which parts are straightforward information about bears, probably based on Stephen Herrero's book, and which are Bill Bryson's comments on that information. The first three paragraphs have been annotated to show this. What is the balance between the information and the comment? Be prepared to present your findings.

As you've discovered, the writer moves in and out of providing information about bears by commenting on it in an entertaining manner. This has established two levels of formality:

- a more formal and serious tone for the information from the academic, Stephen Herrero
- a more informal and entertaining tone for Bryson's comments.

Making telling use of descriptive detail

Information text often includes powerful description to make the topic come alive for the reader. This technique is often used in information texts like children's encyclopaedias or in travel writing like Bill Bryson's.

Task 6 Annotating

Identify the powerful words and phrases that Bill Bryson has used to comment on the academic's information in the following passage. Explain in your annotations what makes each word/phrase effective in entertaining or interesting the reader. A few examples have been completed for you.

Now imagine reading a non-fiction book packed with stories of bear attacks – true tales soberly related – just before setting off alone on a camping trip of your own into the North American wilderness. The book to which I refer is *Bear Attacks: Their Causes and Avoidance* by a Canadian academic named Stephen Herrero...

Now it is important to establish right away that the possibility of a serious bear attack on the Appalachian Trail is remote. To begin with, the really terrifying American, the grizzly – *Ursus horribilis* as it is so vividly and correctly labelled – doesn't range east of the Mississippi, which is good news because grizzlies are large, powerful and ferociously bad-tempered. When Lewis and Clark went into the wilderness, they found that nothing unnerved the native Indians more than the grizzly, and not surprisingly since you could riddle a grizzly with arrows – positively porcupine it – and it would still keep coming. Even Lewis and Clerk with their big guns were astounded and unsettled by the ability of the grizzly to absorb volleys of lead with barely a wobble...

Annotations:
- "soberly related": Suggests Herrero is a bit dull and doesn't have a sense of humour
- "as it is so vividly and correctly labelled": Makes you think about bear's name
- "good news because grizzlies are large, powerful and ferociously bad-tempered": Light-hearted tone is entertaining – makes you think about author's growing fears

Sustaining the writer's voice

Throughout the extract the reader can hear both the serious tone and style of the academic and Bill Bryson's entertaining tone that often includes the rhetoric of ridicule (language that makes Herrero's ideas sound a bit ridiculous).

Task 7

Below is a range of sentence signposts from the extract. Some signal ridicule (make fun of); others are more balanced. Decide which ones should go under each heading.

- It is worth considering
- This raises the question
- Pardon me
- Surely no one could
- Another interesting point
- It is perhaps worth asking
- Are we talking
- Some people have questioned
- Hold on a minute
- Am I hearing clearly
- This adds further detail
- The main point is that
- Hands up anyone who
- You won't be killed in the rush to

Task 8

Reread the final paragraph of the extract aloud in the tone you think the author intended. Annotate the extract to show how the author has used one example of the following rhetorical techniques to make the most of the humour of the passage. The first technique has been annotated for you. See page 74 for a more detailed list of rhetorical techniques.

- Using language to play down the situation to underline its seriousness
- Sentence signposts signalling ridicule
- Rhetorical questions
- Mocking suggestions
- Exaggeration
- Listing points to build up a case

Mismatch of language ('modest' and 'rampage') plays down image, making it even funnier

Pardon me, but what exactly is a light bite? Are we talking a playful wrestle and gummy nips? I think not. And is 500 certified attacks really such a modest number, considering how many people go into the North American woods? And how foolish must one be to be reassured by the information that no bear has killed a human in Vermont or New Hampshire in 200 years? That's not because the bears have signed a treaty, you know. There's nothing to say they won't start a modest rampage tomorrow.

Using the rhetoric of ridicule

Imagine this scenario:

Lee, whose favourite lessons are Art and Drama, is sitting in a Year 9 assembly listening to Mr Jones (the Head of Year) explain about the options that are available to choose for their GCSEs in Years 10 and 11. She has just realised that Art and Drama only appear in option 1 – thus she will not be able to take both subjects. To make matters even worse, Mr Jones explains that option 3 includes the following subjects: PE, Music, History, Geography, IT, French. Lee loathes PE, is bored by History and Geography, is useless at French and IT and is not at all musical.

Task 9 **Writing**

Rewrite the information above in three paragraphs so that the reader can hear both the serious tone of the Head of Year and Lee's sense of disbelief and ridicule. Be prepared to present your version in the appropriate tones. You may want to begin with the following paragraph:

Lee was listening hard now. So far Art and Drama had only appeared in option 1. All her hopes of doing both subjects depended on Drama ...

Text structure and organisation

Getting the structure right

AIMS

- Analyse how a writer has shaped ideas into cohesive paragraphs using a variety of devices such as topic sentences, sentence signposts, connectives and repetition of word or sentence structure to make links within and between paragraphs.
- Consider why text skeletons are a good way to sum up the key content of a passage.

In this section you will shape information into cohesive paragraphs.

Organising ideas coherently

Information skeletons are an excellent way of seeing the sections (categories) that the information has been divided into and how the writer has structured these sections.

Below, the key points of *Bear Attacks* are summed up in an information text skeleton. The notes in the circles are the focus of each section based on the topic sentences (underlined).

BEAR ATTACKS
1. Context: reading book about bear attacks before camping trip in North America
'Bear Attack' by Stephen Herrero
2. Chances of serious attack are remote
Most terrifying bear – grizzly – not found on Appalachian Trail
Grizzlies big and ferociously bad-tempered, and keep on attacking despite arrows/bullets
3. If attacked would be by a black bear
Common on AT, smaller than grizzlies – but can still weigh 650 pounds, more retiring
4. Black bears rarely attack but sometimes do
Agile, strong and always hungry – could kill and eat you and once is enough
5. Herrero stresses attacks rare
In 80 years only 23 confirmed killings of humans and most out west or Canada
6. Not calmed by these assurances
Herrero points out only 25 attacks a year and most injuries not severe – 'light bites'
7. What is a light bite?
Not many people in woods so not so low a number – bears haven't signed peace treaty

Task 10 Discussing

Discuss the following questions and be prepared to feed back your answers:

- Why is it important to begin with a paragraph giving the context for the information?
- Why do you think Bryson includes information about grizzly bears before the information about black bears?
- Why do you think he covers key information about black bears before focusing on black bear attacks?
- What piece of information triggers Bryson's strongest sense of ridicule?
- Would the last paragraph of pure ridicule have been more effective earlier on?

Making a text coherent[1] and cohesive[2]

Bryson confidently guides the reader through the extract using topic sentences, sentence signposts, connectives, repetition of word or sentence structure, and his comments. Look at the annotations below that illustrate all of these features.

[1] **coherent** – well organised across the whole text
[2] **cohesive** – with individual paragraphs that are linked and well organised

Task 11 Annotating

Complete the annotations of the following paragraphs to provide one more example of each of the ways Bryson has made his text coherent and cohesive.

Annotations: Topic sentence; Sentence signpost; Repetition of key words; Authorial comment; Beginning clause with 'they'; Connectives

If I were to be pawed and chewed – and this seemed to me entirely possible, the more I read – it would be by a black bear, *Ursus americanus*. There are at least 500,000 black bears in North America, possibly as many as 700,000. They are notably common in the hills along the Appalachian Trail (indeed, they often *use* the trail, for convenience), and their numbers are growing. Grizzlies, by contrast, number no more than 35,000 in the whole of North America, and just 1,000 in the mainland United States principally in and around Yellowstone National Park. Of the two species, black bears are generally smaller (though this is a decidedly relative condition; a black bear can still weigh up to 650 pounds) and unquestionably more retiring.

Black bears rarely attack. But here's the thing. Sometimes they do. All bears are agile, cunning and immensely strong, and they are always hungry. If they want to kill you and eat you, they can, and pretty much whenever they want. That doesn't happen often, but – and here is the absolutely salient point – once would be enough.

Practising cohesion

Look at the final paragraph of *Bear Attacks* on page 44. Here is the key information from the next paragraph laid out in logical order:

- **Topic:** What should you do if attacked by a black bear?
- **What Herrero suggests:** make a lot of noise, e.g. bang pots and pans together, also throw sticks and rocks and, finally, run at the bear. Note that these tactics could provoke the bear.

Task 12 Writing

Discuss what comments a walker might make to these suggestions. Jot down your ideas.

Use the key information and your comments to create a coherent and cohesive paragraph using a topic sentence, sentence signposts, connectives and repetition of sentence structure. Your paragraph should have a similar tone and voice to the rest of the passage.

You may want to begin like this:
And what advice does Mr Herrero have to offer us if we're atttacked by a black bear?

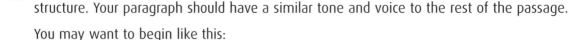

Sentence structure and punctuation

Making the sentences work

AIMS

- Use the full range of punctuation to clarify and emphasise meaning for a reader.
- Review and develop the meaning, clarity, organisation and impact of complex sentences in own writing.

In this section you will consider different ways of structuring sentences and practise punctuating complex sentences to separate off additional information.

Spinning your sentences

Effective writers can vary the structure of their sentences to suit the purpose of their writing. 'Spinning' complex sentences so that the position of subordinate clauses is varied helps keep writing interesting. (See the grammar panel on the range of sentence structures and subordinate clauses, page 18.)

For example, look at these differently-ordered versions of one sentence from the *Bear Attack*s extract.

1. Now imagine reading a non-fiction book packed with stories of bear attacks – true tales soberly related – just before setting off alone on a camping trip of your own into the North American wilderness.
2. Now imagine reading a non-fiction book – true tales soberly related – packed with stories of bear attacks just before setting off alone on a camping trip of your own into the North American wilderness.
3. Just before setting off alone on a camping trip of your own into the North American wilderness, imagine reading a non-fiction book – true tales soberly related – packed with stories of bear attacks.

Task 13

Writing

Respin the sentence below so that the clauses are in a different order but the meaning remains the same.

> 'The typical black bear-inflicted injury,' he writes blandly, 'is minor and usually involves only a few scratches and light bites.'

Check that you have punctuated your sentences correctly.

Separating off additional information

GRAMMAR

There are three ways of separating off additional information inserted into the middle of sentences.

- You can use two commas, e.g. 'The bear, on seeing the man, walked slowly towards him.'
- Or two dashes, e.g. 'The bear – on seeing the man – walked slowly towards him.'
- Or two brackets, e.g. The bear (on seeing the man) walked slowly towards him.

If a sentence already contains commas, e.g. 'The very hungry, tired, old bear – on seeing the man – walked slowly towards him', then dashes or brackets are often selected to make the sentence easier to follow.

Task 14 Annotating

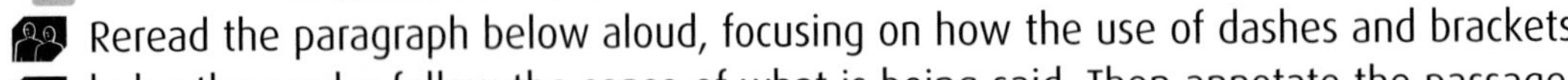

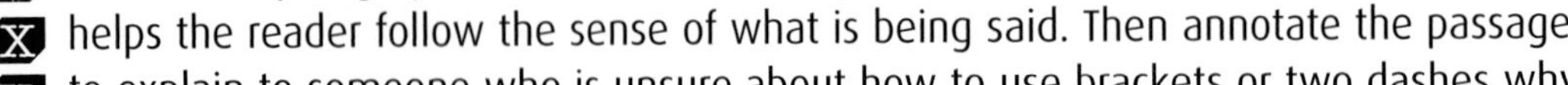

Reread the paragraph below aloud, focusing on how the use of dashes and brackets helps the reader follow the sense of what is being said. Then annotate the passage to explain to someone who is unsure about how to use brackets or two dashes why the writer has selected the punctuation. Be prepared to present your findings.

> If I were to be pawed and chewed – and this seemed to me entirely possible, the more I read – it would be by a black bear, *Ursus americanus*. There are at least 500,000 black bears in North America, possibly as many as 700,000. They are notably common in the hills along the Appalachian Trail (indeed, they often *use* the trail, for convenience), and their numbers are growing. Grizzlies, by contrast, number no more than 35,000 in the whole of North America, and just 1,000 in the mainland United States principally in and around Yellowstone National Park. Of the two species, black bears are generally smaller (though this is a decidedly relative condition; a black bear can still weigh up to 650 pounds) and unquestionably more retiring.

The rewriting challenge

As shown on page 49, sentences can be rewritten in a wide range of ways depending on the effect the writer wants to achieve.

Task 15 Writing

Try rewriting the paragraph above, using the same information and tone and the same number of sentences, but altering the structure and order of each sentence. This will involve altering some of the words used and punctuating your sentences appropriately to bring out their meaning.

You may want to begin like this:

> It seemed entirely possible to me, the more I read, that if I were to be pawed and chewed, it would be by a black bear – *Ursus americanus*. Possibly as many as 700,000 black bears lived in North America, there being at the very least 500,000 of them.

Composing your own information text

AIMS

- Integrate diverse information into a coherent and comprehensive account making telling use of descriptive detail.
- Explore how non-fiction texts can convey information in amusing or entertaining ways by using a sustained narrative voice to achieve a particular effect.
- Write a well-structured information text.

Write an entertaining and informative account of the range of wildlife in the Smoky Mountains.

Audience and purpose

Your account will introduce the range of wildlife and discuss how tourism is changing the bears' lives in the Smoky Mountains. Your audience is young people/adults who enjoy travel writing.

Discuss the effect the audience and purpose of this account will have on its style. In particular consider:

- how you will put across the key information as well as making the piece entertaining
- what difference purpose and audience will make to the tone and style and vocabulary of the piece.

2 Sorting the content

TR Below is the key information to include in your account and the four sections (categories) that it will fit into. Sort the information under the four headings.

Key information

- Around nine million people visit Smoky Mountains a year – many to picnic
- Bears associate people with food
- Sometimes people try to stroke the bears or feed them from their hands
- Smoky Mountains, North America, home to 67 varieties of mammal, 200 types of bird and 80 of reptile – all larger numbers than found in comparable-sized areas almost anywhere else in temperate world
- About a dozen people a year are injured by bears in Smoky Mountains
- Bears don't seem to mind being photographed
- Smoky Mountains most famous for bears – estimated 400–600
- The bears have lost their fear of people
- People like taking pictures of bears
- One woman smeared honey on toddler's fingers for bear to lick off for video – bear ate hand

Section headings

Why bears have lost fear of people

Animal and plant life of Smoky Mountains

Examples of stupid human behaviour around bears

Information about bears – for which the Smokies are famous

3 Planning the content

Using your sorted list, plan the points in an information skeleton, like the one begun below. Arrange the information in the four sections, using memory joggers to organise the detailed information appropriately. If a section has more than one memory jogger, put them in the most logical order.

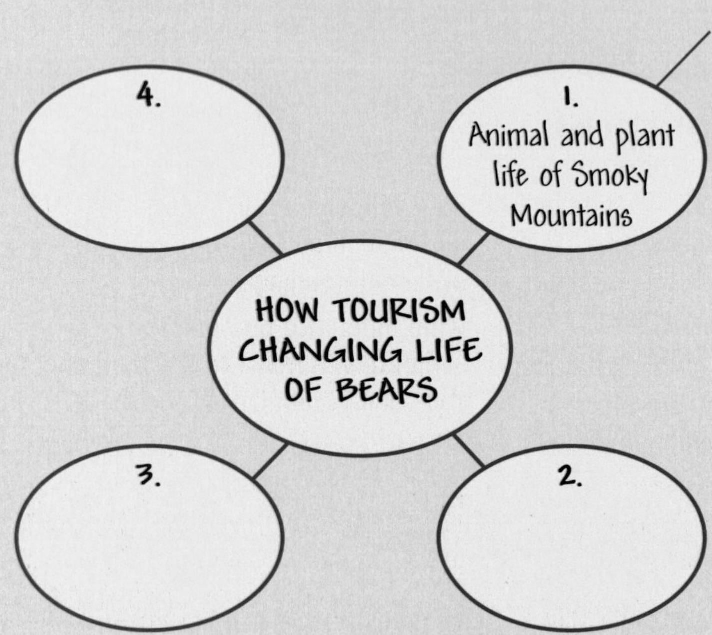

The Smokies are the home of ...
North America, home to 67 varieties of mammal, 200 types of bird and 80 of reptile – all larger numbers than found in comparable-sized areas almost anywhere else in temperate world
4.
1.
Animal and plant life of Smoky Mountains
HOW TOURISM CHANGING LIFE OF BEARS
3.
2.

Then:

- highlight which of the memory joggers you are going to present as straight information and which will lend themselves to entertaining comment. Jot down any phrases you might use to help the reader see the entertaining side of the information.
- decide on the topic sentences/sentence signposts that would be best to introduce each section and add these to your plan. One suggestion has been completed for you.
- decide on the writer's voice you will use in the account (see page 6).

Top tip You will probably have to adjust your plan when you start writing the paragraphs.

4 Discussing what you are going to write

Talk through each other's version with a partner, bringing out the contrasting writer's voices. Help each other to get a sense of the contrast between the information and the comments upon it. Use your topic sentences/sentence signposts to help you.

Composing your piece

Now you are ready to write.

Points to remember

- Bear your audience and purpose in mind while you write (see page 51).
- Integrate the information effectively into the passage (see page 44).
- Comment on the information effectively using the rhetoric of ridicule (see page 46).
- Use powerful effective words to help the reader understand the information or the writer's viewpoint (see pages 44–45).
- Sustain your chosen writer's voice to achieve just the effect you want (see page 45).
- Shape ideas into cohesive paragraphs using a variety of devices such as topic sentences, sentence signposts, connectives repetition of words and sentence structures (see page 48) .
- Vary your sentence structure effectively, remembering to spin some of the sentences to increase variety (see page 49).
- Check that you have punctuated your sentences appropriately (see pages 49–50).

You may want to use some of the sentence signposts and connectives below to help you.

Sentence signposts and connectives

- The Smoky Mountains in North America are
- The trouble is all these picnic baskets mean
- Unsurprisingly
- The all-time award for stupidity
- Where there are bears and people
- The central problem is the bears have
- But what the Smokies are most famous for is
- Unbelievably
- An amazing nine million people visit
- As long as there is food around
- It is a sad reflection on the intelligence of

Peer comment

Swap your draft with your partner's and agree with your partner how to improve your work. Discuss together what really works well and highlight this on your draft. Then decide what needs to be done to improve your account and jot down up to three suggestions on the draft. Redraft the selected sections of the draft using the comments to guide you.

Pulling it all together

Listen to some accounts written by members of your class. Decide on the key features that make these effective. Be prepared to share your ideas.

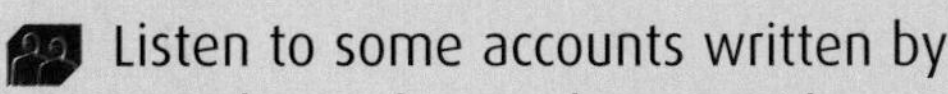

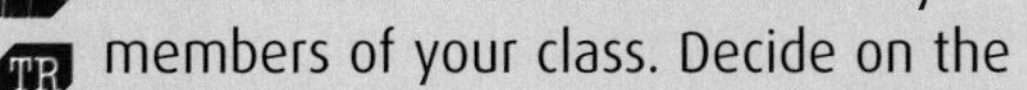

Note down up to three targets for yourself for the next time you write an information text.

D The Art of Explanation Writing

1 Revisiting how explanation text works

AIMS

- Analyse the stylistic conventions of explanation text.
- Compare presentation of ideas in explanation texts.
- Increase the speed and accuracy of note-making skills and use notes for re-presenting information for specific purposes.

In this section you will analyse different explanation texts, decide on the features they share and consider how their structure varies according to the nature of what is being explained.

Different kinds of explanation

Written explanation comes in different shapes and forms, for example:

- a **technical explanation** in a Science textbook explaining how/why things happen
- a **leaflet** explaining why a station is going to close for a month
- a **doctor's note** explaining why someone needs to have time off work.

Although explanation texts often include a lot of information, they differ from information texts. Information texts focus on telling you *what* things are like; whereas explanation texts focus on explaining *how* or *why* they are as they are.

[1] **causal** – stating or implying a cause (why or how something happens)

[2] **generalisation** – a general statement (e.g. about all cats) rather than about one example (e.g. my cat)

Task 1 Reading and annotating

Read the explanation texts on pages 54–55. The first one has been annotated to show some of the features that make it an explanation text. Annotate the text allocated to your pair in a similar way.

Text 1

What causes thunderstorms

Thunderstorms usually occur when moist air rises. In summer this is often triggered by the ground becoming very warm. The air in contact with the ground warms and begins to rise – this is called convection. As the air rises it cools and condenses to form cloud. The rising air forms a towering cloud which often spreads out at the top to form a shape like a blacksmith's anvil. Strong currents of air develop in the cloud which release electrical charges. This is how lightning occurs. The lightning flash causes a sudden heating of the air which causes thunder… Sound travels at a speed of one kilometre in three seconds so it is possible to work out how far away a storm is.

Formal impersonal language – including the third person passive

Causal[1] language – helps reader understand how one thing leads to another

Sentence signpost – helps reader understand what is being explained

Topic sentence – introduces focus of paragraph and directs reader

Generalisation[2] – helps reader categorise information. Uses present tense

Technical vocabulary explained as it is introduced

Structure – a series of logical steps building up the explanation

Powerful language and imagery – helps reader picture what is being explained

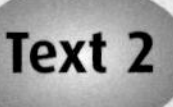

Why Anthony was always late

Anthony found it impossible to keep to deadlines. As a consequence, he was always late for school. The reasons varied from his faulty alarm, to the hours spent by his sister in the bathroom, and the fact that he liked chatting to people on his way to school. In addition, he couldn't get homework done on time. His favourite excuse was that this was because of football training or even because 'The dog ate it'. As a result, he often had several detentions a week.

How polluting are aircraft?

Jetliners may be getting less noisy and more fuel efficient, but they are undoubtedly the fastest growing source of CO_2[1] greenhouse gas emissions.[2] Because they are injected straight into the upper atmosphere, CO_2 emissions from aircraft are three times more damaging in their 'warming' effect than those from cars, homes and industries. And because of the huge growth in passenger air traffic from the UK, such emissions are likely to be more than double by 2030, rising from 5% to 30% of the UK's total contribution to global warming.

[1] **CO_2** – carbon dioxide
[2] **emissions** – discharges

Text 4

How does sand and shingle get onto a beach?

Sand and shingle are washed onto beaches by waves. When a wave breaks, it surges up the beach carrying particles of sediment with it – this is called 'swash'. When the wave draws back toward the sea, the particles are also dragged back towards the sea. This is called backwash.

Waves often approach beaches at an angle. When this happens, swash and backwash cause pebbles to move in a zigzag course along the beach. This is called longshore drift.

Using text skeletons

In order to understand the structure of a text, it can be useful to draw a diagram or 'text skeleton'. Text skeletons represent the bare bones of the text.

Straightforward (linear) explanation text can be summed up by the explanation text skeleton which suggests:

But much explanation is not linear. Many things can contribute to something at the same time, for example the causes of global warming. In which case it is **multicausal** and its skeleton might look like this:

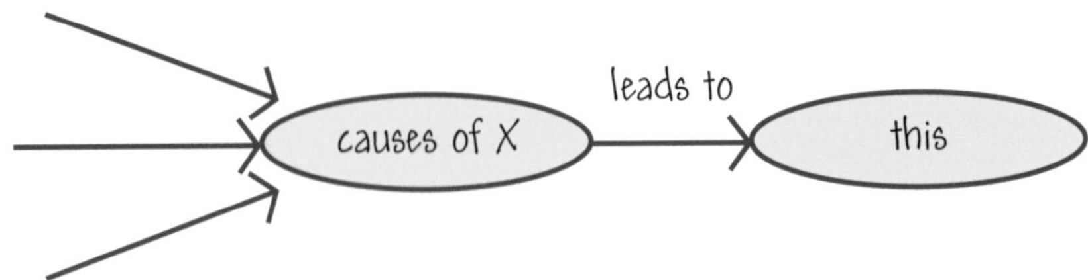

Or the explanation may be **cyclical** like the causes of rain, the food chain or the life cycle of a duck. In which case, the skeleton will represent the shape of the explanation and move round in a circle:

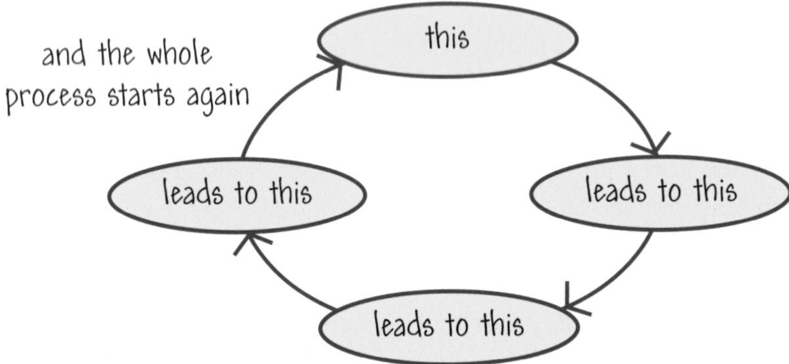

Task 2 Note-taking

Discuss which explanation skeleton would best sum up the text that you have annotated. Then sketch out the skeleton you decide on. It may be different from any of the structures suggested here. Be prepared to present your ideas.

Task 3 Discussing and recording

Each person in the group will have focused on a different text. Discuss what is similar and what is different, and why, in the three texts, comparing the features in the grid like the one below.

	Text 2: Anthony	Text 3: Aircraft	Text 4: Sand
What shape does the explanation take?	Multicausal, leading to particular outcomes		
Do sentence signposts and causal connectives guide the reader through the explanation?			"When a wave breaks..." This shows the reader
Is the writer's voice formal and distant, with some technical terms being used?		No – formal but lively	
Audience			
Purpose			

Are the differences in the explanations linked to audience and purpose or to the nature of what is being described?

Composition and effect

Learning from example

AIMS

- Consider how writers write sustained Standard English with the formality, vocabulary and grammar suited to reader and purpose.
- Consider how explanation writers make telling use of descriptive detail and imaginative and figurative language.
- Analyse how a sustained narrative voice can affect meaning.

In this section you will focus on what helps engage the reader's interest in an explanation text.

Discussing audience and purpose

The following extract is from the natural history text *Life on Earth* by David Attenborough.

Task 4 Reading and discussing

As you read the extract, consider what its purpose is and who the audience would be. Discuss the following question and think about what evidence you have to support your ideas:

- Do you think the book is just aimed at those studying animal life, or at a wider audience?

Causal language – helps reader understand how one thing leads to another

Topic sentence – introduces focus of paragraph which directs reader and helps establish writer's voice

Sentence signpost – helps reader understand what is being explained

Structure – a series of logical steps building up explanation

The Hunters and the Hunted

In order to catch the grazers,[1] the predators on the plain have had to improve greatly their own running techniques. They have not taken to moving on the tips of a reduced number of toes perhaps because they have always needed their toes, armed with claws, as offensive weapons. Their solution is different. They have effectively lengthened their limbs by making their spine extremely flexible. At full stretch, travelling at high speed, their hind and front legs overlap one another beneath the body just like those of a galloping antelope.

The cheetah has a thin elongated body and is said to be the fastest runner on earth, capable of reaching speeds, in bursts, of over 110 kph. But this method is very energy-consuming. Great muscular effort is needed to keep the spine springing back and forth and the cheetah cannot maintain such speeds for more than a minute or so. Either it succeeds in outrunning its prey within a few hundred yards and makes a kill or it has to retire exhausted while the antelope, with their more rigid backs and long lever-legs, continue to gallop off to a safer part of the plains.

[1] **grazers** – grass-eating animals. In this text it covers family of animals, including zebras and antelopes.

Technical vocabulary – explained if necessary

Generalisation – helps reader categorise information. Present tense expresses this

Formal language including the passive

Powerful language and imagery – helps reader picture what is being explained

Lions are nowhere near as fast as the cheetah. Their top speed is about 80 kph. A wildebeest can do about the same and keep it up for much longer. So lions have had to develop more complicated tactics. Sometimes they rely on stealth, creeping towards their victims, their bodies close to the ground, utilising every bit of cover. Sometimes, an individual works by itself. But on occasion, members of a pride will hunt as a team – and they are the only cats that do so. They set off in line abreast.[2] As they approach a group of their prey – antelope, zebra or wildebeest – those lions at the ends of the line move a little quicker so that they encircle the herd. Finally, these break cover, driving the prey towards the lions in the centre of the line. Such tactics often result in several of the team making kills and a hunt has been watched in which seven wildebeest were brought down.

Hyenas are even slower than lions. The best they can manage is about 65 kph and in consequence their hunting methods have to be even more subtle and dependent on teamwork. The females have separate dens where they rear their pups, but the pack as a whole works together and holds and defends a territory. They have a rich vocabulary of sound and gesture with which they communicate among themselves. They growl and whoop, grunt, yelp and whine and at times produce a most terrifying chorus of orgiastic[3] laughs. In gesture, their tails are particularly eloquent.[4] Normally they are carried pointing down. An erect tail indicates aggression; pointed forward over the back, social excitement; held between the legs tight under the belly, fear. By hunting in well-co-ordinated teams, they have become so successful that in parts of the African plains, they make the majority of kills and the lions merely use their bigger size to bully their way on to a carcass, the reverse of the popular conception of the relationship between these two species.

[2] **abreast** – side by side

[3] **orgiastic** – very excited

[4] **eloquent** – able to speak or write skilfully

Using topic sentences

Consider what the text is explaining. Good writers guide the reader through explanation texts by using clear topic sentences (the first two have been highlighted in orange for *The Hunters and the Hunted*. Remember, topic sentences are not always found at the beginning of the paragraph - sometimes paragraphs build up towards their key point.

Task 5 Analysing

Identify the topic sentences in the two remaining paragraphs. Then confer with a partner to see if you have chosen the same sentences.

Task 6 Annotating

The first two paragraphs of the extract have been annotated to illustrate some of the language features of explanation text. Annotate the third paragraph to illustrate another example of as many of these features as possible.

Using powerful language

Effective explanation makes clever use of descriptive detail and imaginative language to help the reader picture what is being explained and to maintain interest. The opening of the final paragraph from the extract has been annotated to show how the writer has selected words to 'paint' images for the reader.

Task 7 Annotating

Complete the annotations begun below to bring out any powerful words or images used.

Range of precise descriptive terms – help reader picture situation

Hyenas are <u>even slower</u> than lions. The best they can manage is about 65 kph and in consequence their hunting methods have to be <u>even more subtle</u> and dependent on teamwork. The females have separate dens where they rear their pups, but the pack as a whole works together and holds and defends territory. They have a <u>rich</u> vocabulary of sound and gesture with which they communicate among themselves. They <u>growl and whoop, grunt, yelp and whine</u> and at times produce a <u>most terrifying chorus of orgiastic laughs</u>. In gesture, their tails are particularly eloquent. Normally they are carried pointing down. An erect tail indicates aggression; pointed forward over the back, social excitement; held between the legs tight under the belly, fear. By hunting in well-co-ordinated teams, they have become so successful that in parts of the African plains, they make the majority of kills and the lions merely use their bigger size to bully their way on to a carcass, the reverse of the popular conception of the relationship between these two species.

Description builds to powerful image helping reader imagine the sounds and feelings they evoke

Series of powerful, precise verbs – helps reader understand range of sounds used

Writer's voice and levels of formality

David Attenborough's book was based on the BBC Television's successful *Life On Earth* series. Having built up a large popular audience, the book was then aimed at that same audience. Just as Attenborough's voice guides the viewer when he comments on the television, so his voice, as a writer, guides the reader.

One sentence from the extract has been reprinted below and annotated to reflect its audience. It has then been rewritten for two very different audiences.

Original

The cheetah has a thin elongated body and is said to be the fastest runner on earth, capable of reaching speeds, in bursts of over 110 kph.

Straightforward formal English – helps reader feel they will be able to understand

Writer not exaggerating his own knowledge – helps reader feel that they can trust the writer

Powerful precise words selected and explained, if difficult, interest a wide range of readers

Version 1

Hey, just look at Cheeky the cheetah go go go! Dream on, Olympic gold medal winners, because he's the all-time winner at 110 kilometres an hour. And, man, that's fast!

Version 2

The cheetah (whose name derives from the Sanskrit term for speckled – *citra*) is a large feline frequenting Africa and south-west Asia. It has an elongated body and is the swiftest known mammal, with the potential to achieve a velocity of over 110 kph for curtailed periods of time.

Task 8 Annotating

Annotate Versions 1 and 2 to show the audience and purpose that would suit their formality. You may want to consider the following audiences: toddlers; teenagers; watchers of popular daytime television; old-age pensioners; specialists in natural history.

Spinning formality

Task 9 Writing

Below is another sentence from *Life on Earth*.

By hunting in well-co-ordinated teams, hyenas have become so successful that in parts of the African plains, they make the majority of kills and the lions merely use their bigger size to bully their way on to a carcass.

Rewrite it in the style of Versions 1 and 2 above so that very different writers' voices guide the reader. Use a dictionary to help you with the more formal version or use the suggestions below:

hyena – any flesh-eating mammal of the order of *Hyaenidae*, with hind limbs shorter than forelimbs

bully – coerce or force **hunting** – seeking prey **carcass** – carrion

Text structure and organisation

Getting the structure right

AIMS

- Consider how the writer has integrated diverse information into a coherent and comprehensive account explaining the precise connections between ideas with clarity.
- Analyse how a writer has shaped ideas into cohesive paragraphs using devices such as signposting and connectives.

In this section you will analyse how David Attenborough has structured a coherent[1] and cohesive[2] explanation, and plan your own explanation text effectively.

[1] **coherent** – well organised across the whole text
[2] **cohesive** – with individual sections/ paragraphs that are linked and well organised

See pages 91–92 for a fuller explanation of these terms.

Integrating information

Well-written explanation looks deceptively easy to write. Structuring explanations clearly and signposting how one section relates to another is vital to help the reader understand the process being explained. Clear signposting is also necessary within paragraphs to help the reader follow how ideas are grouped, connected or developed.

On page 59 you identified how Attenborough has used topic sentences to signpost the main ideas of the text, and show how one paragraph is related to another.

Task 10 Discussing

 Discuss together why you think the extract is divided into four paragraphs.

Structuring writing effectively

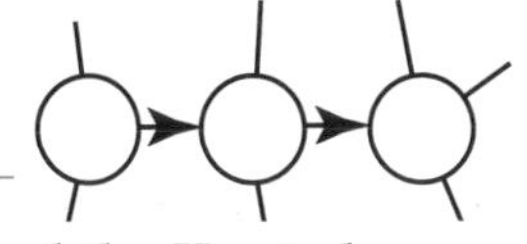

Below is a partially-completed explanation text skeleton for *The Hunters and the Hunted*, summing up how the points relate to each other. The bubble on the left-hand side indicates a possible solution that the predators did not adopt, before focusing on the solution they did find.

HOW CAN PREDATORS CATCH FAST-MOVING GRAZERS?

Rejected moving on tips of toes – need toes (claws) as offensive weapons

Solution – lengthened limbs by making spine flexible – at full-stretch, hind and front legs overlap like galloping antelope

a) Cheetahs – fastest – 110 kph but v. energy-consuming – keep up speed for only 1 min: either – succeeds quickly / retires exhausted – antelope gallops off

b) Lions

c)

Task 11 Note-making

  Complete the skeleton by making notes on the final two paragraphs.

Making paragraphs cohesive

Effective use of topic sentences, sentence signposts and connectives all help link and develop ideas within sections of a text (see page 92 for a fuller explanation of these terms).

Task 12 Annotating

The first half of the paragraph below has been annotated to show how the writer helps the reader follow the sense of what is being explained. Annotate the second half to show how each sentence builds on previous sentences, to help the reader understand.

Linking sentence connecting to previous paragraph

Causal connective introducing lions' solution

Repetition of sentence signpost – helps reader see connection

Evidence backing up opening statement

Sentence outlining problem from lions' perspective

Lions are nowhere near as fast as the cheetah. Their top speed is about 80 kph. A wildebeest can do about the same and keep it up for much longer. So lions have had to develop more complicated tactics. Sometimes they rely on stealth, creeping towards their victims, their bodies close to the ground, utilising every bit of cover. Sometimes an individual works by itself. But on occasion, members of a pride will hunt as a team – and they are the only cats that do so. They set off in line abreast. As they approach a group of their prey – antelope, zebra or wildebeest – those lions at the ends of the line move a little quicker so that they encircle the herd. Finally, these break cover, driving the prey towards the lions in the centre of the line. Such tactics often result in several of the team making kills and a hunt has been watched in which seven wildebeest were brought down.

Task 13 Planning practice

Your task is to plan a one-paragraph explanation summing up the reasons why trains have failed to run on time recently. Below are a range of reasons. Start by grouping the reasons under the following headings:

- Weather conditions
- Human or mechanical error
- Vandalism

Then place the groupings into a logical order. Once you have decided on the order, discuss what topic sentences could introduce each set of reasons.

Reasons for train delays

Leaves on the line
Shortage of drivers
Ice on the rails
Someone shooting airgun at train
Carriages in wrong place
Flooding
Engine failure
Guard not turned up for work
Children throwing things onto line.

Sentence structure and punctuation

Making the sentences work

AIMS

- Review and develop the meaning, clarity, organisation and impact of complex sentences in writing.
- Use the full range of punctuation to clarify and emphasise meaning for a reader.

In this section you will focus on how the variety of sentence structure and use of punctuation help maintain the reader's interest and understanding.

Analysing complex sentences in explanation

As you can see from the example below, David Attenborough has chosen mainly complex sentences to explain how the hunters of the plains have evolved. Refer to the grammar panel on page 18 to remind yourself about the main sentence types.

> In order to catch the grazers, the predators on the plain have had to improve greatly their own running techniques. They have not taken to moving on the tips of a reduced number of toes perhaps because they have always needed their toes, armed with claws, as offensive weapons. Their solution is different. They have effectively lengthened their limbs by making their spine extremely flexible. At full stretch, travelling at high speed, their hind and front legs overlap one another beneath the body just like those of a galloping antelope.

Below is the same passage rewritten in simple sentences.

> The predators want to catch the grazers. They have had to improve their own running techniques. They do not move on the tips of a reduced number of toes. They have always needed their claws as offensive weapons. Their solution is different. They have effectively lengthened their limbs. They have made their spine extremely flexible. At full stretch, travelling at high speed, their hind and front legs overlap one another beneath the body. This is just like those of a galloping antelope.

Task 14 Discussing

Use the rewritten passage to help you decide the answers to these questions.

- What difference do causal connectives and signposts make to the sense of the passage?
- Why is explanation text usually written in complex sentences?
- What makes the simple sentence in the middle of the original extract so effective?

Scan *The Hunters and the Hunted* on pages 57–58 and decide whether the short extract above is typical of the sentence structure used throughout the passage. Find evidence to support your viewpoint.

Using punctuation to guide meaning

Throughout the passage, the punctuation helps the reader follow the clause structure so that the meaning remains clear.

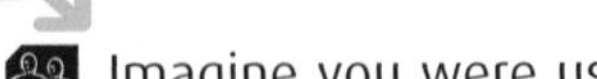

Task 15 Discussing

Imagine you were using the last two paragraphs of the passage to illustrate to a group of Year 8 students how good punctuation helps the reader understand a text. Decide which examples you would focus on (including some for the semicolon) and what you would say. Be prepared to present your examples.

You may want to use the summary of the uses of different punctuation marks below to help you.

GRAMMAR

Full stop .	Ends a sentence
Colon :	Marks a strong pause and used in lists
Semicolon ;	Indicates a stronger pause than a comma
Brackets ( )	Separate additional information inserted into the middle of sentences
Comma ,	Separates words, phrases or clauses that provide extra information; indicates pauses
Hyphen -	Shows that a word continues on the next line; links words to make a compound word or phrases to make an adjective
Dash –	Shows a short pause, or separates out information in a sentence
Elipsis ...	Shows missing text
Question mark ?	Makes a question
Apostrophe ’	Indicates possession or a missing letter(s)
Exclamation mark !	Makes an exclamation or command
Speech marks “ ”	Show direct speech or quotations

Task 16 Writing

Write an entertaining but clear explanation for why the trains were delayed, using the plan developed in Task 13. Remember to:

- use complex sentences including causal language effectively
- make certain you have punctuated your paragraph correctly.

You may find some of the following sentence signposts and causal connectives useful.

Casual sentence signposts and connectives		Connectives and signposts of addition
• Because	• Owing to	• In addition
• Since	• Consequently	• Moreover
• When	• So	• Not only ... but also
• As a result of	• If	• Furthermore
• Therefore	• Thanks to	• Plus
• Thus	• This means	• And

Composing your own explanation

AIMS

- Explain the precise connections between ideas with clarity and an appropriate degree of formality.
- Integrate diverse information into a coherent and comprehensive account.
- Make telling use of descriptive detail.

Your task

Write a clear, lively explanation about why having a vegetarian diet can be dangerous for an animal and how the West African rat solves the problem.

1 Audience and purpose

Your audience is teenagers and adults who are interested in nature. Discuss what effect the audience and purpose will have on the style of this explanation. In particular consider these questions:

- Should the style be informal and friendly, formal but still friendly, or very formal and distant?
- How will you engage the reader and sustain their interest?

2 Sorting the content

TR Sort the information listed below into a logical order. The first few points have been sorted into an order to start you off; the remaining points on page 66 are still jumbled up.

Information for explanation on West African rat

1. Staying alive by eating plants is not easy for animals.
2. Plants not very nutritious.
3. Have to eat vast quantities of plants to get enough calories to live.

A When rat's pouches are full, it can hardly close its mouth and its face blows up to a large size.

B When the rat's pouches full, it returns to burrow and sorts through food.

C Giant West African rat comes out of burrow at night and loads its pouches with anything it can eat.

D One solution is to pick up as much as possible at one time and run off with it.

E West African rat eats the parts that it can eat and rejects anything it can't.

F Some plant-eating animals spend three-quarters of their waking hours eating leaves.

G Eating leaves exposes animals to attack.

H West African rats have very large pouches that can hold 200 or so seeds, nuts, fruits, roots, etc. at one time.

3 Planning the structure

Use an explanation skeleton, like the one begun below, to help sketch out a plan. Complete the skeleton to help you sort out where to fit in each piece of information.

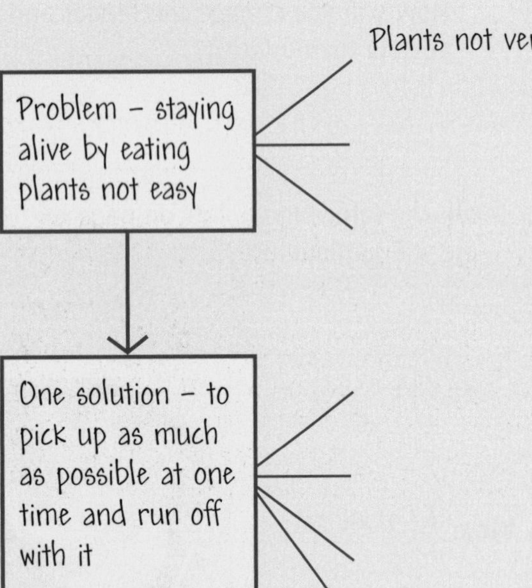
Plants not very nutritious
Problem – staying alive by eating plants not easy
One solution – to pick up as much as possible at one time and run off with it

Now decide on some key topic sentences that will guide the reader through the explanation. Remember to put these in the appropriate writer's voice for this type of explanation (formal but friendly).

4 Discussing what you are going to write

Take it in turns to practise talking through what you think you are going to write for each stage. When you are not presenting, listen carefully to your partner and be prepared to offer advice on how to express the explanation clearly in the appropriate writer's voice.

5 Composing your piece

Now you have organised and discussed your ideas, you are ready to write.

Points to remember

- Keep your audience in mind (teenagers and adults interested in natural history – see page 65).
- Use topic sentences to guide the reader (see page 59).
- Sustain the formal but friendly writer's voice throughout to guide the reader through the explanation and maintain their interest (see page 60).
- Select just the right precise words and images and explain any technical terms so the reader can picture what is being explained (see page 59).
- Use causal connectives and sentence signposts to help the reader follow the explanation (see pages 62 and 64).
- Keep the sentences as straightforward as possible while bringing out the causal links (see page 56).
- Use the passive if that helps makes the explanation clear (see page 57).
- Use punctuation to help the reader follow clause structure in any complex sentences (see page 64).

You may want to use the sentence signposts and connectives below to help you.

Sentence signposts and connectives

- Eating plants is no easy
- This strategy has been chosen
- Under cover of darkness
- For one thing
- Its pouches are
- When
- An animal has to
- Some enthusiastic vegetarians
- That, it itself, may be dangerous because
- One solution

6 Peer comment

Swap your draft with your partner's. Discuss together what really works well and highlight this on your draft. Now discuss what needs to be done to improve each explanation and jot down up to three suggestions on the draft. Redraft the selected sections using these comments to guide you.

7 Pulling it all together

Listen to some of the explanations written by members of the class.

Decide what are the key features that make these explanations effective. Set yourself three targets for the next time you write an explanation.

E The Art of Persuasive Writing

1 Revisiting how persuasive writing works

AIMS

- Analyse the stylistic conventions of persuasive text.
- Compare the presentation of ideas in related persuasive texts.

In this section you will analyse different examples of persuasive writing to remind yourself of its typical features.

Different kinds of persuasion text

Persuasion comes in different forms, for example:

- an **advert** *persuading* you to buy a package holiday
- a **letter** to a **newspaper** *arguing* against fox-hunting
- a **leaflet** *advising* you where best to invest your money.

These are all types of persuasion. However, they all have a different purpose and audience so their language features will be slightly different, too.

Task 1 Reading and analysing

Read the four examples of persuasive writing on pages 68–70. Text 1 has been annotated to show some of the features of persuasive text. Annotate the other three texts in a similar way. As their features will be slightly different, depending on their specific purpose, discuss their purpose and audience first.

Text 1

Series of points to lead reader to required action

Quotation to give the advert authority/status

Emotive language to worry reader

FEARS GROW OF A LARGE-SCALE TERRORIST ATTACK INVOLVING CHEMICAL OR BIOLOGICAL WEAPONS

"In the event of any such large-scale attack, emergency services will find it difficult to cope – <u>especially in the crucial first 12 hours</u>"

<u>You can NOT rely solely on the authorities to protect your family against attack.</u>

Take action now to ensure your family's safety.

Download your copy of 'How to Survive a Chemical or Biological Attack' by Nathalie Hopkins <u>for just $17</u>, and equip yourself with the knowledge and insight <u>you'll</u> need to remain calm and get yourself and your family through unscathed.

Use of different font sizes and colours for effect

Words used for emphasis imply book is cheap

Use of direct address to involve reader

Text 2

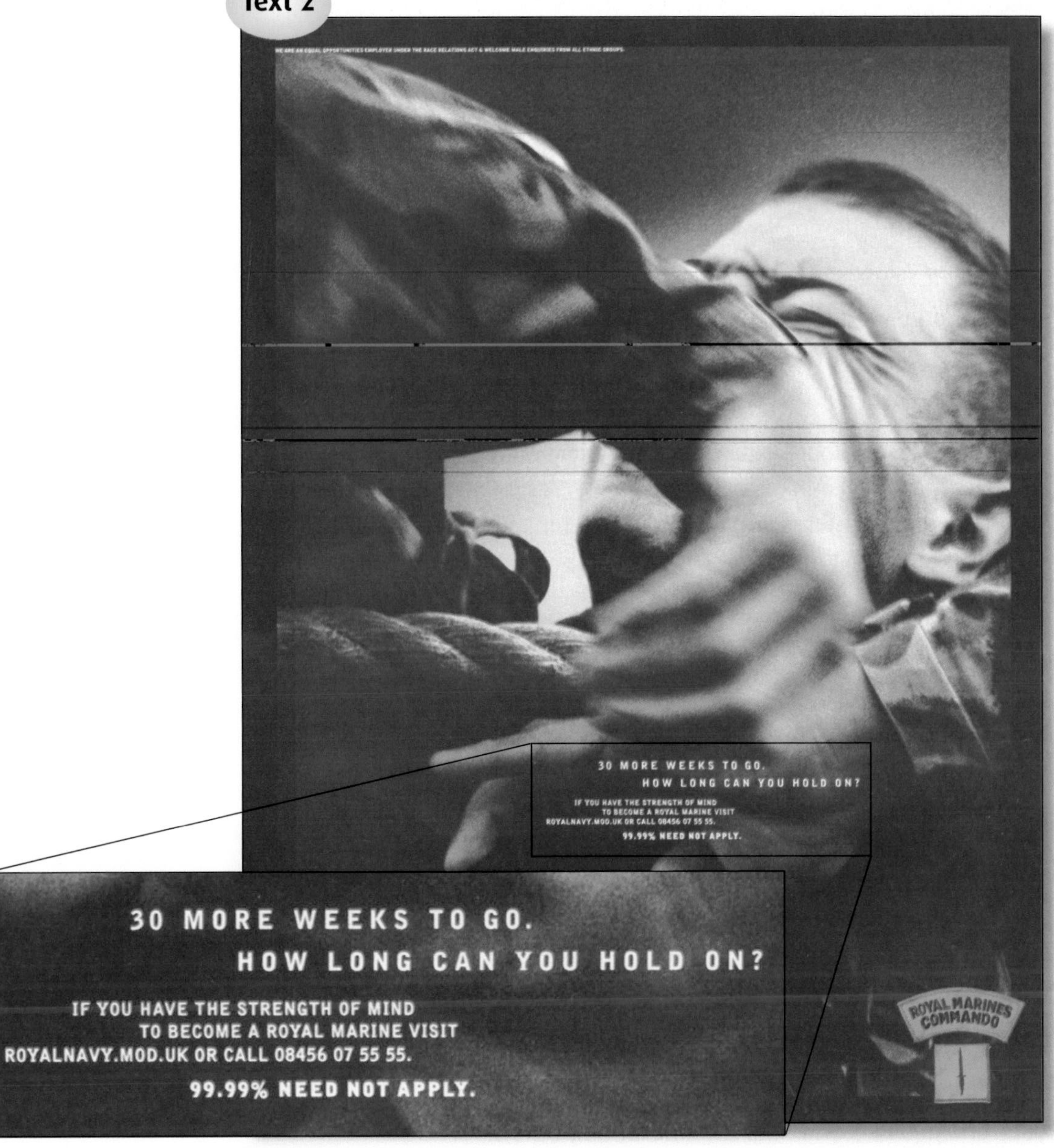

WE ARE AN EQUAL OPPORTUNITIES EMPLOYER UNDER THE RACE RELATIONS ACT & WELCOME MALE ENQUIRIES FROM ALL ETHNIC GROUPS.
30 MORE WEEKS TO GO.
HOW LONG CAN YOU HOLD ON?
IF YOU HAVE THE STRENGTH OF MIND
TO BECOME A ROYAL MARINE VISIT
ROYALNAVY.MOD.UK OR CALL 08456 07 55 55.
99.99% NEED NOT APPLY.
ROYAL MARINES COMMANDO

Text 3

"What should we do?" The question should be: "What have we done?" The US and the UK couldn't care less about the Iraqi people. We've been killing them for years, through sustained bombing and the brutal sanctions which have deprived hundreds of thousands of children of essential medicines. Many of them are dying and are dead from the effects of depleted uranium, used in the Gulf war. The west has shown total indifference to these facts.

What is now on the cards is further mass murder. To say we will rescue the Iraqi people from their dictator by killing them and by destroying the threadbare infrastructure[1] of their country is an insult to the intelligent. We have no moral position in this matter whatsoever.

[1] **infrastructure** – how something is made or put together, e.g. the infrastructure of a country is its factories, schools, roads, etc.

Text 4

What to do after the attack:

After a nuclear attack, there will be a short period before fall-out starts to descend. Use this time to do essential tasks. This is what you should do.

- Do not smoke.
- Check that gas, electricity and other fuel supplies and all pilot lights are turned off.
- Go round the house and put out any small fires using mains water if you can.
- If anyone's clothing catches fire, lay them on the floor and roll them in a blanket, rug or thick coat.
- If the mains water is still available also replenish water reserves. Then turn off at mains.
- Do not flush lavatories, but store the clean water they contain by taping up the handles or removing the chains.

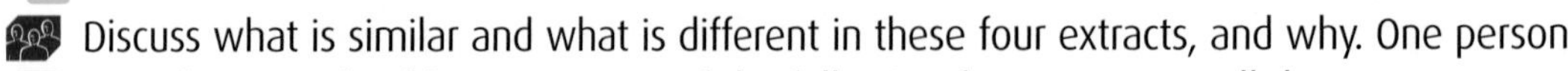

Task 2

Discussing and recording

Discuss what is similar and what is different in these four extracts, and why. One person in each group should compare one of the following features across all the extracts:

- **visual presentation**, e.g. use of images, font size and style
- **style and tone of language**, e.g. how formal, use of emotive words
- **attitude to audience**, e.g. whether direct address ('you') is used
- **structure**, e.g. how logical or clear the structure is.

Record your findings in a grid, like the one begun below.

	Text 1	Text 2	Text 3	Text 4
Visual presentation • What use is made of font sizes/style? • What use is made of images/graphics? • Consider the effect of the overall presentation.		Large, striking image of marine dominates advert		
Language • How formal is the language?				

The group should then discuss what five features they would include in a list of 'Key Features of Persuade Texts'. Be prepared to present your findings and your key features table to the class.

Composition and effect

Learning from example

AIMS

- Analyse the stylistic conventions of persuasive text.
- Comment on the authorial perspective offered in a text from a different culture, and how the author's standpoint can affect its meaning.
- Analyse and discuss the use made of rhetorical devices in a text, and use them to present a case persuasively.

In this section you will analyse what makes a famous speech so effective, focusing on its use of personal pronouns and rhetorical techniques.

Speaking persuasively

The extract below is the final part of Martin Luther King's speech given in Washington DC, America, in 1963. King was an African-American Baptist pastor (priest) who campaigned for equal rights for black Americans.

Task 3 Reading

As you read the speech, consider these questions:

- What is the purpose of the speech?
- Who do you think the audience is?

I Have a Dream

I have a dream that one day even the state of Mississippi, a desert state, sweltering with the heat of injustice and oppression, will be transformed into an oasis of freedom and justice. I have a dream that my four children will one day live in a nation where they will not be judged by the color of their skin but by the content of their character.

I have a dream today.

I have a dream that one day the state of Alabama, whose governor's lips are presently dripping with the words of interposition and nullification,[1] will be transformed into a situation where little black boys and black girls will be able to join hands with little white boys and white girls and walk together as sisters and brothers.

I have a dream today.

Powerful opening

Rhetorical effect – 'injustice and oppression' is echoed below by 'freedom and justice' in next line

Structure – each new paragraph gives new example of what he dreams

Formal language – emphasises seriousness of subject

Figurative language – contrasting heat with oasis

Sentence structure – second sentence echoes length and structure of first to give strong pattern

Repetition – opening phrase repeated, but in short sentence on its own for rhetorical effect

Emotive language – referring to boys and girls rather than men and women

[1] **interposition and nullification** – refers to the legal efforts of the governor of the state of Alabama to oppose equal rights for black people

I have a dream that one day every valley shall be exalted,[2] every hill and mountain shall be made low, the rough places will be made plain, and the crooked places will be made straight, and the glory of the Lord shall be revealed, and all flesh shall see it together.

This is our hope. This is the faith with which I return to the South. With this faith we will be able to hew[3] out of the mountain of despair a stone of hope. With this faith we will be able to transform the jangling discords[4] of our nation into a beautiful symphony of brotherhood. With this faith we will be able to work together, to pray together, to struggle together, to go to jail together, to stand up for freedom together, knowing that we will be free one day.

This will be the day when all of God's children will be able to sing with a new meaning, "My country, 'tis of thee, sweet land of liberty, of thee I sing. Land where my fathers died, land of the pilgrim's pride, from every mountainside, let freedom ring."

And if America is to be a great nation, this must become true. So let freedom ring from the prodigious[5] hilltops of New Hampshire. Let freedom ring from the mighty mountains of New York. Let freedom ring from the heightening Alleghenies of Pennsylvania!

Let freedom ring from the snowcapped Rockies of Colorado! Let freedom ring from the curvaceous[6] peaks of California! But not only that; let freedom ring from Stone Mountain of Georgia! Let freedom ring from Lookout Mountain of Tennessee! Let freedom ring from every hill and every molehill of Mississippi. From every mountainside, let freedom ring.

When we let freedom ring, when we let it ring from every village and every hamlet, from every state and every city, we will be able to speed up that day when all of God's children, black men and white men, Jews and Gentiles,[7] Protestants and Catholics, will be able to join hands and sing in the words of the old Negro spiritual, "Free at last! free at last! thank God Almighty, we are free at last!"

[2] **exalted** – made high, i.e. things will be turned upside down. This and the rest of the paragraph is a quotation from the Bible

[3] **hew** – dig

[4] **jangling discords** – horrible clashing sounds

[5] **prodigious** – mighty

[6] **curvaceous** – curving

[7] **Gentiles** – non-Jews

Task 4 Summarising the content

Read the speech aloud and write down a one-sentence summary of each paragraph. You could begin like this:

1. I have a dream of freedom and justice.
2. I have a dream.
3.

Task 5 Discussing

Discuss the purpose of this speech and its audience. Consider the following questions in your discussion, noting down the evidence for your ideas:

- The language is very persuasive, but what exactly is King trying to persuade the audience to do, think or feel?
- Does your summary of the content suggest that he is making a series of logical points? If not, what is he doing?
- What can you say about the audience from the evidence of this extract?
- What does King's use of quotations tell us about his background and the background of the audience? (Think about ethnic group, religion, profession.)
- How does the formality of King's language help him achieve his purpose?

Task 6 Annotating

The first section of the speech has been annotated to highlight some of the language features of a persuasive text. Annotate the next section (lines 15–52) to bring out further features, and explain what effect they have.

Using personal pronouns

Texts that persuade aim to win the audience over to the writer's viewpoint. One effective way of doing this is to use personal pronouns.[1] This makes the text more personal and includes some groups and excludes others:

- Using the **first person** ('I', 'we') brings in the person of the speaker/writer, or includes the audience on their side, e.g. 'I have a dream', 'We know that…'
- Using the **second person** ('you') addresses the audience, to engage with them on a personal level, e.g. 'You will never regret it', 'You are mistaken if…'
- Using the **third person** ('she', 'he', 'they') often excludes a group by making them separate from 'you' or 'us', e.g. 'He thinks that …, but you know better', 'We are united, but they are divided'.

[1] **personal pronouns** – words that take the place of a name, e.g. 'I', 'me', 'you', 'it', 'we', 'they', 'them'

Task 7 **Analysing**

 Look through the extract from *I Have a Dream* and make a note of the ways in which King has used personal pronouns. How effective are these techniques in his speech? Note down three or four examples and be prepared to feed back to the class.

Rhetorical techniques

'Rhetoric' was originally the art of public speaking, which was taught as a skill as long ago as the fifth century BC in ancient Greece. Rhetorical techniques,[1] therefore, are particularly common (and important) in persuade texts that are meant to be heard rather than read. The panel below lists ten of the most effective rhetorical techniques.

[1] **rhetorical techniques** – techniques used to persuade an audience

Ten great rhetorical techniques

1. **Emotive language** Using language with strong positive or negative bias to get the audience on your side, e.g. 'Protect your innocent children', 'He has something of the night about him'.
2. **Sound devices** Using sound effects, such as alliteration, assonance and rhyming, to make the message or point more attractive, e.g. 'Fight a fair fight, my friends', 'the green fields of home', 'It's not a bad law, just a mad law'.
3. **Figurative language** Using metaphors, similes or personification to draw a picture in the audience's mind, e.g. 'This war is a cancer', 'like vultures circling over their prey'.
4. **Exaggeration** Overstating a view or statistic to impress the audience, e.g. 'There are thousands of cases where…', 'in every city in England'.
5. **Contrast** Putting two opposing ideas or facts next to each other to show up how different they are, e.g. 'Should we support the tiny groups of protesters or the vast armies of the police?'
6. **Using personal pronouns** Using 'I', 'you', 'they', etc. to make the text more personal, and to include or exclude groups (see above), e.g. 'I strongly believe', 'We cannot allow this to happen'.
7. **Repetition** Repeating the same word, phrase or sentence structure to hammer home the point, e.g. 'We shall fight them on the beaches; we shall fight them on land and in the air.'
8. **Making a list** Listing different examples of the same thing emphasises the point and builds up momentum, e.g. 'Do this for your children, for your mothers and fathers, and for your sisters and brothers.'
9. **Rhetorical question** A question which does not need to be answered but which is asked for effect, e.g. 'Are we going to give up before we've even started?'
10. **Using quotations** Quoting other people or famous lines from books to show that your view is backed up by others, or to appeal to a shared culture, e.g. 'As the prime minister himself remarked…', 'in John Donne's words, "No man is an island".'

Task 8 Analysing

Look through the *I Have a Dream* speech on pages 71–72 and identify the rhetorical techniques that King has used. Discuss how effective they are. Draw up a grid like the one below to record your findings.

Example	Rhetorical technique	Effect
'sweltering with the heat of injustice and oppression'	Figurative language	The concrete picture is more powerful than the abstract 'an unjust and oppressive state'
'an oasis of freedom and justice'	Figurative language/contrast	

You may find it helpful to read the speech out loud to yourself or to others in your group.

The importance of the writer's voice

Whenever you write anything, you have to decide what role you are taking as you write, just as in role play you have to know what your character is. This role is known as the 'writer's voice', and always depends on the audience and purpose of the writing.

In the *I Have a Dream* speech, both the use of personal pronouns and rhetorical devices play a key part in sustaining a distinctive and persuasive writer's voice throughout the piece.

Task 9 Writing

You have been asked to contribute to a public protest against closing your school, where you are very happy. (The school has only 150 students.) Below is an early draft of the final paragraph of your speech. Redraft the paragraph so that it has more persuasive power. Try to include at least three of the rhetorical techniques from page 74 and use them to sustain a persuasive writer's voice. You will need to change words and sentence types, and add or delete material.

As a student, I am expected to meekly accept this decision to close Challington School. But we must fight for our rights. The facts are plain: this is an excellent school, and everyone here is happy. It also serves the community around it. Closing the school is a ridiculous policy. But it would be a tragedy. I really don't want this to happen.

Text structure and organisation

Getting the structure right

AIMS

- Compare and use different ways of opening, developing, linking and completing paragraphs.
- Analyse and exploit the stylistic conventions of persuasive text.

In this section you will use a text skeleton to help you analyse the structure of *I Have a Dream* and think about how powerful endings and repetition give a text coherence and cohesion. You will also plan a speech of your own.

Text skeletons

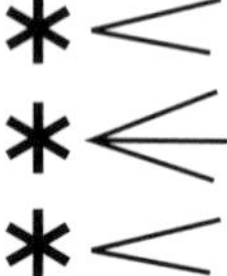

Text skeletons are a useful way of analysing the structure of a text, making notes on a text and planning your own text. The persuade text skeleton lists each main point on the left, and adds any supporting points or examples on the right as memory joggers.

Task 10 Structuring

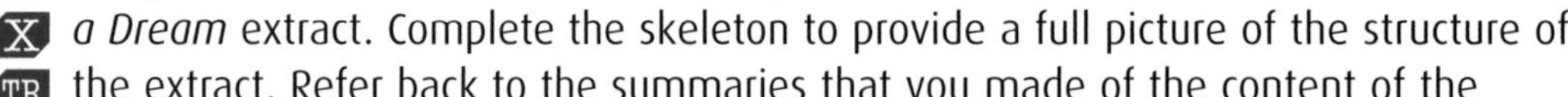

The persuade text skeleton below analyses the structure of the start of the *I Have a Dream* extract. Complete the skeleton to provide a full picture of the structure of the extract. Refer back to the summaries that you made of the content of the speech (see Task 4, page 73) to help you.

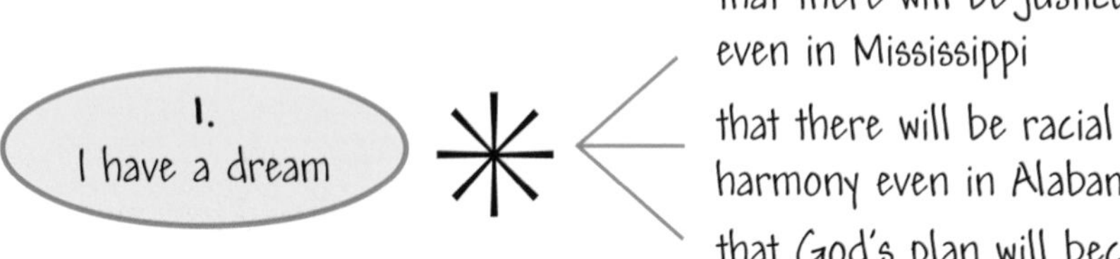
1.
I have a dream
that there will be justice even in Mississippi
that there will be racial harmony even in Alabama
that God's plan will become true

The speech seems to be organised in three main sections (lines 1–19, 20–33 and 34–52). You may find it helpful to identify a single main point for each section.

Good endings

A text will increase its power of persuasion if it begins and ends powerfully. There are various techniques for ending a persuade text effectively:

- With a rhetorical 'flourish', using one or more of the rhetorical techniques outlined on page 74.
- By referring back in some way to the beginning, to give it a satisfying ring composition.[1]
- With a particularly long (or short) sentence after building up the momentum of the previous section.

[1] **ring composition** – beginning and ending a text with the same idea or image so that they 'join up' to form a 'ring'. This is also known as an echo.

Task 11 Discussing

Discuss how effectively you think Martin Luther King ends his *I Have a Dream* speech (see page 72). Which of the three techniques highlighted on page 76 does he use? Prepare a detailed answer to present to the class.

Repetition as a structural tool

Some persuade texts, such as *I Have a Dream*, do not have a logical point-by-point argument to give them cohesion[1] or structure. They therefore have to rely on other devices. King relies on the rhythm of repetition to provide the backbone of his speech. Repetition is used in several ways:

1 **Repetition of words and phrases** which act as a 'chorus', e.g. 'Let freedom ring', each followed by a different place in America.

2 **Repetition of sentence types**, to give an underlying pattern to the words, e.g. the long sentences 'I have a dream that…' alternating with the short sentence 'I have a dream'.

3 **Picking up a key word** in one sentence or paragraph and using it again near the beginning of the next sentence or paragraph, e.g. 'This is the *faith* … With this *faith* …'; 'we will be free one *day* …This will be the *day*…'.

[1] **cohesion** – how the individual sections of the text are linked or organised
(For a fuller explanation, see page 92.)

Task 12 Writing

Practise using repetition in your own writing. Below are four sentences from four different speeches. Write the *next* sentence of the speech, using repetition effectively. In each case, decide if you are going to repeat a phrase, the sentence structure or a key word. The first one has been done for you.

1 If they demand that we hand over our belongings, we must refuse.
In fact, we must refuse to give in to any of their demands.

2 We promise to lower the voting age to sixteen.

3 Trust in our strength and courage, and we will not fail.

4 Are more mothers going to lose their sons in this war?

Task 13 Planning practice

There is to be a mock general election at your school, in which you are standing as a candidate for the 'Youth Party'. You have to give a speech persuading students to vote for you. To help you with your planning, some key topics (in bold) and some supporting points are given below.

- Rearrange these points into a logical or effective order.
- Then, using the points, draw up a text skeleton to plan your speech.
- Finally, think of a word or phrase that you could repeat in one section, to give it structure and rhetorical impact. Write this word or phrase next to the relevant section on your plan.

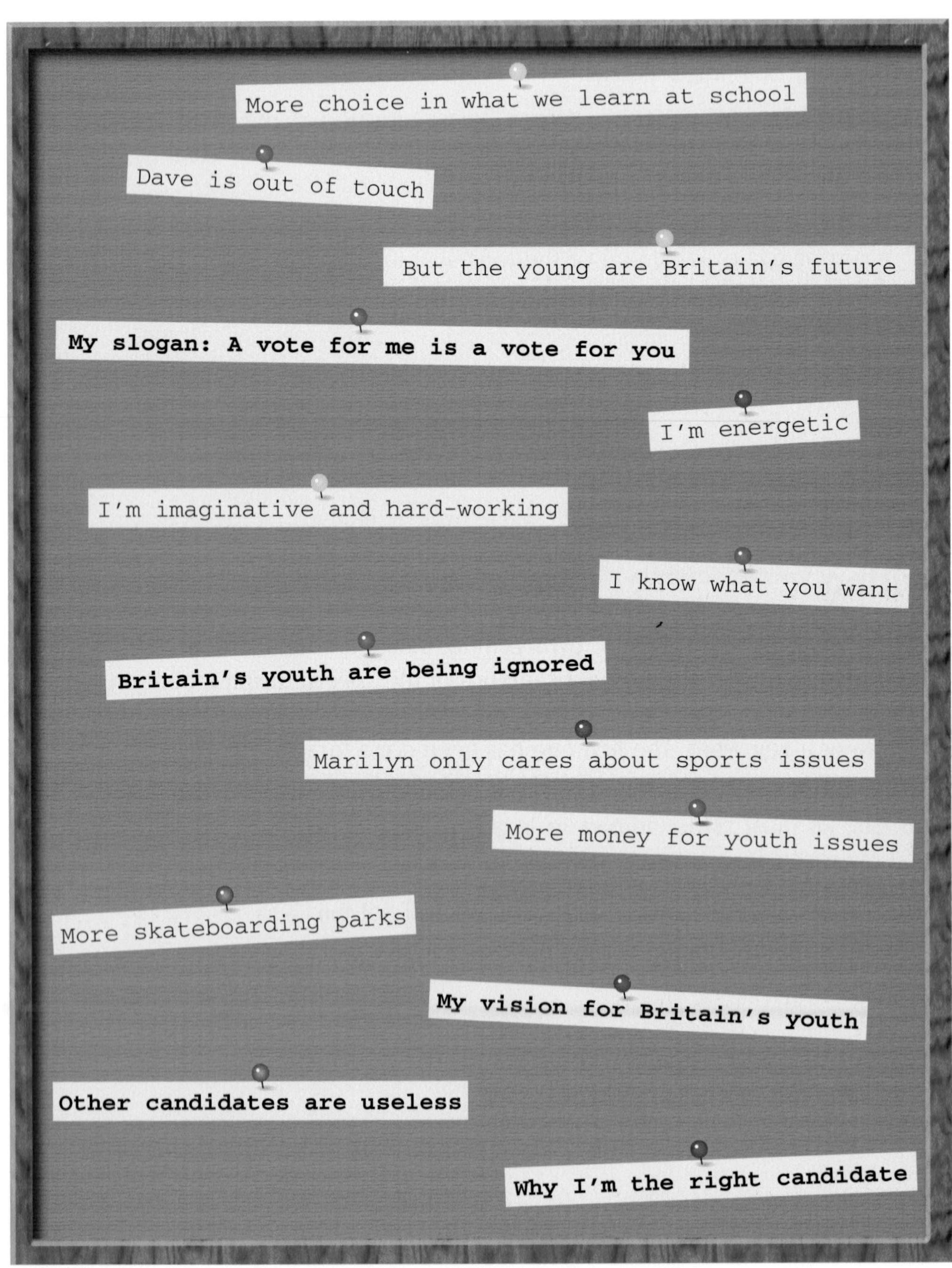

Sentence structure and punctuation

Making the sentences work

AIMS

- Develop your use of sentences of different lengths and structures.
- Use commas to clarify meaning.
- Use sentence signposts effectively.

In this section you will explore how to add emphasis to your writing by varying the length and structure of your sentences. You will also review the uses of the comma.

Varying sentence length

The length and rhythm of your sentences is especially important in a text that is going to be heard rather than read. If your sentences all have the same length and/or structure, you are in danger of boring your audience.

Task 14 Discussing

Look at how Martin Luther King varies the length of his sentences in the *I Have a Dream* extract on pages 71–72. Discuss these questions:

- What pattern is used in the first five paragraphs, and how effective is it? (lines 1–19)
- How does this pattern change in paragraph six? Why does King change the pattern here? (lines 20–28)
- Why does King make the sentences in paragraphs eight and nine the same length? (lines 34–45)
- Where is the longest sentence and why has King put it there?

Emphatic sentence signposts

King often brings a key word or phrase up to the beginning of a sentence, and signposts it with 'It is…' or 'This is…' or 'With this…'. This is an effective way for a writer of persuasive texts to both vary the structure of their sentences and add emphasis. (It also shows very clearly where the line of thought is going.)

Compare this pair of sentences, for example:

- *This is the faith with which I return to the South.*
- *I return to the South with this faith.*

and this pair:

- *With this faith we will be able to hew out of the mountain of despair a stone of hope.*
- *We will, with this faith, be able to hew out of the mountain of despair a stone of hope.*

The first sentence in each pair is more powerful because it emphasises the key noun 'faith'.

Task 15 Writing

Rewrite sentences 1 to 4 to make them more effective by emphasising a key noun, as described on page 79. One way of beginning the new sentence has been suggested in each case.

1 Defending our title is a matter of honour.
It ...

2 After Wednesday's game, their team is exhausted.
This ...

3 We will win this game if we show courage and determination.
With ...

4 We will show them today why we are top of the league.
This ...

Using commas

Commas are used to indicate a pause, and to separate words, phrases and clauses. Look at the grammar panel for a more detailed explanation.

GRAMMAR

Indicating a pause

Commas are often used after adverbials[1] at the beginning of the sentence, to indicate a pause, though omitting the comma is also correct:

Adverbial
- *At the end of the match, it began to rain.*
- *At the end of the match it began to rain.*

You should *not* put a comma between the subject and verb of a clause, even if the noun phrase is very long:

noun phrase = subject — Verb
- *The thirty-fifth and final contestant to enter the ring won the fight.*

Separating clauses

When a complex sentence begins with a subordinate clause, a comma marks the end of that clause. (For example, 'If you return the book tomorrow, I will be in.')

When the subordinate clause ends the sentence, a comma is not used if the clause adds some information necessary for the full understanding of the sentence:

- *It doesn't happen unless you turn the switch to number 3.*
- *I'm returning the book that you lent me last week.*

Compare this sentence, where the subordinate clause simply adds more information:

- *I'm returning the book, which was excellent.*

Noun phrases or relative clauses which describe a word are separated off from the rest of the sentence by commas at either end:

- *I'm returning the book, which was excellent, and borrowing another one.*
- *He sold his bicycle, a Trek 2500, and bought a moped.*

[1] **adverbial** – a group of words acting as an adverb[2]

[2] **adverb** – usually gives more information about a verb, an adjective or another adverb, e.g. 'easily', 'very', 'happily'

GRAMMAR

Separating items in a list

Commas must be used to separate words, phrases or even clauses in a list:

- *He is loud, lazy, and dreadful to live with.*
- *Put it in the pan, heat it up, keep stirring and bring it to the boil.*

Note that the comma before the final item is optional.

In direct speech

Commas are used to separate the reporting clause ('he said', etc.) and the actual words of direct speech:

- *'Over there,' he said.*
- *She replied, 'Why did you do that?'*

Task 16 Punctuating

The two extracts below from the *I Have a Dream* extract are missing their commas. Discuss where you would put the commas and why. You may like to refer back to the grammar panel above.

Extract 1

I have a dream that one day even the state of Mississippi a desert state sweltering with the heat of injustice and oppression will be transformed into an oasis of freedom and justice. I have a dream that my four children will one day live in a nation where they will not be judged by the color of their skin but by the content of their character.

Extract 2

When we let freedom ring when we let it ring from every village and every hamlet from every state and every city we will be able to speed up that day when all of God's children black men and white men Jews and Gentiles Protestants and Catholics will be able to join hands and sing in the words of the old Negro spiritual "Free at last! free at last! thank God Almighty we are free at last!"

5 Composing your own persuasive speech

AIMS

- Write sustained Standard English with the formality suited to reader and purpose.
- Present a case persuasively enough to gain the attention of a specified audience.

Write a speech, thinking carefully about how it will sound to your audience and including the techniques of persuasive writing that you have explored in this unit.

1 Audience and purpose

Tomorrow is the under-15s national championship finals in your favourite team sport, and you are captain of your local team. You are writing a speech to encourage the team, and because the local newspaper want to print it alongside the match report.

Discuss what effect the audience and purpose of this text will have on the style. In particular, consider these questions:

- How formal should the language be?
- What kind of feelings do you want to evoke, and how will you do this?

2 Brainstorming the content

In groups sharing the same favourite sport, brainstorm all the approaches you can think of to encourage your team. Think up some details about your team and the opposition so that your speech isn't too general but has real impact. Put an asterisk against the ideas and phrases that you think are the most effective.

3 Planning the form and structure

TR

Select the three or four ideas that you think are the strongest and list them in the most effective order. Use these ideas as the main points in a persuasion skeleton, and jot down some supporting points as memory joggers.

Now decide on possible key sentence signposts that will guide the reader through the speech. Remember to keep these in the appropriate writer's voice for your persuasive speech.

4 Discussing what you are going to write

Take it in turns to practise talking through your speech plan. When you are not presenting, listen carefully to your partner and be prepared to offer constructive comments on his or her plan. Does it begin effectively? Do the sections build up to a powerful ending? Is the writer's voice consistent throughout?

5 Composing your piece

Now you are ready to write your speech.

Points to remember

- Use personal pronouns to emphasise your relationship with the audience (see page 73).
- Make sure the formality of the language is suited to the reader and purpose (see page 68).
- Use as many of the ten great rhetorical techniques as you can, especially emotive words and sound effects (see page 74).
- Add an attention-grabbing beginning and a rousing ending (see page 76).
- Repeat key words, phrases or sentence types where effective to give structure and impact to your speech (see page 77).
- Vary the length and structure of your sentences to make the writing as powerful as possible (see page 79)
- Bring key words and phrases to the front of your sentences for emphasis (see page 79)
- Use punctuation, especially the comma, effectively (see pages 80–81).

You may like to use some of the sentence signposts and key phrases below.

Sentence signposts and key phrases

- This is the day when
- We know that we can
- It's up to all of you to
- How will you live it down if
- Think of the England rugby team
- If they think we're a pushover
- Tackle hard, run hard, and shoot hard
- Listen to the cheers as
- Let them throw all they've got at us!
- This will be our finest hour

6 Peer comment

Swap your draft with a partner's and read it carefully. Decide what really works well and highlight this on the draft. Discuss what you need to do to improve your work. Jot down up to three suggestions on the draft.

Redraft the selected sections of your speech, using your partner's comments to guide you.

7 Pulling it all together

Listen to some of the speeches written by members of your class. Discuss what are the key features that make these effective. Write down three targets to aim for the next time you do some persuasive writing.

F The Art of Presenting an Argument

1 Revisiting how to write an argument

AIMS

- Analyse the stylistic conventions of persuasive argument.
- Compare the presentation of ideas in related texts.

In this section you will analyse different examples of argument texts to remind yourself of their typical features.

Different kinds of argument

Arguments come in different shapes and forms, for example:

- a **government document** outlining the case for London to host the Olympic Games
- a **newspaper editorial** arguing for a ban on fox hunting
- a **letter** from a mother to a school head arguing that her son should not be excluded.

Argument text is a particular kind of persuasion, as the aim is to persuade one or more people – but this time to a particular point of view. Argument texts do this by constructing a series of logical points to demonstrate and back up that view.

Task 1 Reading and analysing

Read the two texts below; Text 1 argues that boxing should be banned, Text 2 that it should not. Half of Text 1 has been annotated to show some of the features that make it an argument text. Annotate the rest and the whole of Text 2 in a similar way.

Text 1 *The final part of a speech given in the House of Lords*

I have broadly two reasons for supporting the Bill. The first I can put this way. All of us in the course of our lives, whether long like mine or shorter, have hoped that our society would become more civilised as time went on. Alas, however, violence has increased and become part of the way of life of so much of our community in recent years and we must be careful to try to prevent the attitude among people that violence is a legitimate part of life. We must try to dissuade them from it. Boxing seen on television gives people, especially the young, the impression that violence is acceptable in certain circumstances. That is my first reason for supporting the Bill, put as briefly as I can.

Clear topic sentence – indicates what conclusion consists of

Sentence signpost – introduces first reason

Formal language throughout

Sentence signpost – shows what point of conclusion he has reached

Inclusive use of first person – gets audience on his side

Hint of humour – gets audience on his side

Sentence connective – shows that this sentence contradicts the last

Reasonable and restrained tone

Simple logical argument
A There is too much violen
B Boxing encourages violence, therefore
C Ban boxing

My second reason has been mentioned, the medical reason. There is now strong scientific evidence and medical proof that heavy blows to the human head – whether to a heavyweight boxer like Muhammad Ali whose head suffered through his contests, or a middleweight, or any boxer – can destroy some of the brain cells.

Text 2 *A contribution to an e-mail forum*

front page
features
reviews
recommended
watch & listen
community
my space
search and find
email updates
about forums
help and faqs

It is true that something needs to be done to improve the image and safety record of boxing, but banning it is totally the wrong idea. Firstly, it would drive the sport underground and lead back to a time where bare-knuckle fights didn't end till one person was killed. Secondly, it's not just grown men who box. Young people all over the country are boxing in organised conditions, some for better self-defence, others for the love of the sport. Many of these kids wouldn't have any other hobby if boxing were banned, which could lead to them becoming involved in crime. Do we really want more hooligans on the streets?

Task 2 Discussing and recording

Discuss what is similar and what is different in these two texts, and why. One person should compare one of the following features across both texts, recording examples and giving reasons for their use:

- the writer's voice – that is, the voice that will be telling the story, and the tone and style of that voice, e.g. how formal, use of emotive words
- attitude to audience, e.g. whether direct address is used
- structure, e.g. how logical or clear the structure is, use of connectives.

Record your findings in a grid like the one begun below.

	Text 1	**Text 2**
Language • How formal is the language? • Have powerful nouns ...	Formal language, e.g. words like 'legitimate' Carefully constructed sentences, e.g. the final sentence	

Now discuss the following questions:

- Can you explain the similarities and differences? Consider the audience and context[1] of each extract in your analysis.
- Is one extract a more effective argument text than the other?

Finally, draw up a list of 'Key Features of Argument Texts'. Be prepared to present your findings to the class.

[1] **context** – background and purpose

Composition and effect

Learning from example

AIMS

- Analyse the stylistic conventions of persuasive argument.
- Explore the rhetorical devices in a text, and use them to present a case persuasively.
- Explore the aesthetic features of language, and how texts can convey ideas in an entertaining way.
- Analyse different ways of attacking the opposition, and make a counter-argument to a view that has been expressed.

In this section you will analyse what makes a magazine editorial effective as an argument, focusing on how it conveys ideas in an entertaining and forceful way.

News editorials

The editorial below is from the *New Statesman* magazine. It defends the increased use of speed cameras and the strict policing of speed limits.

Task 3 Reading and considering

As you read the editorial, consider these questions:

- What is the purpose of the argument?
- Who do you think the audience is?

Topic sentence – clearly states first point in argument

Formal language throughout – shows seriousness of issue and writer

Third person generally used – though sometimes first person ('we') to get audience on side

What a strange attitude we have to lawbreakers in cars. Attempts to enforce speed limits are denounced as interference with our ancient freedoms. Motorists who drive too fast are excused on the grounds that they are 'otherwise law-abiding', a description that may as easily be applied to murderers. Upright citizens boast of victories over breathalysers, speed cameras and parking tickets. *The Sun* launches a 'stop the highway robbery' campaign against the cameras, while a lunatic fringe attacks them with hammers and airguns, and threatens explosives. Ministers tremble at the tabloids' wrath and agree to consider proposals to remove cameras where they do not 'protect' the public. This is an incoherent[1] thought even by today's standards. If a legal limit on speed exists, it is worth enforcing.

Ridiculing the opposing argument – a series of sentences presenting opponents in an exaggerated way

Emotive language – to arouse strong feeling in reader

Vivid language – to engage interest of reader

Reason for view given – in a reasonable tone

Sentence signpost – links with previous sentence

[1] **incoherent** – illogical, not making sense

The Art of Presenting an Argument

Our love affair with the motor car blinds us to logic and common sense. We strain every sinew to protect children from paedophile murderers. Yet, the number of child pedestrians killed on the roads annually is ten times greater than the number killed by perverted strangers. It is also higher than in France or Germany. The yearly toll of death on the roads exceeds that exacted by Osama Bin Laden's madmen in New York in 2001, and is vastly higher than the number of Britons killed in all recent terrorist attacks. On any sane risk assessment, speed cameras on roads, which have been shown to cut deaths and serious injuries by 35 per cent, are more necessary than armed marshals[2] on aeroplanes.

There is no argument whatever for treating errant[3] motorists more leniently than any other class of offender, or for making less determined efforts to catch them. Even an ignored 'no right turn' sign can cause death or injury to innocent people. An illegally parked car, which may itself lead to an accident, is simply theft of road space, an expensive and scarce commodity. Retailers stuff their stores with cameras to deter shoplifters, who cause no physical harm to anybody. It is hardly possible to walk a hundred yards along a high street or a few feet across an airport lounge without surveillance.[4] Why should it be different when we get into a motor vehicle?

The argument that exceeding the speed limit is acceptable when the road is deserted or the schools are on holiday is preposterous. Children are more, not less, likely to be wandering around in the holidays, and pedestrians may unwittingly[5] put themselves at risk in the belief that the limit is being observed. In any case, a pedestrian hit by a vehicle travelling at 40mph will almost certainly be killed, while one hit at 20mph will almost certainly survive. Cars seem to create a state of arrested adolescence[6] in many users. Behind the wheel, middle-class, middle-aged men (and the worst drivers are nearly always men) become as reckless and heedless as teenagers. They resemble naughty schoolboys not only in their determination to flout authority, but in their resentment when they are 'picked on'. Yet a car is potentially a lethal weapon. The use of it is a privilege, not a right; the minority who forget that deserve to be hounded as mercilessly as any housebreaker or teenage vandal.

[2] **armed marshals** – a form of police carrying guns on aeroplanes. These were proposed in 2003 as a way of deterring terrorist attacks on aeroplanes

[3] **errant** – making an error with knowledge

[4] **surveillance** – being watched (by CCTV)

[5] **unwittingly** – without knowing

[6] **state of arrested adolescence** – i.e. they continue to act as teenagers

Task 4 Using topic sentences

Scan the newspaper editorial together for the topic sentences (the first is highlighted in orange). Then write down a five-sentence summary of the whole piece.

Why is it important for a written argument to have clear topic sentences?

Task 5 Annotating

The first paragraph of the editorial has been annotated to highlight some of the language features of a written argument. Annotate lines 16–28 to bring out further features, and explain what effect they have.

Exploiting the cadence of sentences

Good writers of arguments listen to the cadence[1] of their sentences. The *New Statesman* editorial uses this technique in several ways, including:

- **Using a similar length of sentence and rhythm**, e.g. in lines 3–13, where five examples of the 'strange attitude' to cars are hammered out, each beginning with a noun (or noun phrase) plus verb ('Upright citizens boast...', '*The Sun* launches ...').
- **Using a contrasting length of sentence which breaks the rhythm**, e.g. the short sentence 'This is an incoherent thought even by today's standards' (line 13) after the list of examples.

[1] **cadence** – rhythm, in this case within a piece of writing

Task 6 Discussing and analysing

Discuss why each of the cadences described above is effective. Scan the rest of the editorial and find further examples of where the writer has paid attention to the cadence of the sentences. Be prepared to present your findings.

Using rhetoric to argue and entertain

Rhetorical techniques are not only useful when delivering a speech (see page 74), but also to make an argument more forceful and more entertaining. As long as they are not over-used, rhetorical techniques can win the reader over to the writer's side.

Here are four rhetorical techniques used by the editorial writer:

- **Using emotive language** – 'a lunatic fringe', 'perverted strangers', 'Osama Bin Laden's madmen', 'stuff their stores', 'a lethal weapon'.
- **Using first person to get reader on side** – 'what a strange attitude we have', 'our love affair with the motor car', 'we strain every sinew'.
- **Stacking up the nouns and adjectives** (using two or three examples when one would do) – 'attacks them with hammers and airguns', 'logic and common sense', 'higher than in France or Germany', 'can cause death or injury', 'reckless and heedless', 'as any housebreaker or teenage vandal'.
- **Asking a rhetorical question** – 'Why should it be different when we get into a motor vehicle?'

Task 7 Writing

Read the 'Arguments for the Internet' below. Choose *one* of these arguments and discuss how to write a short paragraph (two or three sentences) to make it much more forceful. Include at least two of the rhetorical techniques listed in the bullet points above. Then draft your paragraph.

Arguments for the Internet

- It provides easy access to lots of information.
- It allows communication with people across the world.
- You save time and effort by shopping on the Internet.

Here's an example of how the first argument could be made more forceful and entertaining:

The Internet is a vast treasure house of information. We would be crazy to ignore all the opportunities and possibilities it offers for providing us with the facts that we need. The facts are literally at our fingertips!

Countering the opposition

'Attack is the best form of defence' is a principle that often applies to writing powerful arguments as well. Look at the different ways in which the editorial writer attacks the opposing argument:

- **The head-on attack**. An opposing point is stated only to be immediately countered or denied, e.g. 'the argument… is preposterous', 'there is no argument whatever for…'.
- **Saying it is illogical**. The idea is to make your argument the only reasonable one, e.g. 'blinds us to logic and common sense', 'on any sane risk assessment', 'this is an incoherent thought'.
- **Ridiculing the opposition**. Emotive or biased language is used to put the opposition in a bad light, e.g. 'a lunatic fringe', 'as reckless and heedless as teenagers', 'naughty schoolboys'.
- **Exaggerating the opposition's case**. Putting the opponents' points in an exaggerated way, which undermines them by making them sound silly or extreme, e.g. most of the first paragraph, which consists of examples of our 'strange attitude'.

Top tip The word HIRE will help you remember the ways of countering the opposition:

Head-on attack
Saying it's **I**llogical
Ridiculing the opposition
Exaggerating the opposition's case

The importance of the writer's voice

'Writer's voice' is the role a writer takes on for a piece of writing, in this case an editorial. The voice may range from very friendly and informal to very distant and formal. The voice always depends on the audience and purpose of the writing. The style of the writing reflects or matches this voice and should be sustained throughout.

Task 8 Discussing

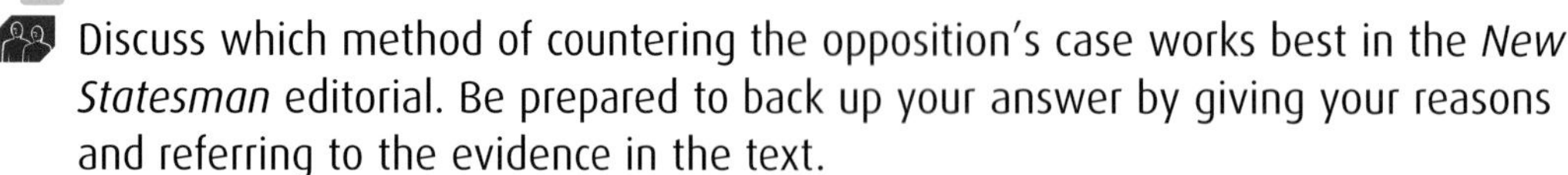

Discuss which method of countering the opposition's case works best in the *New Statesman* editorial. Be prepared to back up your answer by giving your reasons and referring to the evidence in the text.

Task 9 Writing

You are now going to improve your argument in favour of the Internet by attacking the opposition. Read the 'Arguments against the Internet' below – this is the opposition's case. Draft a second short paragraph for your own piece which demolishes all three arguments. Use at least two of the HIRE techniques outlined above. Try to sustain a formal writer's voice throughout your argument.

Arguments against the Internet

- Much of the information on the Internet is inaccurate or rubbish.
- Phoning or writing are better forms of communication.
- It is dangerous to shop on the Internet.

You could begin your second paragraph like this:

Opponents criticise the quality of the information on the Internet, as if cyberspace is the only place where you have to sift through mountains of rubbish...

Text structure and organisation

Getting the structure right

AIMS

- Analyse how a writer has shaped ideas into cohesive paragraphs using devices such as signposting and connectives to make links within and between paragraphs.

In this section you will think about how to signpost an argument and shape your ideas effectively into paragraphs. Then you will use a text skeleton to analyse the structure and coherence of the *New Statesman* editorial.

Signposting the argument

When your argument includes lots of references to the opposing argument, you need to make it clear that you approve of your argument and disapprove of theirs. One way of doing this is to signpost your attack very forcibly, using one-sided sentence connectives and signposts.

Task 10 Discussing

Discuss what makes these sentences from the editorial effective:

- 'There is no argument whatever for treating errant motorists more leniently than any other class of offender' (lines 29–30).
- 'The argument that exceeding the speed limit is acceptable when the road is deserted or the schools are on holiday is preposterous' (lines 41–43).

Identify a) how the sentences are signposted, and b) their position in the text as a whole.

Shaping ideas into paragraphs

The *New Statesman* editorial may be passionately argued, but the writer doesn't lose control of his material. One important way in which he organises his material is by shaping the ideas into paragraphs:

- Each paragraph has a slightly different approach to the main argument;
- The approach is stated clearly in the topic sentence;
- The rest of the text in that paragraph backs up the main idea.

Organising material in this way makes the paragraphs cohesive and the argument easier to follow.

Coherence and cohesion

The features of text structure and organisation studied so far in this section contribute to the **coherence** and the **cohesion** of the argument. Argument texts have to be particularly coherent and cohesive. A muddled argument in which the points are not clearly explained will not convince anyone.

The table below summarises what these terms mean and how you can make a text both coherent and cohesive:

Coherence	Cohesion
Definition: How the whole text is organised	*Definition:* How the individual sections of the text are organised
Key features: • the main points of the text are covered in a logical/sensible order • text includes structural features, e.g. an introduction and conclusion • paragraph breaks are used to show movement to a new main point • sometimes presentational devices used to aid the organisation	*Key features:* • the points in each paragraph are organised logically, e.g. main point then supporting points • ideas developed effectively within each paragraph, e.g. main point supported in different ways • topic sentences used to introduce the main point of a paragraph • signposts and connectives used to show links between the points, and between the paragraphs

Using text skeletons

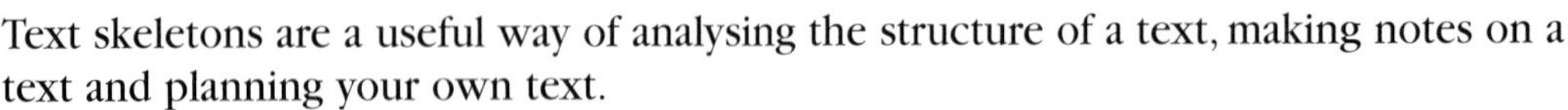

Text skeletons are a useful way of analysing the structure of a text, making notes on a text and planning your own text.

The persuade text skeleton is best suited to argument texts: it lists each main point on the left, and adds any supporting points or examples on the right as memory joggers.

Task 11 Analysing

The text skeleton on page 93 shows structure of the first three paragraphs of the *New Statesman* editorial. The first two paragraphs have been annotated (comments in boxes) to bring out the key features of coherence and cohesion and to comment on how effective they are.

Complete the whole skeleton and the annotations for paragraph 3 to provide a full analysis of the structure of the editorial. Refer back to the text of the editorial when analysing sentence connectives and signposts.

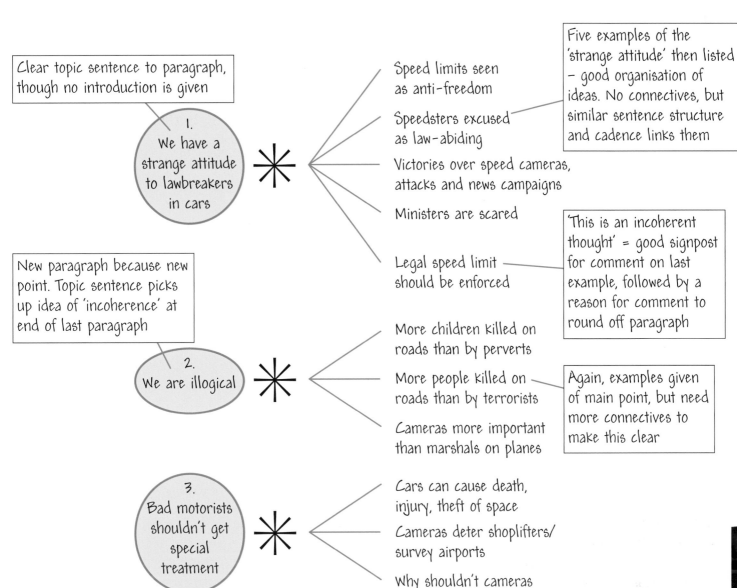

Clear topic sentence to paragraph, though no introduction is given

1. We have a strange attitude to lawbreakers in cars

- Speed limits seen as anti-freedom
- Speedsters excused as law-abiding
- Victories over speed cameras, attacks and news campaigns
- Ministers are scared
- Legal speed limit should be enforced

Five examples of the 'strange attitude' then listed – good organisation of ideas. No connectives, but similar sentence structure and cadence links them

'This is an incoherent thought' = good signpost for comment on last example, followed by a reason for comment to round off paragraph

New paragraph because new point. Topic sentence picks up idea of 'incoherence' at end of last paragraph

2. We are illogical

- More children killed on roads than by perverts
- More people killed on roads than by terrorists
- Cameras more important than marshals on planes

Again, examples given of main point, but need more connectives to make this clear

3. Bad motorists shouldn't get special treatment

- Cars can cause death, injury, theft of space
- Cameras deter shoplifters/survey airports
- Why shouldn't cameras survey cars?

Task 12 Planning practice

Using the work that you did last lesson arguing for the benefits of the Internet, your task is to plan two paragraphs of argument, but this time *against* the Internet.

- First, decide which two main points you want to make. (You may want to refer back to the list of arguments on page 90.)
- Then discuss with a partner how you could expand those points, perhaps by adding examples or by attacking the opposing argument.
- On your own, draw up a detailed text skeleton for your two paragraphs. If you group relevant ideas together, the paragraphs will be cohesive.
- Finally draft a topic sentence for each paragraph, and jot down a couple of sentence signposts that you could use, preferably including one-sided connectives like the ones below.

- Surely nobody thinks that...
- How is it possible that...
- It's beyond belief that...
- The argument that...is laughable
- Obviously...
- Everybody knows that...

Sentence structure and punctuation

Making the sentences work

AIMS

- Review the use and form of relative clauses.
- Practise punctuating relative clauses.

In this section you will remind yourself of how to construct and punctuate different kinds of relative clause, which can add variety to your sentence structures.

Using relative clauses

A relative clause is a type of subordinate clause which gives extra information about the noun phrase to which it is attached. Several relative clauses appear in the *New Statesman* editorial, as they are useful for organising ideas within a complex sentence. In each case the relative clause has been underlined, and the noun to which it is attached is in bold:

1 **Motorists** <u>who drive too fast</u> are excused on the grounds…

2 **… a description** <u>that may as easily be applied to murderers</u>

3 **speed cameras on roads**, <u>which have been shown to cut deaths and serious injuries by 35 per cent</u>, are more necessary than…

4 **An illegally parked car**, <u>which may itself lead to an accident</u>, is simply theft of road space

5 **… to deter shoplifters**, <u>who cause no physical harm to anybody</u>

6 **the minority** <u>who forget that</u> deserve to be hounded…

GRAMMAR

There are two main types of **relative clause** – **defining clauses** and **non-defining** clauses.

Defining relative clauses add information that is necessary for a full understanding of the sentence, e.g.:

The boy *<u>who came first</u> was presented with a medal.*

Here it is not clear who 'the boy' is without the relative clause: the clause 'defines' which boy you are writing about.

Note that defining relative clauses must *not* be separated from the main clause by a comma.

Non-defining relative clauses add information that is *not* necessary for a full understanding of the sentence, e.g.:

The boy, *<u>who had now recovered his breath</u>, took his medal.*

Here the relative clause does not define which boy we mean, but simply adds some information about him. 'The boy took his medal' makes sense on its own.

Note that non-defining relative clauses *are* separated from the rest of the sentence by commas. The commas show that the whole clause can be removed from the sentence without major loss.

Task 13 Discussing and analysing

Read the six relative clauses used in the *New Statesman* editorial carefully (listed on page 94).

- Discuss whether they are defining or non-defining. How can you tell?
- Do any of the sentences alter in meaning if a different type of relative clause is used instead?

Task 14 Writing

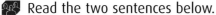

Read the two sentences below.

- *The bus driver who often speeds down our road has been sacked.* (Defining relative clause, no commas)
- *Mr Davidson, who often speeds down our road, has been caught on camera.* (Non-defining relative clause, with commas)

Work together to construct three more sentence pairs, each pair with the same relative clause except that one is a defining relative clause and one a non-defining. Make sure your sentences are grammatically correct and make sense, and that they are punctuated correctly. Be prepared to present your sentences.

Top tip Proper names are usually followed by non-defining relative clauses, as the name already defines exactly who (or where) you mean, e.g. 'Bristol, where I used to live,…';'Greg, who was absent yesterday,…'.

Reduced relative clauses

Reduced relative clauses, also called **non-finite clauses**, act almost as adjectives describing the noun they are attached to.

Look at this example from the *New Statesman* editorial:

A pedestrian hit by a vehicle travelling at 40 mph will almost certainly be killed.

The clause underlined is a reduced relative clause, which describes the noun 'vehicle'. The writer could have used a full relative clause instead:

A pedestrian hit by a vehicle which is travelling at 40 mph will almost certainly be killed.

Here is another example:

Yet the number of child pedestrians killed on the roads annually is ten times greater than…

Reduced relative clauses offer the writer another tool with which to construct complex sentences.

Task 15 Discussing and analysing

Discuss these questions:

- How could you turn the second example above into a full relative clause?
- Can you identify another reduced relative clause in the first example above?
- Are these defining or non-defining clauses? How can you tell?
- Why should a writer want to use reduced clauses when he or she can simply use full relative clauses?

Composing your own argument

AIMS

- Write sustained Standard English with the formality suited to reader and purpose.
- Make a counter-argument to a view that has been expressed, addressing weaknesses in the argument.
- Use rhetorical devices to add force to an argument.

Write your own argument for or against a ban on fox hunting, using the techniques that you have explored and practised in this unit.

1 Audience and purpose

Your local newspaper has a 'Comment' section to which young people are invited to send their opinions on a range of issues. Next week they want your opinions on whether fox hunting should be banned. The most persuasive and well-written Comment piece will be published by the editor of the paper next week.

Discuss what effect the audience and purpose of this text will have on the style of your argument. In particular, consider these questions:

- How formal should the language be?
- How reasonable or emotive do you want your piece to be?

2 Brainstorming the content

In groups who want to argue the same line (i.e. either for or against), brainstorm all the arguments that you can think of in favour of your position. You may like to build on the arguments in the panels below and on page 97.

Arguments FOR a ban

- Killing wild animals for pleasure should not be acceptable in this day and age.
- Foxes are terrified by the chase and then torn apart by the hounds – not a civilised way of protecting lambs and chickens.
- The fact that people are employed in fox hunting doesn't make it right: some people make a living selling drugs or weapons.
- There are other ways of controlling foxes, such as shooting or snares.
- As Oscar Wilde said, fox hunting is 'the unspeakable in pursuit of the uneatable'.

Arguments AGAINST a ban

- Fox hunting is a traditional country pursuit supported by 60% of people in hunting areas – city-dwellers should not interfere.
- Fishing is just as cruel as fox hunting, yet fishing is not banned.
- A foxhound kills a fox quickly and cleanly; shooting can cause foxes slow and painful deaths.
- Fox hunting is a practical method for controlling the fox population.
- The Countryside Alliance says that 16 000 jobs will be lost if hunting is banned – people who work for the hunts, breed dogs, make saddles, etc.

3 Planning the form and structure

Select three or four arguments that you think are the most powerful and list them in the most effective order.

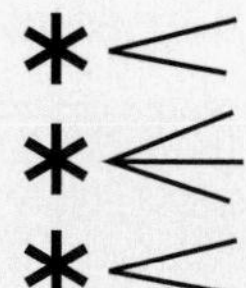

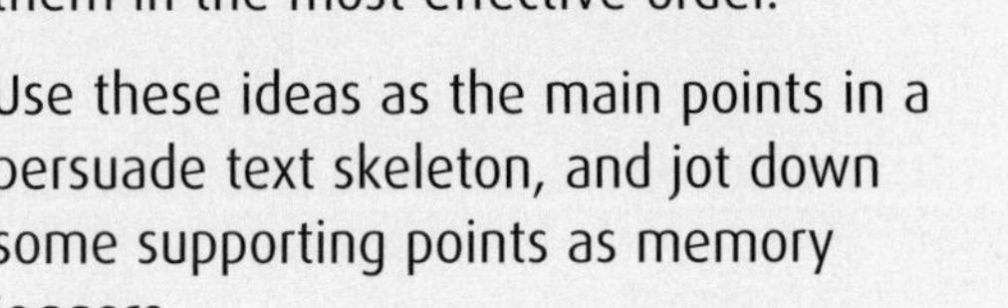

Use these ideas as the main points in a persuade text skeleton, and jot down some supporting points as memory joggers.

If you can think of any powerful phrases that can be used in support of any of these arguments, jot these down too.

4 Discussing what you are going to write

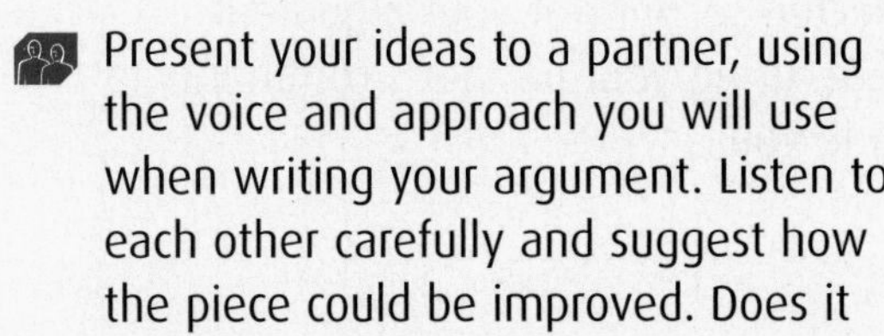

Present your ideas to a partner, using the voice and approach you will use when writing your argument. Listen to each other carefully and suggest how the piece could be improved. Does it hang together well? Do the sections include attacks on the opposing argument? Is the chosen writer's voice appropriate and sustained throughout? Jot down any useful points on your plan.

5 Composing your piece

 Now you are ready to write.

Points to remember

- Include clear topic sentences to show the point you are making in each paragraph (see page 88).
- Think of the cadence, or rhythm, of your sentences (see page 88).
- Use some rhetorical techniques to make your argument more forceful (see page 88).
- Counter the opposing argument (remember the HIRE techniques), as attack is often the best form of defence (see page 89).
- Sustain a consistent writer's voice, using a tone appropriate to your audience and purpose.
- Signpost the argument to clarify the point you are making (see page 90).
- Shape your ideas into effectively organised paragraphs (see page 91).
- Use connectives to show the connection between points, and between paragraphs (see pages 91–92).
- Use a range of complex sentences, including relative clauses (see page 94).
- Punctuate your sentences correctly, especially when distinguishing defining and non-defining relative clauses (see page 95).

You may like to use some of the sentence signposts and connectives below.

Sentence signposts and connectives

- Fox hunting is an established part of
- How is it possible that in the 21st century
- The argument that... is beyond belief
- We all know what really happens when
- Just because the fox hunting industry employs
- It is illogical to condemn fox hunting when
- Surely nobody can enjoy
- To argue that
- However
- Yet
- Furthermore

6 Peer comment

 Swap your draft with a partner's and read it carefully. Decide what works well and highlight this on the draft. Discuss what you need to do to improve your work. Jot down up to three suggestions on the draft. Redraft the selected sections of your argument piece, using your partner's comments to guide you.

7 Pulling it all together

Listen to some of the comment pieces written by members of your class. Decide what are the key features that make these extracts effective as arguments. Write down three targets to aim for the next time you compose an argument.

G The Art of Writing Advice

Revisiting how to write advice

AIMS

- Analyse the stylistic conventions of advice: a particular form of persuasion text.
- Compare the presentation of ideas in related texts.

In this section you will analyse different examples of advice texts and decide what typical features they share.

Different kinds of advice

Written advice comes in different shapes and forms, for example:

- an **advice leaflet** on how to protect your house from the risk of fire
- a **self-help book** on controlling your anger.

Advice text aims to persuade the reader to take a recommended course of action. However, the audience of advice texts is usually looking for help in the first place. Heavy persuasive techniques, such as emotive language, are therefore usually not appropriate.

Task 1 Reading and analysing

Read the two advice texts below. Text 1 has been annotated to show some of the features that make it an advice text. Annotate Text 2 in a similar way.

Text 1 *Online advice given by Relate, an organisation which specialises in relationship problems*

Home | Want Advice? | Take Charge | Family Life

• About us • Support us • Media Centre • Business Centre

"We keep having the same old arguments. How do we stop going round in circles?"

When you keep regurgitating the same old issues it means that nothing is getting resolved. Both of you will feel unheard and frustrated. It becomes a battleground where neither of you will back down, and this can become really destructive. There are no winners in this scenario, only losers – the relationship being the biggest loser of all. For a different outcome try a few basic rules: Stick to only one subject – don't keep saying 'And another thing!'; Don't point the finger of blame – there are usually three fingers pointing back at you; Don't name call – it really isn't very grown up; Take it in turns to talk – listen to what's being said and check out anything you don't understand.

Not all rows are destructive. They can be healthy, especially if you both learn ways of negotiating ways forward. Relate counsellors can help you to stop going round in circles.

• Back to Top

Layout – problem needing advice is in bold, with quote marks. This acts as hook for reader

Direct address – second person used

Informal language (including contractions) – to get reader onside

Commands used for the 'rules'. Each rule has same **format**, with reason or further point given after dash

Informal tone – answer uses some of same language to show it is addressing question

Signposting – 'it means that' signposts the reason

Sentence signpost shows this is where writer suggests acting in a new way

Clear topic sentence to introduce new point

Causal connective signposts reason for statement

Text 2 *An extract from a book on violence, aimed at young teenagers*

12 things you can do about violence

1. **SAY NO!**
   If someone tries to hurt you or forces you to do something you know is wrong, say NO! Say it loudly, clearly and repeatedly.

2. **BREAK THE SILENCE**
   If you are being hurt or know that someone else is being hurt by someone, tell an adult you can trust. Make it clear to people who ask you to keep secrets about violence that you won't.

3. **DEMAND A BULLYING POLICY**
   Find out if your school has a policy about bullying. If it doesn't, get together with your classmates and teachers, talk to your head teacher or write to the board of governors at your school and demand a bullying policy.

Task 2 Discussing and recording

Discuss what is similar and what is different in these two texts, and why. One person in each group should compare one of the following features across both texts, recording examples and giving reasons for their use:

- visual presentation, e.g. use of bold and colour
- writer's voice, e.g. how formal, use of emotive words
- attitude to audience, e.g. whether direct address is used
- structure, e.g. how logical or clear the structure is.

Record your findings in a grid like the one begun below.

	Text 1	Text 2
Visual presentation Font sizes/style Colour and overall design	Font size the same, as it's an electronic text. Question in bold, to be clear and hook reader.	
Language		

Now discuss the following questions:

- Can you explain the similarities and differences? Consider the audience and context of each extract in your analysis.
- Is one extract a more effective advice text than the other?

Finally, draw up a list of 'Key Features of Advice Texts'. Be prepared to present your findings.

Composition and effect

Learning from example

AIMS

- Analyse the stylistic conventions of persuasion text, seeing how it relates to advice text.
- Write with different degrees of formality to suit the audience and purpose.
- Analyse how the author's standpoint can affect meaning in an advice text.

In this section you will analyse what makes an advice text effective, focusing on the mix of formal/informal and personal/impersonal language.

Task 3 Reading and considering

Read the advice below, which is taken from the Raising Kids website. As you read the extract, consider these questions:

- What is the purpose of the advice?
- Who do you think the audience is?

raising kids

If it's about raising kids... ...it's here | Sitemap | Parents' news | Win prizes! |

Beat The Bickering Between Siblings

Do your children squabble all the time? Is it driving you mad? How can you stop it?

It's unlikely that anyone will get hurt but they're not the only ones who get wound up by their constant needling and bickering. It's so irritating for innocent bystanders!

'You're on a yellow card!'

Give them a warning that if they don't play together peacefully – or at least quietly – then you will stop the game. The football metaphor 'You're on a yellow card!' is a graphic way to issue a warning and works particularly well with boys. Fear of the subsequent 'red card' and 'sending off' may just be enough to stop them bickering.

'If you're going to squabble, go outside'

Bickering and squabbling often bothers the listener more than the antagonists. Faced with low-level warfare of the most irritating kind, try moving the battlefield to somewhere where you can't hear them. As long as you're sure that no one will get hurt, this could solve your problem.

Separate them

If the bickering starts again, separate them. If they can't play together, they'll have to play alone. Each will claim to be delighted at this prospect, but playing alone is seldom as much fun as playing with someone else. They now have an incentive to sort things out between themselves.

Powerful title to attract attention – note use of alliteration

Subheading – draws reader in by listing problems they may have. Three questions for rhetorical effect

Conversational/informal tone – note use of contractions

Subheading marks first piece of advice

Command – used for first rule

Reason why advice should be followed

Informal language – gets on side of audience

Sympathetic remark to get audience on side

Direct address for impact

Sentence signposts – structures advice clearly and logically

Let them solve their own problems

If you want them to sort out the cause of the problem, different tactics are required. Tell them they have a certain amount of time to get the matter sorted, after which you'll take away the toy, turn off the television or remove whatever is causing the disagreement. The best long-term solution to squabbling and bickering is to help your children develop their own ways of settling their differences. Reaching a compromise provides excellent lessons in negotiating and problem solving. When the agreement breaks down – as it undoubtedly will – make them go back and work things out again.

Life skills

Conflict and disagreements are facts of life. When peace finally breaks out between brothers and sisters, it's because they have used problem solving and negotiation skills instead of fighting. These will be very useful when they have to deal with other children at school and in the peer group.

Task 4 Topic sentences

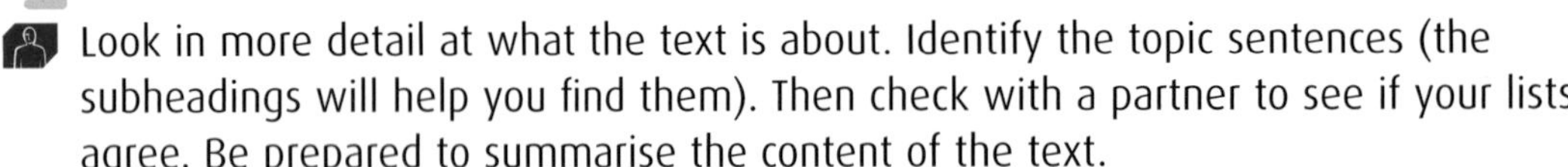

Look in more detail at what the text is about. Identify the topic sentences (the subheadings will help you find them). Then check with a partner to see if your lists agree. Be prepared to summarise the content of the text.

Task 5 Annotating

The first part of *Beat the Bickering* has been annotated to show some of the language features that make it an advice text. Annotate the rest of the extract in a similar way, to bring out the typical features of advice texts.

Formal or informal?

The writer of a piece of advice has to decide how formal the language is going to be. Remind yourself of the main features of each style of language given in the grid below.

Formal	Informal
More complex/compound sentences	More simple sentences
Often impersonal language	Often personal language
Does not use contractions/abbreviations	Uses contractions/abbreviations
Uses Standard English	Uses non-Standard English: colloquialisms, slang, dialect
Includes specialist/difficult vocabulary	Mainly straightforward vocabulary

Task 6 Discussing

Look at the grid on page 102, then discuss:

- What are the advantages and disadvantages of using formal language in an advice text?
- What are the advantages and disadvantages of using informal language?

The importance of the writer's voice

'Writer's voice' is the role a writer takes on for a piece of writing, in this case a piece of advice. The voice may range from very friendly and informal to very distant and formal. The voice always depends on the audience and purpose of the writing. The style of the writing reflects or matches this voice and should be sustained throughout.

Task 7 Analysing

Many successful advice texts combine the advantages of both informal and formal language. Read through *Beat the Bickering* together and highlight or draw up a list of places where each style is used.

- Is the balance between informal and formal a good one for the purpose and audience of the text?
- Is the writer's voice consistent throughout this piece of advice?

Task 8 Writing

The final paragraph of the advice text, headed 'Life skills', is quite formal in style. Your task is to rewrite it for a different audience of 10- to 12-year-olds. You will, therefore, need to make the style more informal.

For example, you could begin:

> Let's face it, if you've got a brother or sister you're going to get into a fight with them sometime or other.

Text structure and organisation

Getting the structure right

AIMS

- Compare and use different ways of opening paragraphs.
- Integrate diverse information into a coherent account.

In this section you will use a text skeleton to analyse the structure of *Beat the Bickering*, and think about the order of advice and how to begin your paragraphs effectively. You will also plan an advice text of your own.

Using text skeletons

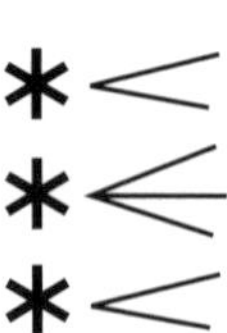

A useful way of analysing the structure of any text, and of planning your own text, is to construct a text skeleton. The persuade text skeleton is most useful for advice texts. It lists each main point on the left, and adds any supporting points or examples on the right as memory joggers.

Task 9 Structuring

The persuade text skeleton has been used below to start the analysis of *Beat the Bickering*. Complete the skeleton to provide a full picture of the structure of the extract. Refer back to the summaries that you made of the content of the extract (Task 4, page 102) to help you.

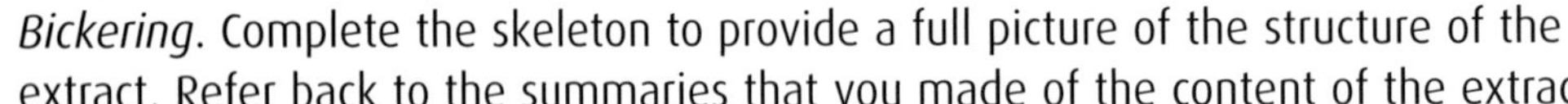

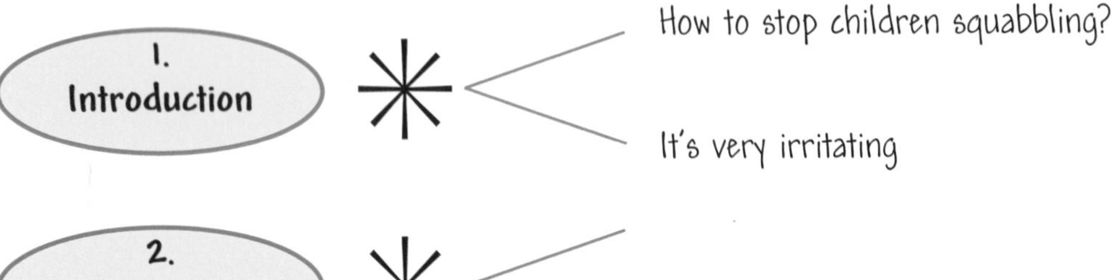

What is the main presentational device that the author of the extract has used to organise their material?

Ordering the advice

When you are writing advice, you must consider the best order in which to put your tips. In some texts you may want to put the most important pieces of advice first, whereas in others you may want to build up to it.

Task 10 Discussing

Discuss why you think the author of *Beat the Bickering* ordered their advice in the way they did. How is the chosen order effective?

Effective openings

To be effective, advice texts must be clear and direct. In particular, the reader needs to know what the topic of each paragraph or section is as soon as possible. *Beat the Bickering* uses three main types of opening sentence in its paragraphs:

- **A statement of how things are**, often beginning with a noun phrase to act as a sentence signpost, e.g. '*Bickering and squabbling* often bothers the listener…'
- **A command** – telling the reader to do something, e.g. '*Give* them a warning…'
- **A conditional clause** followed by a command, e.g. '*If the bickering starts again*, separate them'.

Task 11 Discussing

Consider the following questions:

- What purpose does each of these types of opening sentence have? Identify different examples of these in the text to help you.
- What would the effect be if the author had used one type throughout?

Task 12 Planning practice

You are writing an advice leaflet aimed at windsurfers. Below is a list of topics that you could cover, and five main headings for your five paragraphs (in bold).

- Construct a text skeleton to plan your leaflet using this material. Make sure you put the paragraphs in an effective order.
- Think of a clear opening sentence for each paragraph, and write this on your plan. You may like to use one of the three types discussed above.

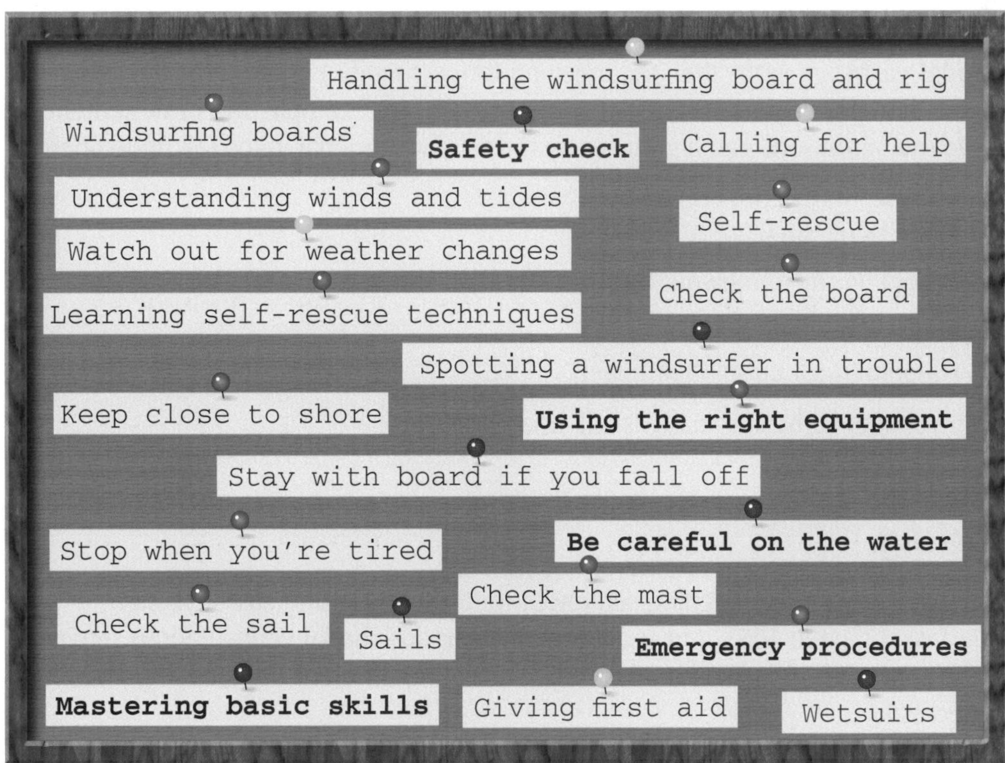

Handling the windsurfing board and rig
Windsurfing boards
Safety check
Calling for help
Understanding winds and tides
Self-rescue
Watch out for weather changes
Check the board
Learning self-rescue techniques
Spotting a windsurfer in trouble
Keep close to shore
Using the right equipment
Stay with board if you fall off
Stop when you're tired
Be careful on the water
Check the mast
Check the sail
Sails
Emergency procedures
Mastering basic skills
Giving first aid
Wetsuits

4 Sentence structure and punctuation

Making the sentences work

AIMS

- Develop your sentences by using modal verbs.
- Use punctuation effectively to clarify meaning.

In this section you will explore how to use modal verbs to add degrees of possibility or necessity to your sentences. You will also review the different uses of punctuation.

Using modal verbs

Look at these three sentences from *Beat the Bickering*:

- Fear of the subsequent 'red card' and 'sending off' may just be enough to stop them bickering.
- As long as you're sure that no one will get hurt, this could solve your problem.
- These will be very useful when they have to deal with other children at school and in the peer group.

The underlined words are **modal verbs** (see grammar panel below). Modal verbs are particularly useful when writing advice, as they show *how likely* it is that something will happen when you act in a certain way.

likely	more likely	most likely	necessary
MAY/MIGHT	CAN/COULD	WILL	SHOULD/MUST

GRAMMAR

Modal verbs are verbs that add meaning to (or 'modify') other verbs by giving them different degrees of possibility or necessity. For example, the basic sentence 'I do my homework' can be altered by the following modal verbs (all underlined):

- I might do my homework
- I can do my homework
- I could do my homework
- I will do my homework
- I should/must do my homework.

Other modal verbs are 'may', 'shall' and 'would'.

Task 13 Writing

Look back at your five opening sentences for the windsurfing advice leaflet (see Task 12, page 105), and see if they include any modal verbs. Redraft three of the sentences to include modal verbs, indicating different degrees of possibility or necessity.

For example:

Check your equipment regularly to make sure it is in good working order

could be redrafted as:

You should check your equipment regularly to make sure it is in good working order.

Swap sentences and check if your partner's are effective. If not, suggest different modal verbs, giving reasons why your suggestion is an improvement.

Punctuation for clarity and meaning

The main purpose of punctuation is to make the meaning of a text clear. It does this by indicating:

- where there should be a pause (e.g. semicolon, comma)
- where clauses and sentences end (e.g. comma, full stop)
- how different parts of a word or sentence are connected (e.g. apostrophe of omission, brackets, dashes)
- what function a word or sentence has (e.g. apostrophe of possession, question mark, inverted comma).

Task 14 Analysing

 Scan *Beat the Bickering* (see page 101) and identify six different punctuation marks. Discuss the reason why each one is used, and draw up a table to show your findings.

Punctuation mark	Examples of use/effect
Apostrophe of omission	Line 3 'It's unlikely' – contraction of 'it is' to give informal tone

Task 15 Writing

TR

The extract below about competition between siblings (brothers and sisters) is hard to follow because it contains several punctuation errors. Rewrite the passage, correcting the mistakes. Be prepared to explain why you have added, deleted or changed the punctuation in each case.

> Everyone has special qualities and talents and each of your children have qualities, that are different from their siblings'. Is he or she artistic; practical; a good cook, a natural comic; a great socialiser or sporty. Help competitive children by identifying their strength's and developing their confidence, in their own unique abilities. Make sure they understand – that their talents though different are equally valued by you

5 Composing your own advice

AIMS

- Write sustained Standard English with the formality suited to reader and purpose.
- Offer advice or guidelines for action, adopting an impersonal style to suggest impartiality and authority.

Write an advice text on the subject of teenage safety, adopting a formal style.

1 Audience and purpose

The local council is sending a booklet on practical crime prevention to all households. Your job is to write the section entitled 'Safety tips for teenagers'.

Discuss what effect the audience and purpose of this text will have on the style. In particular, consider these questions:

- How formal and impersonal should the language be?
- What tone should you adopt?

2 Brainstorming the content

Brainstorm the topics that you may want to include in your section, and any pieces of advice that occur to you. You may want to consider the following areas:

- going out at night
- looking for casual jobs, like babysitting
- using internet chatlines
- making emergency phone calls
- self-defence
- being harassed.

Your brainstorm may begin like this:

3 Planning the form and structure

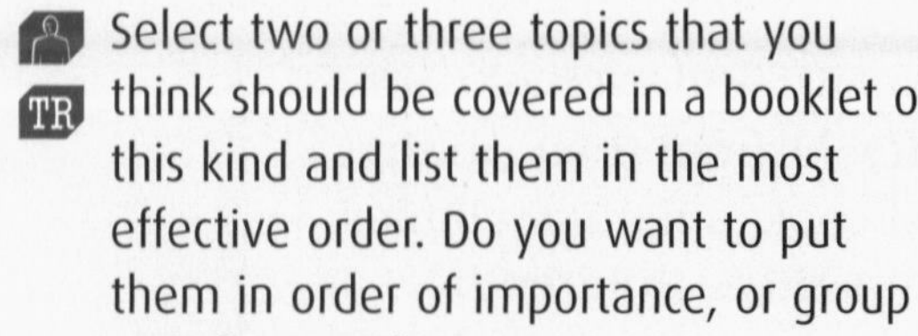

Select two or three topics that you think should be covered in a booklet of this kind and list them in the most effective order. Do you want to put them in order of importance, or group together similar topics?

Use these ideas as the main points in a persuasion skeleton, and jot down some supporting points as memory joggers. Remember that supporting points can give further examples, provide reasons for the advice, or go into more detail. Add the focus for a short introduction and conclusion.

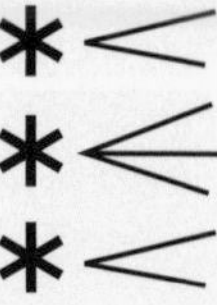

Think about the visual presentation. Will you use devices such as subheadings and bullet points to organise the text?

4 Discussing what you are going to write

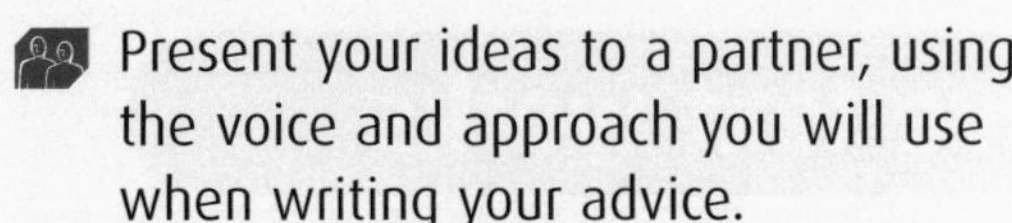

Present your ideas to a partner, using the voice and approach you will use when writing your advice.

Listen to each other carefully and suggest how the advice could be improved. Check that the chosen writer's voice is appropriate and sustained throughout. Jot down any useful points on your plan.

5 Composing your piece

Now you are ready to write.

Points to remember

- Think about the right balance of formal and informal language and your chosen writer's voice (see page 102).
- Give reasons, where appropriate, why each piece of advice should be followed (see page 104).
- Give each paragraph or bullet point an effective opening sentence (see page 105).
- Use modal verbs to show the right degree of possibility or necessity (see page 106).
- Make sure the punctuation is varied, accurate and effective (see page 107).

You may like to use some of the sentence signposts and connectives below.

Sentence signposts and connectives

- There are some basic rules
- If you go out at night
- If you walk home
- Knowing some self-defence
- Screech alarms can be useful
- Don't take a lift
- Of course, you will want
- Wherever you are,
- On a paper round,
- Don't be afraid to
- One way of
- These simple rules should

6 Peer comment

Swap your draft with a partner's and read it carefully. Decide what works well and highlight this on the draft. Discuss what you need to do to improve your work. Jot down up to three suggestions on the draft. Redraft the selected sections of your advice, using your partner's comments to guide you.

7 Pulling it all together

Listen to some of the advice texts written by members of your class. Discuss what are the key features that make these extracts effective. Write down three targets to aim for the next time you write advice.

H The Art of Discursive Writing

Revisiting how discursive text works

AIMS

- Analyse the stylistic conventions of discursive writing.
- Compare the presentation of ideas in related texts.

In this section you will analyse different examples of discursive texts to remind yourself of their typical features.

Different kinds of discursive text

Discursive texts come in different shapes and forms, for example:

- **newspaper articles** covering controversial issues, e.g. whether smacking children should be banned
- **magazine articles** listing the good and bad points of a product, shop or activity
- **textbook discussions** of ethical issues, e.g. the advantages/dangers of cloning
- **compare-and-contrast or 'discuss' essays**, particularly in English, History or RE.

Discursive texts present arguments and information from different points of view. As their purpose is to help someone understand an issue, they present the arguments as fairly as possible, although the writer often states their own viewpoint in a concluding paragraph.

Task 1 Reading and analysing

In groups of six, read the four different texts below. Text 1 has been annotated to show some of the features that make it a discursive text. One pair in each group should annotate Text 2, 3 or 4 in a similar way, then join up to discuss their findings.

Text 1

How much influence do adverts have on you?

Some people argue that adverts have less influence than is often made out. They say that most people are suspicious of the claims that advertisers make. They suggest that the most popular TV ads are enjoyed because they are entertaining and funny, rather than because they are informative about the product, and that they don't really influence people to buy the product.

However, there is plenty of evidence to suggest that advertising does work. Retailers are often informed before a TV advertising campaign is about to take place in their area, so that they can stock up on the product in advance, and be in a position to meet the demand for the product that a campaign is likely to generate. Successful campaigns do lead to increased sales.

Sentence signpost – shows which point of view is being put

Present tense and third person used throughout

Logical connective – shows opposing case is being put

Structure – each paragraph presents a different viewpoint

Title – often raises question to be discussed

Sentence signpost – introduces evidence to back up claim

Formal language – note use of passive

New paragraph – to show we are moving on to opposing view

Restrained tone throughout

Text 2

Euthanasia – for and against

Euthanasia (literally, 'a good death') means a death brought about by a doctor providing drugs or an injection to bring a peaceful end to someone who is terminally ill or in great pain.

Some people believe that only God can give and take away life. Many religious people, therefore, do not agree with suicide and assisted dying. However, there are many religious people who do support voluntary euthanasia. In the Netherlands, Catholic or Dutch reformed clergymen may be present at assisted deaths.

Opponents of euthanasia believe that it is the slippery slope to involuntary euthanasia – that soon we will be killing the sick or elderly against their will. Supporters of euthanasia assert that voluntary euthanasia is based on the right to choose for yourself, which is totally different from murder.

Those who disagree with euthanasia also believe that it would damage society if it were legalised, as it would remove the traditional principle that man should not kill. Supporters of euthanasia, however, point out that we already let people die when they refuse treatment which could save their life.

Text 3

Compare and contrast Alfred Lord Tennyson's poem 'The Charge of the Light Brigade' and Wilfred Owen's 'The Sentry'. Which do you prefer as an example of war poetry?

Two poems about war – but they could hardly be more different. They seem to come from different eras, yet Tennyson wrote his poem only sixty years before Owen. The differences are partly to do with their historical context, therefore, which makes the tone of the poems almost poles apart, but also to do with different techniques that the 20th-century poem had to offer.

Tennyson's poem describes an incident at the Battle of Balaklava in 1854, when six hundred cavalrymen (the 'light brigade') ride into a trap and half of them are killed. The poem starts breathlessly in the midst of this fateful cavalry ride, the rhythm of the lines mimicking the thunder of the horses' hooves:

Half a league half a league
Half a league onward
All in the valley of Death
Rode the six hundred.

Wilfred Owen's poem, by contrast, describes an ordinary incident in the First World War, when one of the writer's companions is blinded by a shell.

Text 4

Sony Walkman

Some really **GOOD** points

* The beautiful, elegant and light MD player fits perfectly into a pocket, and looks really good on your desk or on your lap on the train!
* It comes with a rechargeable battery and a neat little stand to charge it on.
* It can plug into the car and play all your favourite tunes out loud on a basic car stereo.
* The loading and unloading pop up system is flawless.

Some **BAD** points (worth considering)

* The headphones, in my opinion, are almost pointless (but they still play the tunes!).
* The charger-come-stand is the only way to charge the batteries, so if you run out and don't have the stand with you, you will need to rely on normal batteries.

If I were you I would definitely go with Sony, all of the Net MDs are ace!, but stay away from other makes unless you're spending a lot of money.

Task 2 Discussing and recording

In fours, discuss what is similar and what is different in these discursive texts, and why. One person in each group should compare one of the following features across all four texts, recording examples and giving reasons for their use:

- writer's voice, e.g. how formal, use of descriptive/emotive words
- how fairly the arguments are presented, e.g. balance of coverage, writer's own viewpoint
- structure, e.g. how logical or clear the structure is, use of connectives
- presentation, e.g. use of subheadings, design devices.

Record your findings in a grid like the one begun below.

	Text 1	Text2	Text 3	Text 4
Language • How formal is the language? • Have powerful nouns and verbs, and emotive language been used? • How are sentences constructed? • What is the tone of the writer?	Formal language, e.g. 'are often informed' (passive) Plain words, not emotive, e.g. 'plenty of evidence'			Some informal language, e.g. contraction 'don't', and exclamation marks
Balance/fairness				

Now discuss the following questions:

- Can you explain the similarities and differences? Consider the audience and purpose of each extract in your analysis.
- Is one extract a more effective discursive text than the others?

Finally, draw up a list of 'Key Features of Discursive Texts'. Be prepared to present your findings to the class.

Composition and effect

Learning from example

AIMS

- Analyse the stylistic conventions of discursive writing.
- Compare the presentation of ideas in related texts.
- Integrate speech, reference and quotation effectively into a discursive essay.

In this section you will analyse a compare-and-contrast essay, focusing on the choice of topics to be compared, how it uses evidence from the text, and the effectiveness of the introduction.

Comparing openings

The following discursive essay compares and contrasts two openings of recount texts about footballers. You may like to reread the original texts on pages 24 and 25 to refresh your memory before starting work on the essay.

Task 3 Reading and considering

As you read the essay, think about its purpose and audience, and how this affects the content, structure and style.

Compare and contrast the opening paragraphs of Tony Adams' autobiography, *Addicted*, and Ian Hamilton's biography of Paul Gascoigne, *Gazza Antagonistes*. Which passage is the more effective opening?

Books about footballers – aren't they just all the same? Well, yes and no. These accounts of Tony Adams and Paul Gascoigne begin in equally arresting ways, but their style is markedly different. Their titles give us a clue as to what is to follow: what could be more pithy and hard-hitting than *Addicted*, and what could be more stylish and playful than *Gazza Antagonistes*?[1] In their different ways, therefore, the books manage to engage the reader even before they have been opened. This attention-grabbing continues with the first few paragraphs of text.

Both writers begin their books by plunging us into the middle of the action. Adams describes – or rather hints at, and later describes – the famous penalty shoot-out with Germany in Euro '96, and Hamilton takes us onto the pitch with Gazza on a particular day in 1987. This method is direct and effective. The structure of the passage from *Addicted* is particularly interesting and complex. We begin with a key moment of anticipation – Adams is expecting disaster both on the football field and

Question clearly sets out two texts being compared

Interesting opening hook – grabs reader

Topic sentence

Formal and impersonal language, but not dull. Note rhetorical questions and balanced clauses

Present tense and third person, as describing books

Question ends by asking writer to decide between texts

Reference to two texts early on – shows that writer is answering question

Causal connective – shows that this statement follows on from previous sentences

Sentence signpost – leads reader to expect more on this in next paragraph

[1] **Antagonistes** – a play on the title of John Milton's verse drama *Samson Agonistes*

in the bar afterwards – then, in the second paragraph, look back over several years to give this moment real meaning and context, and finally, in the third paragraph, return to the detail of the shoot-out. Hamilton's structure is remarkably similar: he begins with a key moment (emphasised by the single-sentence paragraph), fills that out in the second paragraph and gives some context in the third.

As one passage is from a biography and one from an autobiography, their narrative perspective is different. *Addicted* is written in the first person – indeed, the very first word of the book is 'I'. Adams describes the events of Euro '96, and his feelings about drink, from personal experience – from 'within'. *Gazza Antagonistes,* however, is a biography, so the main subject of the book is described in the third person. Again, this is made clear in the first sentence, where Gazza's full name is given. And the long description of him in the second paragraph has an objectivity about it, as if a camera were tracking him from the side of the pitch. Five sentences in a row begin 'He'. Despite the very real presence of the biographer, who seems to sidle onto the pitch alongside his hero, we are left in no doubt as to the subject of this book, and of how he commands our attention.

There is, therefore, a personal aspect to both passages, which affects the formality of the language. Although both are predominantly written in formal Standard English, the occasional informality creeps in. (And why not? Football fans don't stand on formality.) Adams refers to drink as 'booze' in line 12, and uses the phrase 'right now ... was as bad as it got' shortly afterwards. The rest of his language is strangely formal: the third paragraph, for example, begins with the stilted 'We had not actually planned for this' instead of the more natural 'We hadn't actually planned for this.' Hamilton, by contrast, is not afraid of contractions ('I didn't' begins the second sentence) and other informalities, such as the colloquialism 'nutmeg' in line 8.

This difference affects the tone too. Hamilton may be in love with his subject but he treats it with a light touch. There is gentle mockery in his description of Gazza as 'plump, twitchy and pink-faced', and of his huge hunger for the ball. He can end his sentence in a throwaway phrase, which almost undercuts what he has just said: 'He talked a lot, played to the crowd, or tried to', where the final three words undermine Gazza's efforts. Adams, on the other hand, is as grim as his real subject, alcohol addiction. There is little room for humour here, though the bleakness and fatalism, right from the first sentence ('I just knew what would happen'), has its own power and attraction.

In their different ways, each author knows how to sustain an effective style. Adams focuses on the harsh facts. The sentences are often as plain and hard as a red card waved in the face: 'I needed to numb the pain. And so I would drink. For the next seven weeks.' Longer sentences add variety: the contrast between the final two sentences, for example, is very effective, and the repetition of 'I just knew what would happen' at the beginning and end of the first paragraph is also well managed. His vocabulary is not rich, however: 'joyous moments of achievement' and 'balmy summer night' are bland and verge on the cliché.

Hamilton is the greater stylist. The description of Gazza in the second paragraph draws the reader in, point after punchy point being emphasised by the repeated 'He's. The similar lengths of the sentences add to this effect. Nor is he afraid of uncommon words such as 'unprepossessing', 'puerile' and 'wags'. Finally, there is the delightful imagery of 'He would bring sunshine to our drizzly field of play', followed immediately by the contrast of 'What he actually brought was a repertoire of muttered curses'.

As both passages have their strengths, I find it hard to judge between them. Hamilton's command of language is surer, but Adams' psychological insight and cliffhanger beginning is hard to beat. In their own way, therefore, they are both very effective openings to draw the crowds to the bookshop terraces.

Task 4 Topic sentences

Look in more detail at what the text is about. Identify the topic sentences, then check with a partner to see if you agree. The first one has been highlighted in orange for you. Be prepared to summarise the content of the text. Why are topic sentences so important in a discursive text?

Task 5 Annotating

The first part of the essay has been annotated to show some of the features that make it a discursive text. Annotate the next section (lines 14–26) to bring out further features, and explain what effect they have.

Comparing and contrasting

In English you are often asked to 'compare and contrast' two stories, poems, playscripts, adverts or other kinds of text. But what aspects of the two texts are you actually being asked to compare?

Task 6 Scanning and discussing

Scan the essay and make a note of the all the different features of the texts, that the writer compares and contrasts. Your list of topic sentences will help you with this task. Then discuss:

- Have these features been covered in an appropriate order? What other order(s) would have worked just as well?
- Are there any other features that you would have covered, or that you would have missed out?
- The second part of the question asks the writer to focus their comparison on a particular aspect of the texts. What is this aspect, and how does it differ from the main question in terms of personal response?

Task 7 Thinking about content

Imagine that one of you has to write an essay comparing two films, and the other to write an essay comparing two novels. Brainstorm with your partner what features you would compare in each essay. Choose from the list of muddled features started below. Then add your own additional features.

- The quality of the acting
- The music/special effects
- The style and tone of the language
- The characters/characterisation
- How entertaining they are

Be prepared to present your two lists of features.

Writing an effective introduction

Most forms of text need a good introduction, and compare-and-contrast essays are no exception. These are some of the things that a good introduction will do:

- Show that you understand the question and key issues by including some of the words or ideas from the question in your introduction;
- Introduce the two texts that you are comparing, even if only briefly;
- Make the reader want to read on by using powerful language or providing an interesting angle or hook;
- Use Standard English appropriate to a formal essay.

Task 8 Analysing

Read the two versions of the opening paragraph below and discuss which is more effective. Be prepared to explain in detail how well they fulfil the criteria outlined in the bullet points above.

Version 1

Books about footballers – aren't they just all the same? Well, yes and no. These accounts of Tony Adams and Paul Gascoigne begin in equally arresting ways, but their style is markedly different. Their titles give us a clue as to what is to follow: what could be more pithy and hard-hitting than *Addicted*, and what could be more stylish and playful than *Gazza Antagonistes*?[1] In their different ways, therefore, the books manage to engage the reader even before they have been opened. This attention-grabbing continues with the first few paragraphs of text.

Version 2

You can hardly compare the great Tony Adams with poor old Gazza, can you. Adams has been one of the greatest captains and players for Arsenal. When I was six I saw Tony Adams score the last goal against Everton in a fantastic 4–0 victory. What Gazza is famous for is blubbing on the pitch. Where is the contest? Comparing the two books is a more difficult question, but you can see straight off that one is a biography and one is an autobiography, so that makes a difference. Adams' book is from his point of view.

Quoting the evidence

When you are writing an essay about a text or texts, you need to back up your comments by referring to evidence in the text itself. This can be done directly or indirectly:

- **Direct references** must consist of the actual words used in the text, which are enclosed in inverted commas to show that they are quotes, e.g. 'Finally there is the delightful imagery of "He would bring sunshine to our drizzly field of play".'

- **Indirect references** are statements about the text backed up by paraphrased[1] evidence, e.g. 'Hamilton is the greater stylist. The description of Gazza in the second paragraph draws the reader in, point after punchy point being emphasised by the repeated 'He's'.

[1] **paraphrased** – summed up

In either case, you must have a *purpose* in quoting evidence, which means you must use it as evidence to back up a particular point you are making, for example:

Point

Hamilton's structure is remarkably similar: he begins with a key moment, fills that out in the second paragraph and gives some context in the third.

Evidence

Point

His vocabulary is not rich, however: 'joyous moments of achievement' and 'balmy summer night' are bland and verge on the cliché.

Comment

Evidence

Top tip Make your **P**oint and back it up with **E**vidence (do your **PE**).

Often adding a further **C**omment can explain how the evidence relates to the point, or emphasises the point further: **P**oint, **E**vidence, **C**omment (flex your **PEC**s).

Task 9 Analysing

Read the two extracts below, and discuss why Version 1 makes better use of quotation than Version 2.

Version 1

Hamilton may be in love with his subject but he treats it with a light touch. There is gentle mockery in his description of Gazza as 'plump, twitchy and pink-faced', and of his huge hunger for the ball. He can end his sentence in a throwaway phrase, which almost undercuts what he has just said: 'He talked a lot, played to the crowd, or tried to', where the final three words undermine Gazza's efforts.

Version 2

Hamilton may be in love with his subject but he treats it with a light touch. 'His appearance was unprepossessing. He was plump, twitchy and pink-faced, and on the small side. And he was cheeky in a puerile sort of way. He was always looking to nutmeg defenders when it would have been easier to pass them by.' He can end his sentences in throwaway phrases.

Text structure and organisation

Getting the structure right

AIMS

- Compare and use different ways of developing paragraphs.
- Analyse and exploit the stylistic conventions of discursive text.
- Analyse how a writer has shaped ideas into cohesive paragraphs using devices such as signposting and connectives to make links within and between paragraphs.

In this section you will use a text skeleton to analyse the structure of the compare-and-contrast essay. You will also explore different ways of shaping ideas into paragraphs and signposting which text or argument you are discussing.

Using text skeletons

Text skeletons are a useful way of analysing the structure of a text, making notes on a text and planning your own text. The discursive text skeleton lists the main points of one argument or text on one side, and the main points of the other argument or text on the other side. Any supporting points or examples are added on the right as memory joggers.

Task 10 Structuring

The discursive text skeleton below shows the start of the structure of the compare-and-contrast essay in Section 2. Complete the skeleton to provide a full picture of the structure of the essay. Refer back to the summaries that you made of the content of the essay (Task 6, page 116) to help you.

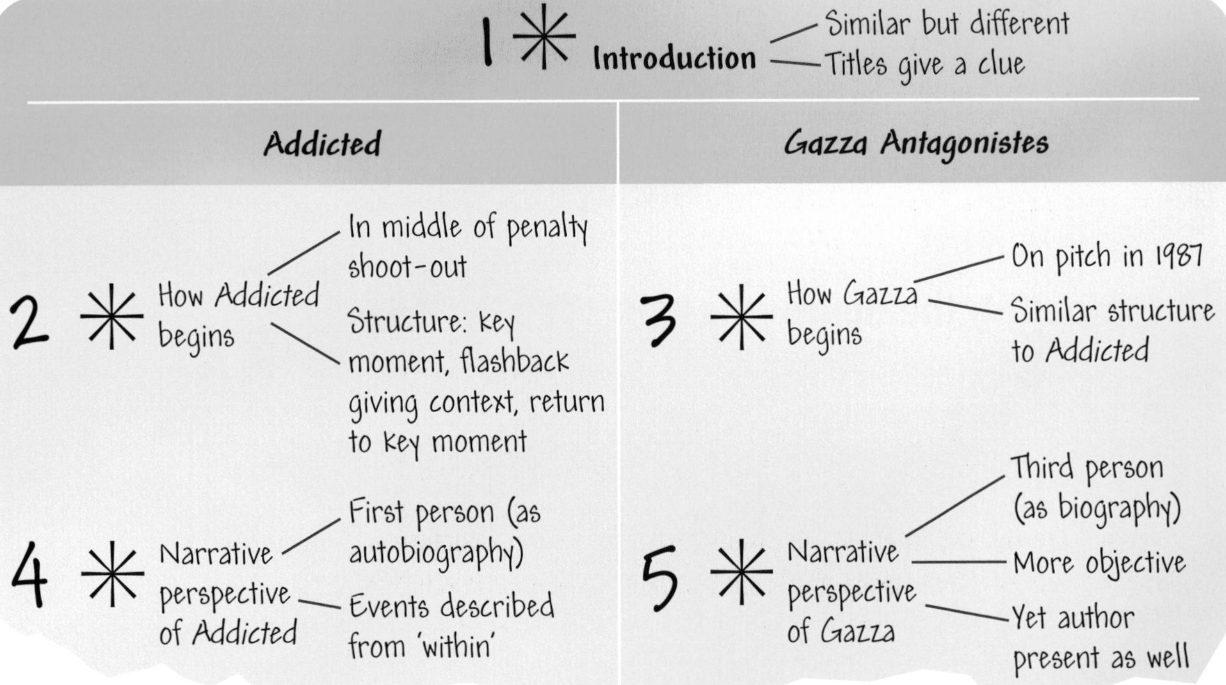

Check how your main points relate to the paragraphing of the essay.

Using a different approach

The author of this essay has chosen to focus on both texts at the same time, comparing and contrasting the key features in turn. The essay is, therefore, organised **by feature** rather than by text (**Structure A**).

Another way of structuring a discursive essay is to focus first on one text, bringing out each key feature in turn, then on the other text, bringing out the points of comparison or contrast (**Structure B**). This structure organises the essay **by text** rather than by feature.

In this first draft of the essay, the writer used this second approach. Here is the beginning of his plan:

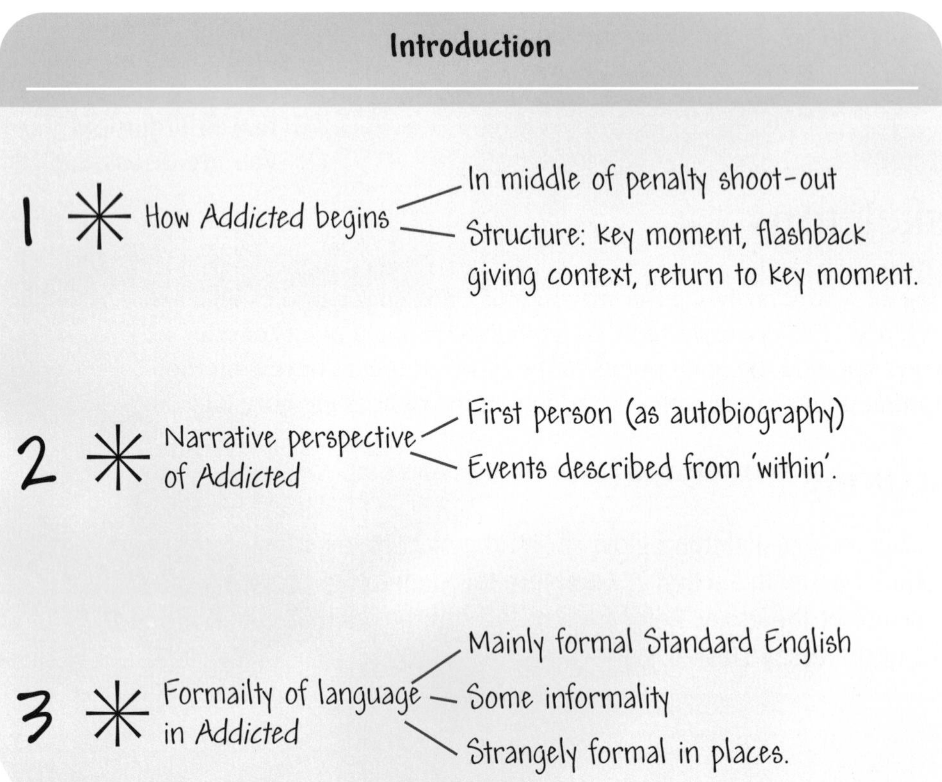

Introduction
1 * How Addicted begins
In middle of penalty shoot-out
Structure: key moment, flashback giving context, return to key moment.
2 * Narrative perspective of Addicted
First person (as autobiography)
Events described from 'within'.
3 * Formailty of language in Addicted
Mainly formal Standard English
Some informality
Strangely formal in places.

Task 11 Comparing the approaches

Using the content of the first skeleton that you completed (see Task 10), complete the plan for this new approach. Then discuss:

- Which features of the two approaches remain the same, and which differ? Why is this?
- What are the advantages and disadvantages of using Structure A?
- What are the advantages and disadvantages of using Structure B?

Signposting the line of thought

When two arguments or texts are being compared in detail in a discursive essay, it is very important to show the reader clearly which viewpoint or text you are talking about, and how it relates to the other one. That means using connectives and sentence signposts.

Connectives are used in the compare-and-contrast essay to show whether the texts are *similar* or *different*:

- 'Hamilton's structure is remarkably similar' (line 25) – this sentence signpost shows (a) that we are now moving on to a discussion of Gazza's biography, and (b) that in the point under discussion (the structure of the opening) it is similar.
- '*Gazza Antagonistes*, however, is a biography' (lines 32–33) – the sentence signpost '*Gazza Antagonistes*' shows that we are now moving on to a discussion of Gazza's biography. The connective 'however' shows that in the point under discussion (narrative perspective) it is being **contrasted** with *Addicted*.

The panel below lists some connectives and sentence signposts that indicate whether a point of similarity or difference is being made.

Connectives of similarity	Connectives of contrast/opposition
Similarly	Text X, however
Author X also	On the other hand
... and text X	A very different effect is created by
Likewise	By contrast
Text X is similar, in that	Author X does it very differently
In just the same way	... whereas text X
Just as	... yet author X

Task 12 Scanning

Scan the whole of the compare-and-contrast essay on pages 113–115. Identify where the author has signposted that he is moving on to discuss the second text in each case. Write down the sentence signpost or connective used. Are these connectives of opposition or similarity? You may like to draw up a table like the one started below:

Connective	Reference	Type
and Hamilton takes us	lines 16–17	similarity
Hamilton's structure is remarkably similar	line 24	similarity
Gazza Antagonistes, however,	lines 31–32	difference

Task 13 Planning practice

You have been asked to plan this essay:

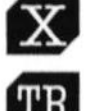

Compare and contrast Alfred Lord Tennyson's poem 'Charge of the Light Brigade' and Wilfred Owen's 'The Sentry'. Which do you prefer as an example of war poetry?

The start of such an essay has been included on page 111, and the first few lines of each poem are given here (though you don't need to read or understand the poems to attempt this task).

Below are some notes that you have written on the two poems. The notes in bold are the main points or features that you want to cover in your essay. Put all the notes in an effective order on a text skeleton so that you have a full plan for your essay.

Remember, there are two different ways in which you can structure a discursive essay (A or B). Choose just one and stick to it!

Charge of the Light Brigade
by Alfred Lord Tennyson (1855)
Half a league, half a league,
Half a league onward,
All in the valley of Death
Rode the six hundred.
'Forward, the Light Brigade!
Charge for the guns!' he said:
Into the valley of Death
Rode the six hundred.

The Sentry
by Wilfred Owen (1918)
We'd found an old Boche dug-out, and he knew,
And gave us hell, for shell on frantic shell
Hammered on top, but never quite burst through.
Rain, guttering down in waterfalls of slime,
Kept slush waist-high and rising hour by hour,

Style/language
'Light Brigade' – rhetorical style – sound effects and repetition
'Sentry' – strong sound effects and word choices/imagery

Introduction
Two poems about war, but very different

Which I prefer
'Light Brigade' – good sound effects, but dislike how it glorifies war
'Sentry' – better example of war poem – strong and true

Content
'Light Brigade' describes a disastrous major cavalry attack
'Sentry' describes a minor incident in First World War

Narrative perspective
'Light Brigade' – third-person omniscient narrator
'Sentry' – first-person narrator – autobiographical

Structure/form
'Light Brigade' – six stanzas of similar length, short lines
'Light Brigade' – very strong rhythm and rhyme
'Sentry' – four stanzas of different lengths, long lines
'Sentry' – rhythm but only some rhyme

You may want to start your text skeleton like this:

1 ✳ **Introduction** Two poems about war but very different	
'Light Brigade'	'The Sentry'
2 ✳ Content — describes a disastrous major cavalry attack	3 ✳ Content — describes a minor incident in First World War

Sentence structure and punctuation

Making the sentences work

AIMS

- Develop and vary the use of reported speech.
- Integrate quotations into your essay effectively and creatively, using punctuation to clarify meaning.

In this section you will explore how to add impact to your writing by varying how you quote words or phrases from other texts, in both direct speech and reported speech. You will also practise punctuating these passages correctly.

Varying reported speech

Discursive texts use a lot of **reported speech** (see panel). This is because they present arguments and summarise views, usually without quoting the exact words of those who hold the views.

The simplest way of introducing reported speech is to use the reporting verb 'say':

Supporters of fox hunting say that 68% of people agree with them. Their opponents say that this statistic is based on too small a survey.

Too many 'say thats' make your writing dull and repetitive, so try varying your approach:

- by using a **different verb** in the reporting clause, e.g. 'assert that' (see box)
- by **interrupting the statement** with the reporting clause, e.g. 'This statistic, they claim, is based …', 'It's immoral, they argue, to …';
- by **rephrasing the sentence** completely, e.g. 'According to their opponents …,' 'Protesters have a different point to make'.

Reporting verbs
- argue that
- claim that
- emphasise that
- point out that
- believe that
- reply that

GRAMMAR

Direct and reported speech

Direct speech is when you quote the exact words that the speaker or writer uses, e.g.:
He said, 'We should be allowed to do what we want.'

Reported speech is when the words used are only referred to, or reported, e.g.:
He said that they should be allowed to do what they wanted.

Note that in **reported speech**:
- no inverted commas are needed
- no comma is needed after the reporting clause 'said that'
- the pronoun and the tense of the verb often need changing ('we want' changes to 'they wanted' above).

Task 14 Analysing and writing

Reread Texts 1 and 2 in Section 1 (pages 110–111). Analyse the different ways in which reported speech is used to refer to people's views. Which passage uses the more varied and effective methods?

Then find two sentences in Text 2 which use 'believe that' to introduce the reporting clause. Rewrite them so that they are less repetitive. Refer back to the three ways of varying reported speech on page 123 to help you. Be prepared to share your ideas.

Quoting from other texts

Discursive essays that analyse texts often have to quote directly from the text to back up points that are made (see also Section 2). Again, it is important to keep the reader's interest not to use only one method of introducing quotations. The writer of the compare-and-contrast essay, for example, wrote this:

He is not afraid of contractions ('I didn't' begins the second sentence) and other informalities, such as the colloquialism 'nutmeg' in line 8.

rather than:

He is not afraid of contractions, like 'I didn't' in the second sentence, and other informalities, like the colloquialism 'nutmeg' in line 8.

Notice how the sentence structure is not varied in the second version because both quotations are introduced by the word 'like'.

Here are some of the different ways in which you can introduce quotations:

- use a colon, e.g. *He can end his sentence in a throwaway phrase: 'He talked a lot, played to the crowd, or tried to'*
- put the quotation in parentheses, e.g. *right from the first sentence ('I just knew what would happen')*
- use different introducing phrases, e.g. *such as, for example* (try to avoid 'like'): *Nor is he afraid of uncommon words such as 'unprepossessing'*
- reword the sentence completely, e.g. *the delightful imagery of 'He would bring sunshine to our drizzly field of play'.*

Punctuating quotations

You punctuate quotations by putting them in inverted commas. Remember:

- enclose only the words used in the text
- quote them exactly; don't paraphrase them
- only include punctuation marks, such as commas and full stops, as part of the quotation if they are in the original text.

If it is a very long sentence, you can miss unnecessary words out of quoted text by inserting a three-dot ellipse instead (...), e.g. *Adams uses the phrase 'right now... was as bad as it got' shortly afterwards.*

Note: Long quotations, including verse quotations longer than one line, are best set off from the text after a line break. Use of inverted commas around them is then optional.

Task 15 Analysing

Discuss what is wrong with the punctuation of this sentence, and write it out correctly:

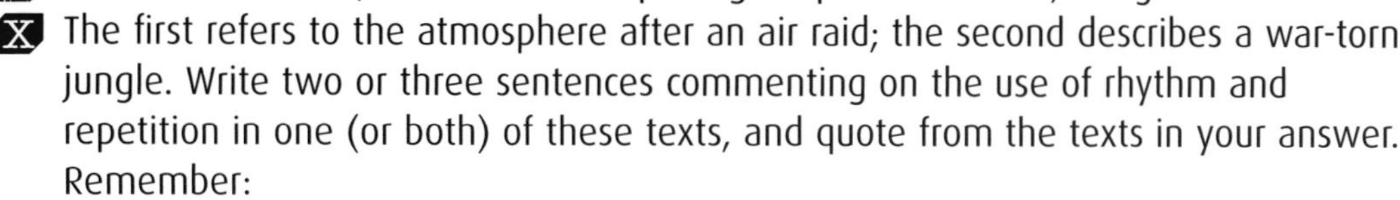

Nor is he afraid of uncommon words such as 'unprepossessing,' 'puerile and wags.'

Task 16 Writing

Two short extracts, each from the opening chapter of a novel, are given below. The first refers to the atmosphere after an air raid; the second describes a war-torn jungle. Write two or three sentences commenting on the use of rhythm and repetition in one (or both) of these texts, and quote from the texts in your answer. Remember:

- vary your method of introducing the quotations
- punctuate them accurately.

If you need help, look back at the different ways in which the writer of the compare-and-contrast essay in Section 2 introduced quotations (pages 113–115).

> Everything was just the same: same whistling milkman, same cart-horse.
> *(Robert Westall, The Machine Gunners)*

> They are forgotten by peace, damaged or impassable, all the tracks disappearing, bit by bit, day by day, into the embrace of the coarse undergrowth and wild grasses.
> *(Bao Ninh, The Sorrow of War)*

You may like to begin like this:

Westall uses rhythm and repetition to good effect when he writes,

5 Composing your own compare and contrast essay

AIMS

- Write sustained Standard English with the formality suited to reader and purpose.
- Present a balanced analysis of two related texts, citing relevant evidence to justify judgements and integrating it effectively into the writing.

Write your own compare-and-contrast essay, thinking carefully about the organisation and content and using the techniques of discursive writing that you have explored in this unit.

Audience and purpose

Your essay will be in answer to the discursive essay question below (the passages to be compared are on pages 127–128). The audience is your teacher.

> Compare and contrast the opening passages of two novels about war, Robert Westall's *The Machine Gunners* and Bao Ninh's *The Sorrow of War*. In your opinion, which is the more effective opening and why?

2 Reading and discussing

Read the two passages carefully, then read the compare-and-contrast question again. Discuss:

- How many parts are there to the question? Which are the key words? How will this affect your approach in the essay?
- How will the audience and purpose of this essay affect the style and formality of your answer? (It will be important to choose your writer's voice carefully and use it consistently.)

When Chas awakened, the air-raid shelter was silent. Grey winter light was creeping round the door-curtain. It could have been any time. His mother was gone, and the little brown attaché case with the insurance policies and bottle of brandy for emergencies. He could hear the milk-cart coming round the square. The all-clear[1] must have gone.

He climbed out of the shelter scratching his head, and looked round carefully. Everything was just the same: same whistling milkman, same cart-horse. But there was too much milk on the cart and that was bad. Every extra bottle meant some family bombed-out during the night.

He trailed round to the kitchen door. His mother had the paraffin heater on and bread frying. It smelt safe. There were two more panes of glass out of the window, and his father had blocked the gaps with cardboard from a Nestlé's Milk box. The lettering on the cardboard was the right way up. Father was fussy about things like that.

Father was sitting by the heater with his pint mug of tea. He looked weary, but still neat in his warden's uniform, with his beret tucked under his shoulder-strap.

'You remember that lass in the greengrocer's?'

'The ginger-haired one?' said his mother, still bending over the stove.

'Aye. A direct hit. They found half of her in the front garden and the other half right across the house.'

'She didn't believe in going down the shelter. She was always frightened of being buried alive.' From the way his mother hunched her shoulders, Chas could tell she was trying not to cry.

Robert Westall, The Machine Gunners *(1975)*
(set in the Second World War)

[1] **all-clear** – siren signalling that bombing has ended

On the banks of the Ya Crong Poco River,[1] on the northern flank of the B3 battlefield in the Central Highlands, the Missing In Action body-collecting team awaits the dry season of 1976.

The mountains and jungles are water-soaked and dull. Wet trees. Quiet jungles. All day and all night the water steams. A sea of greenish vapour over the jungle's carpet of rotting leaves.

September and October drag by, then November passes, but still the weather is unpredictable and the night rains are relentless. Sunny days but rainy nights.

Even into early December, weeks after the end of the normal rainy season, the jungles this year are still as muddy as all hell. They are forgotten by peace, damaged or impassable, all the tracks disappearing, bit by bit, day by day, into the embrace of the coarse undergrowth and wild grasses.

Travelling in such conditions is brutally tough. To get from Crocodile Lake east of the Sa Thay River, across District 67 to the crossroads of Cross Hill on the west bank of the Poco River – a mere fifty kilometres – the powerful Russian truck has to lumber along all day. And still they fall short of their destination.

[1] **Ya Crong Poco River** – a river in Vietnam

[2] **tailgate** – truck boot
[3] **tarpaulin** – large sheet of thick plastic

Not until after dusk does the MIA Zil truck reach the Jungle of Screaming Souls, where they park beside a wide creek clogged with rotting branches.

The driver stays in the cabin and goes straight to sleep. Kien climbs wearily into the rear of the truck to sleep alone in a hammock strung high from cab to tailgate.[2] At midnight the rains start again, this time a smooth drizzle, falling silently.

The old tarpaulin[3] covering the truck is torn, full of holes, letting the water drip, drip, drip through onto the plastic sheets covering the remains of soldiers laid out in rows below Kien's hammock.

Bao Ninh, The Sorrow of War *(1991)*
(set in the Vietnam War)

3 Brainstorming the content

TR Brainstorm all the different aspects of these two texts that you may want to compare in your essay. Refer to Task 6, page 116, if you are stuck, but remember that the two texts compared there are non-fiction. What additional features are relevant to fiction (e.g. dialogue, characterisation)? Draw up a grid like the one begun below and jot down the evidence for your ideas.

	The Machine Gunners	*Sorrow of War*
Author's purpose	– describing the atmosphere after an air raid, to introduce novel	
Theme/content		– body-collecting team in the jungle in Vietnam during a gap in the fighting – power of jungle/weather
Narrative voice	– third person, but identifying with Chas	
Opening hook		
Characterisation		

4 Planning the form and structure

TR Plan your essay by constructing a text skeleton. Choose either:

- **Structure A** – focus on both texts at the same time, comparing and contrasting the key features in turn, *or*
- **Structure B** – focus first on one text, bringing out each key feature, then on the other text, bringing out the points of comparison or contrast.

Either way, the features included in your analysis grid will provide you with your main points. Add some supporting points/evidence as memory joggers. If you can think of any powerful phrases to compare or contrast key points, jot these down too. Add an introduction and a conclusion to your plan.

Discussing what you are going to write

Present your ideas to a partner, using the voice and approach you will use when writing your essay. Listen to each other carefully and suggest how the piece could be improved. Check that the chosen writer's voice is appropriate and sustained throughout.

Jot down any useful points on your plan.

Composing your piece

Now you are ready to write.

Points to remember

- Write an effective introduction (see page 117).
- Use topic sentences and connectives to signpost thoughts clearly (see page 121).
- Give equal coverage to both texts. Reserve your personal opinion on which text is more effective till the final paragraph.
- Back up your judgements by referring to the evidence, and giving a comment where necessary (see pages 117–118).
- Make sure you have compared all the important features of literary texts.
- Stick to your overall plan for the essay, so that the organisation of its ideas is clear to the reader (see pages 119–120).
- Vary the way in which you introduce quotations, and punctuate them correctly (see pages 117–118 and 123–124).
- Write in Standard English appropriate to a formal essay.

You may like to use some of the sentence signposts and connectives below.

Sentence signposts and connectives

- Both of these passages are about war, but
- At the start of *The Machine Gunners* we observe
- Their language and style, however
- Bao Ninh concentrates on
- As for their effectiveness as opening passages
- *The Sorrow of War* is set in
- Westall, in particular
- By contrast
- ... whereas Westall

Peer comment

Swap your draft with a partner's and read it carefully. Decide what really works well and highlight this on the draft. Discuss what you need to do to improve your work. Jot down up to three suggestions on the draft. Redraft the selected sections of your essay, using your partner's comments to guide you.

Pulling it all together

Listen to some of the essays written by members of your class. Discuss what are the key features that make these essays effective. Set yourself three targets to aim for the next time you do some discursive writing.

I The Art of Writing for the Test

1 How to analyse test questions

- Revisit the stylistic conventions of the main text types.
- Review ability to write for a range of purposes and audiences, recognising strengths and identifying skills for further development.

In this section you will revisit the key text types that may be focus of your Year 9 English writing tests, and practise analysing questions and planning your response.

Text analysis game

A key reason for students not doing well in tests is not that they don't have the necessary knowledge but that they don't know how to adapt their knowledge to suit the question asked. In the writing tests, recognising the type of writing required and knowing what ingredients to include is half the battle.

Below and on the next page is a grid of the five key non-fiction text types the Year 9 English test focuses on, as well as one narrative text. The grid includes an example of each text type plus a list of its typical structure and language features and its text skeletons. However, the text examples are in the wrong order.

Task 1

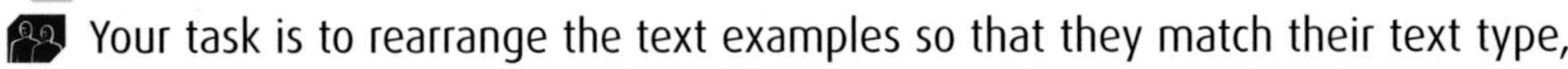

Your task is to rearrange the text examples so that they match their text type, structure and language features. (The text examples may be familiar because they have all been taken from units within this book.)

Be prepared to share your findings with another pair before feeding back your findings.

Text type	Example (in wrong order)	Typical structure	Typical language features
Information	Both writers begin their books by plunging us into the middle of the action. Adams describes – or rather hints at, and later describes – the famous penalty shoot-out with Germany in Euro '96, and Hamilton takes us onto the pitch with Gazza on a particular day in 1987. This method is direct and effective. The structure of the passage from *Addicted* is particularly interesting and complex.	• Paragraphs but NOT in chronological order • Often organised in categories with subheadings • Paragraphs often begin with topic sentences	• Present tense • Third person • Technical vocabulary • Formal language, often impersonal

Recount	I have a dream that one day even the state of Mississippi, a desert state, sweltering with the heat of injustice and oppression, will be transformed into an oasis of freedom and justice. I have a dream that my four children will one day live in a nation where they will not be judged by the color of their skin but by the content of their character.	• Paragraphs organised in chronological (time) order • Time connectives to guide reader through events	• Past tense • First or third person • Figurative, descriptive language • Dialogue
Explanation	As Gregor Samsa awoke one morning from uneasy dreams he found himself transformed in his bed into a gigantic insect. He was lying on his hard, as it were armour-plated, back and when he lifted his head a little he could see his dome-like brown belly divided into stiff arched segments on top of which the bed-quilt could hardly keep in position and was about to slide off completely.	• Series of logical steps explaining how or why something happens • Topic sentences introducing each step • Causal connectives	• Causal language • Formal language, often impersonal
Narrative	Thunderstorms usually occur when moist air rises. In summer this is often triggered by the ground becoming very warm. The air in contact with the ground warms and begins to rise – this is called convection. As the air rises it cools and condenses to form cloud. The rising air forms a towering cloud which often spreads out at the top to form a shape like a blacksmith's anvil.	• Paragraphs organised in chronological (time) order • Time connectives to guide reader through events	• Past tense • First or third person • Figurative, descriptive language
Persuasion	A great white shark's colouring makes it difficult to see in the water, so it is able to sneak up on its victims. When seen from below, this shark's white undersides blend in with a bright sky's reflection at the water's surface. This magnificent shark is sometimes called 'white pointer', referring to its pointed snout which makes it more streamlined.	• Series of points supporting one viewpoint • Logical order • Topic sentences to introduce points	• Personal language using first and second person • Emotive, persuasive language • Often informal
Discussion	I just knew what would happen. Not that Gareth Southgate would fail to score with his penalty, but that if he did miss, and if the Germans then scored with their next one, I was going to get drunk. I had not had a drink all the way through Euro '96, which, for a man coming to realise he was an alcoholic, took some doing. But then, I had been consumed by my first addiction – football.	• Paragraphs in logical order • Often a series of contrasting viewpoints • Logical connectives to bring out similarities and differences	• Present tense • Third person • Formal impersonal language • Language of comparison

Understanding writer's voice

Whenever you write anything you have to decide what role you are taking as you write, just as in a role play you have to know who your character is and act in role. When writing, this role is known as **writer's voice**. The voice may range from very friendly and informal to very distant and formal. Writer's voice includes narrative perspective, for example third-person formal or first-person friendly. The voice always depends on the audience and purpose of the writing. The style of the writing should reflect or match this voice.

Range of writer's voice

very friendly and informal ⟷ very distant and formal

Task 2

 The writer's voice in the six passages varies in the four following ways:

A Very personal and full of feelings (personal and emotive)

B Personal and looking back on past emotions (personal and reflective)

C Telling you about things in a formal but friendly way (formal but friendly)

D Telling you about things in a formal and distant way (formal and impersonal)

The information passage about the shark is an example of C – a formal but friendly writer's voice. Find one example of each of the three remaining writer's voices from the remaining five passages. Be prepared to present your findings with evidence to support your choice.

Question analysis

The **top tip** for English tests:

Never start writing until you have worked out the:

- audience
- purpose &
- form of the task set
- & the writer's voice this requires.

Then plan what you are going to write in the light of this analysis.

On pages 133–134 are six typical writing tasks for the Year 9 national curriculum tests. Writing task has been annotated to show the key words that indicate its:

- **audience (A)**
- **purpose (P)**
- **form (F)**
- as well as its **writer's voice (WV)**.

It also identifies any information that will be useful for the **content** of the response.

Task 3

 Annotate Writing tasks 2–6 in the same way using abbreviations to help you save time when planning under exam conditions. Be prepared to present your conclusions.

Writing task 1

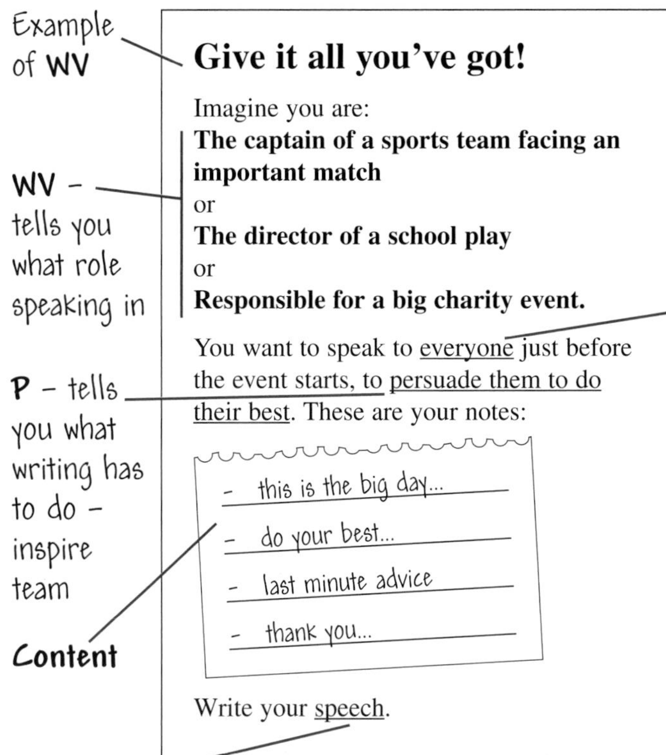

Example of WV
WV – tells you what role speaking in
P – tells you what writing has to do – inspire team
Content
A – tells you who you're speaking to
F – Tells you what sort of writing to do: persuasive speech

Give it all you've got!

Imagine you are:

The captain of a sports team facing an important match

or

The director of a school play

or

Responsible for a big charity event.

You want to speak to everyone just before the event starts, to persuade them to do their best. These are your notes:

- this is the big day...
- do your best...
- last minute advice
- thank you...

Write your speech.

Writing task 2

How important is what you wear?

You read the following announcement in a teenage magazine:

We're looking for your comments on style and image for next month's magazine.

- *Do you worry about image?*
- *Is fashion all a fuss about nothing?*
- *Does the style of clothes you wear affect how people react to you?*
- *What do you think about these issues?*

Write your views for the teenage magazine.

Writing task 3

If you liked *Lord of the Rings...*

You work for Ace Reads, a website that focuses on advising teenagers about books that might appeal to them. You receive the following memo:

Write a review of a book that you think should feature on the website (it can be fiction or non-fiction). Include:

- the title you are proposing and a brief summary of its focus
- why this title would appeal to young people or particular groups of young people
- your personal viewpoint

Write your review for the website.

Writing task 4

To work or not to work

This is an extract from the *Casterbury High School Newsletter*:

Casterbury High School Newsletter

Are part-time jobs a good idea for teenagers?

The leader of the Parents' Association writes:

There are different views on this topic. For example, Janet Day, mother of Sam in Year 10, thinks doing a paper round has helped her daughter to grow up. Jack Kelly, however, is concerned that his son, who is in Year 9, should concentrate on his homework.

Mr Patel, the headteacher, has suggested we have a discussion evening on this subject with opportunities for parents, teachers, pupils and local employers to give their views.

As a Year 9 pupil, write a speech to give at this discussion evening analysing what you think are the advantages and disadvantages of teenagers having part-time jobs.

Writing task 5

An act of bravery!

You are a journalist for the local newspaper. You have just received the following email from your editor:

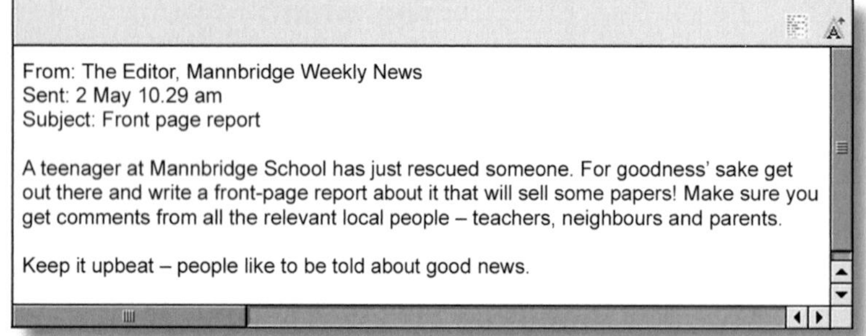

From: The Editor, Mannbridge Weekly News
Sent: 2 May 10.29 am
Subject: Front page report

A teenager at Mannbridge School has just rescued someone. For goodness' sake get out there and write a front-page report about it that will sell some papers! Make sure you get comments from all the relevant local people – teachers, neighbours and parents.

Keep it upbeat – people like to be told about good news.

Write a report about the teenager for the front page of a local newspaper. You should include a headline but do not set your report in columns.

Writing task 6

I regret to inform you

You are the headteacher of Thornberry Comprehensive School, 83 Brewery Road, Tadsworth TD2 4AH.

A severe burst water main today, Thursday 8 May, means that the school will have to be closed tomorrow. The health and safety manual states that it is illegal to open the premises if running water is not available. The water board has informed the school that the burst should be mended by the weekend.

You had been intending to inform parents in your next letter home that for the second year running the school's senior football team has won the local championship.

Write the letter to parents explaining the reason for the emergency closure and informing them when the school will reopen. Also include news of the school's football success.

You should set your writing out like a letter.

Planning practice

You will be given one of the five Writing tasks above that you have just analysed to plan.

Task 4

Focusing on the question you are allocated, decide on the key structure and language ingredients that are appropriate given its audience, purpose, form and writer's voice. Jot these down on a plan, e.g. a text skeleton or planning frame.

Remembering that you should choose and maintain your writer's voice, work out the key topic sentences/sentence signposts (underlined in the bold example below) that will guide the reader through the text in the appropriate voice. Question 1 has been completed for you.

Writing task 1

Give it all you've got! – captain of sports team facing important match

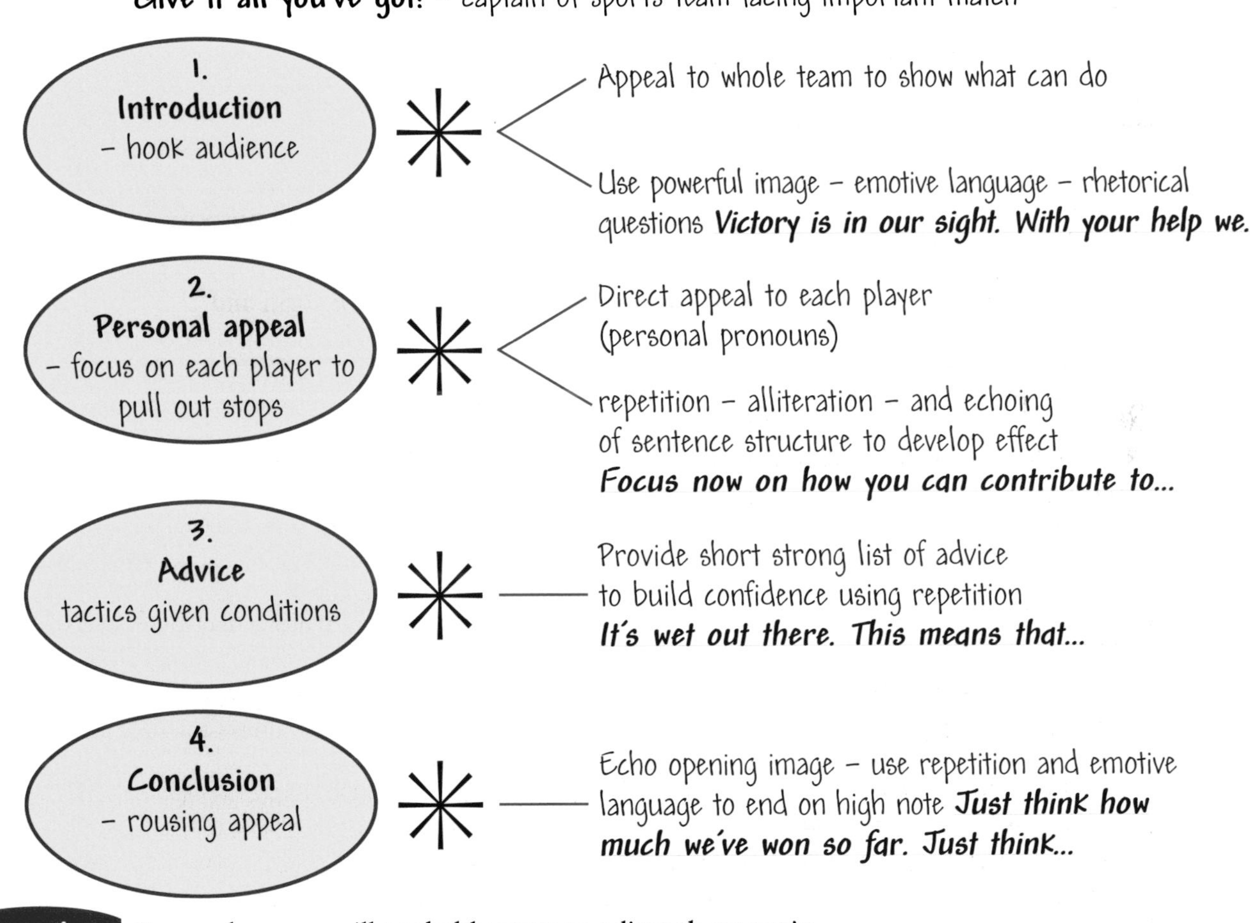
1.
Introduction
– hook audience
Appeal to whole team to show what can do
Use powerful image – emotive language – rhetorical questions ***Victory is in our sight. With your help we...***
2.
Personal appeal
– focus on each player to pull out stops
Direct appeal to each player (personal pronouns)
repetition – alliteration – and echoing of sentence structure to develop effect
Focus now on how you can contribute to...
3.
Advice
tactics given conditions
Provide short strong list of advice to build confidence using repetition
It's wet out there. This means that...
4.
Conclusion
– rousing appeal
Echo opening image – use repetition and emotive language to end on high note ***Just think how much we've won so far. Just think...***

Top tip Remember, you will probably want to adjust these topic sentences/sentence signposts when you start writing.

Task 5

Join up with the other pairs who focused on the same question. Look at all the plans, select the one you think has worked best and, if appropriate, adapt it adding ideas from the other plans.

Be prepared to feed back your group's plan.

The shorter writing task

AIMS

- Produce a formal essay in Standard English under exam conditions, writing fluently and legibly and maintaining technical accuracy.
- Understand the criteria used to mark it and what the examiner is looking for.
- Set targets to improve your writing for the shorter writing task.

In this section you will complete a mock shorter writing task. You will then analyse what makes effective planning and writing using the marking criteria the examiners use, and decide what to focus on to improve your writing.

Background information

The task set will relate to one of the groups of text types below (known as the writing purposes triplets):

- Imagine, explore, entertain
- Inform, explain, describe
- Persuade, argue, advise
- Analyse, review, comment

A different triplet will be focused on for the longer writing task.

The emphasis should be on being precise and concise. No planning guide will be provided but there will be information in the task about structure, audience and purpose so that you can work out the appropriate writer's voice to use.

Remember to analyse the writing task set to establish its audience, purpose, form and writer's voice before planning your writing.

The mock test

Task 6

 Complete the writing task below.

You have 30 minutes in which to answer this question, including planning time.

20 marks, including 4 for spelling

Should healthy eating be compulsory at Northfields?

Northfields School will be discussing banning fattening food like chips and fizzy drinks and only providing healthy food in school at the next governors' meeting in two weeks.

Experts say obesity is rapidly increasing. If present trends continue, one fifth of boys and one third of girls will be obese by 2020.

There is a range of different views on this topic including the following:

- Compulsion is only answer.
- Won't work – many pupils don't like healthy food.
- Lee Wilson (Y9): "I won't bother having any lunch if I can't have burgers and chips. I'll be straight down the local chippie."
- Yasmin Yilmaz (Y8): "I think making us eat healthy food is a good idea. If there's chocolate, we won't be able to resist it."
- The problem is exaggerated.
- Anorexia is also on the increase.

Write a short article for the school magazine, as a Year 9 pupil, presenting this range of views and inviting students to join in the debate by emailing their views to the editor at editor.northfields@hotmail.com

Analysing the planning

Two attempts at planning the answer to the shorter Writing task are given below.

Task 7

Identify what makes the Exemplar 2 plan better than the Exemplar 1 plan. Provide evidence to support your conclusions.

You may want to consider:

- has the writer analysed the question?
- has the writer helped themselves to get going in the right direction?

Planning Exemplar 1

Introduction – lots of different views on issue

Facts

For	Against
Banning only way of changing children's diets	Won't work – don't like veg – Lee
Have to do something – Yasmin	Exaggerated – anyway what about anorexia

Conclusion – not going to be able to make kids eat what don't like – tell us what you think.

Planning Exemplar 2

Composition and effect

A: pupils, parents, staff

P: to get people thinking about whether healthy eating should be compulsory in schools

F: Discursive essay – points for both sides

WV: write as Year 9 student – formal but friendly given audience.

Introduction as hook & outline problem – facts

For	Against
Compulsion only way of changing children's diets	Won't work – pupils will opt out of school dinners L quote
Have to do something – obesity is growing problem – Y quote	Scaremongering – latest fad – increase in anorexia as well

Email your views

In just two weeks' time Northfield's governors will be debating...

This is because...

Those arguing for compulsion believe that...

Whereas, those arguing against compulsion point out...

The compulsion lobby point out that time is not on our side

However, such talk is dismissed as scaremongering...

So what do you think?

REMEMBER

- Vary sentences
- C&C (Coherence & cohesion)
- Check spelling & punctuation, vary vocabulary (Select powerful words)

Analysing the writing

Listen to your teacher as he or she reads the two answers to the shorter writing task below.

Task 8

Discuss what makes the second answer better than the first by referring in detail to the marking criteria on page 140.

Exemplar 1

Should healthy eating be compulsory at Northfields?

Northfields School will be discusing baning fattening food like chips and fizzy drinks and only providing healthy food in school at the next governors' meeting.

Experts say that obesity is rapidly increasing and if this continues, a fifth of boys and a third of girls will be obese by 2020.

The people who suport the ban think it is a good idea and are arguing that providing healthy food will be good for us.

On the other hand the people who are arguing against this point of view argue that many of the pupils just don't like vegetables and healthy stuff like that. Lot's of people agree with Lee Wilson and he said "I won't bother having any lunch if I can't have chips I'll be straight down the local chippie".

Some pupils think that something must be done urgently and Yasmin Yilmaz (Y8) said "I think making us eat healthy food is a good idea. If there's chocolate we won't be able to resist it."

The problem is exagerated and anorexia is also on the increase and this too can be a real problem so maybe we should worry about this to. My friend Jane used to refuse to eat and we couldn't do anything about it.

Anyway why don't you tell us what you think. The email adress is editor.northfields@hotmail.com.

Exemplar 2

Should healthy eating be compulsory at Northfields?

In just two week's time Northfield's governors will be debating the issue that has got the whole school talking: burgers and chips could be banned from the school canteen in an attempt to make us eat healthy food.

This is because experts say that obesity is rapidly increasing. If the present rate continues, a fifth of boys and a frightening third of girls will be obese by 2020.

Those arguing for compulsion believe that banning fattening food, like chips and fizzy drinks is the only way of changing the children's diets.

However, those arguing against the ban point out that many of the pupils just don't like so-called healthy food like green vegetables. Lee Wilson's response sums up the feelings of many students: "I won't bother having any lunch if I can't have chips. I'll be straight down the local chippie."

But such threats don't seem to be affecting the compulsion lobby who point out that time is not on our side. This view is supported by pupils like Yasmin Yilmaz (Y8) who think that something must be done urgently: "I think making us eat healthy food is a good idea. If there's chocolate we won't be able to resist it."

This sort of talk is dismissed as scaremongering by those who see the issue as the latest fad to hit the headlines. They point out that eating disorders like anorexia are also on the increase. Banning fatty foods may lead to an increase in young people becoming obsessed about being thin.

So who's right? We want to know what you think. Do we ban chips and fatty foods? Do we let everyone eat what they like? Or is there another solution? Email us your views at editor.northfields@hotmail.com.

Marking criteria for the shorter writing task

Sentence structure, punctuation and text organisation (6 marks)

1. **Planning and coherence:** Is the writing well structured, given its purpose (i.e. *discursive article*), with an introduction and conclusion, and paragraphs in logical order, reflecting both sides of the argument, with topic sentences that clearly guide the reader?
2. **Cohesion:** Does each paragraph link clearly with those around it, and are the ideas connected and developed within each paragraph? Is a range of connectives used to make points clearly and in a varied manner (e.g. *On the other hand, alternately, moreover*).
3. **Varied effective sentence structure:** Is there an effective mixture of simple, compound and complex sentences? Have sentences of different lengths been used effectively? Do the sentences include statements, questions, commands, different kinds of subordinate clauses, verb forms (e.g. *active/passive, past/present*)? Are they used accurately, and do they achieve particular effects or emphasis?
4. **Punctuation:** Has a wide variety of punctuation been used accurately to vary the pace, make the meaning clear and create interesting effects?

Composition and effect (10 marks)

5. **Sustaining the writer's viewpoint with a clear sense of audience and purpose:** Is the tone appropriate to the task and audience, and maintained consistently through the piece? Has the writer maintained a confident balanced writer's voice throughout (*not favouring one side or the other*) that engages the interest of the reader?
6. **Form and content:** Does the form chosen suit its purpose (e.g. *discursive article format that either deals with all aspects of one viewpoint and then the opposite viewpoint, or that contrasts the two viewpoint throughout*)?
   Is the layout of the writing, and its introduction and conclusion, appropriate?
   Is the content relevant to the task and well-chosen?
7. **Style:** Is the style lively, interesting and appropriate, with vivid vocabulary and imaginative images or expressions being used to make the arguments come alive?

Spelling (4 marks)

8. **Spelling:** Has the writer spelled a range of words – simple, complex and irregular – correctly?

Assessing what you need to focus on

Task 9

Swap your own answer with a partner's and use the marking criteria on page 140 to assess the effectiveness of your partner's work. Focus on up to three areas from the eight listed in the criteria that you feel need improving most, and discuss these with your partner.

Listen to what your partner has to suggest about what has worked really well and how you could improve your own answer. Identify the three areas of improvement that you most need to focus on and annotate your essay accordingly.

The Writing Clinics

Below are five Writing Clinics related to the eight key areas identified by the assessment criteria for the shorter writing task. You will focus on the two or three that will most help you to improve your writing.

Clinic 1: Planning, coherence and cohesion

Planning, coherence and cohesion is all about understanding the best order to say things and guiding your reader clearly through that order. If you are arguing a point, this usually involves making the point, backing it up with evidence and driving it home with a comment. If you are writing a discursive piece, this means balancing a range of points.

The essay you have just written presented the views of those in favour of compulsory healthy eating in school and those opposed to this approach. But there is a third possible position: educate children in the importance of healthy eating.

Below are some points to support this viewpoint:

- Offer healthy food alongside more fattening food and encourage children to eat healthily.
- Al Brown (Y9): "School should help us to want to eat healthy food – otherwise we'll just continue stuffing ourselves with crisps and chocolate at the first opportunity."

Look back at Planning Exemplar 2 on page 137 and decide how you could work this strand into the plan. You may want to consider adding it as an additional perspective just before the conclusion rather than trying to weave it in as a third perspective throughout.

Once you have decided how to amend the plan, work out the sentence signposts that will introduce this new material.

Clinic 2: Sustaining the writer's voice

In order to write with a clear sense of audience and purpose, you need to select a tone that is appropriate to the task and audience, and maintain that voice consistently throughout the piece in a way that will interest the reader.

Many people fall back on a recount style of writing (e.g. *My friend used to refuse to eat and none of us could do anything about it*) because this is the one we are most familiar with: we have been talking about things that have happened to us ever since we learned to talk. The more you can get 'in role' and feel comfortable with the sort of language that is appropriate to the type of writing that is required, the easier it will be to write it.

Brainstorm all the topic sentences, sentence signposts, connectives and phrases that you can think of that could be appropriate for the additional section of the essay that you have just planned in Writing Clinic 1.

Now attempt to present a coherent spoken version of that piece of writing. Take it in turns to see how far you can get. Keep practising until you can present your spoken version to another pair.

Listen to another pair's version and help each other to get the voice right.

Clinic 3: Varying your sentences

Exemplar 2 is much more interesting than Exemplar 1 partly because the writer has used a much greater variety of sentences. Look at the version of the last two paragraphs of Exemplar 2 below which has been annotated to bring out the range of sentence structured used.

This sort of talk is dismissed as scaremongering by those who see the issue as the latest fad to hit the headlines. They point out that eating disorders like anorexia are also on the increase. Banning fatty foods may lead to an increase in young people becoming obsessed about being thin.

So who's right? We want to know what you think. Do we ban chips and fatty foods? Do we let everyone eat what they like? Or is there another solution? Email us your views at editor.northfields@hotmail.com.

Series of short, hard-hitting questions (simple sentences) to draw the reader in to the debate

Series of complex sentences that are varied in structure. The first two begin with the main clause. The third begins with a subordinate clause.

Ends with direct instruction (simple sentence) to reader to join the debate

Any sentence can be rewritten in question form.

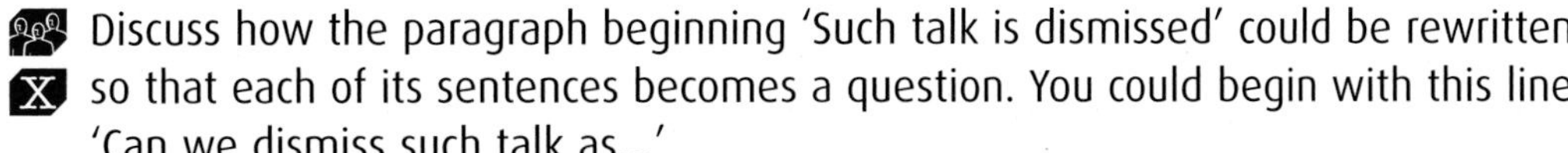

Discuss how the paragraph beginning 'Such talk is dismissed' could be rewritten so that each of its sentences becomes a question. You could begin with this line: 'Can we dismiss such talk as...'

Now rewrite paragraph 3 from Exemplar 2 which includes Lee Wilson's viewpoint. See if you can find a way of beginning with all of or part of the quotation so that the paragraph really comes alive. You may wish to try several versions and see which one works best.

Be prepared to present the version you think works best.

Clinic 4: Punctuating your sentences

The more varied your sentence structure, the more difficult it is to punctuate and the more important punctuation becomes if the reader is to follow the sense you intended.

Analyse all the punctuation errors in Exemplar 1. Then focus on the punctuation errors you have made in your draft essay and list the most significant errors you are making. Use the punctuation guide on page 64 to help you.

Make a mental note to try and look out for the correct use of this sort of punctuation when you are reading so you start to become more familiar with how effective punctuation works.

TR Now look at Exemplar 2. Annotate it to show how the writer has used a variety of punctuation well. Be prepared to present your annotations to another pair.

Clinic 5: Selecting powerful words and phrases

If you want to maintain your reader's interest, your writing style should be lively. This involves selecting powerful yet varied and appropriate vocabulary and images or expressions to make the arguments come alive.

Below are ten words or phrases taken from Exemplar 2. Look at the context for each word carefully, then write down some alternatives for each and highlight the ones you think are powerful. Try to find at least one powerful alternative for each.

- debating
- got the whole school talking
- banned
- attempt
- response
- issue
- supported
- dismissed
- fad
- views

Remember, when you're writing, select powerful words and try not to repeat them unless for deliberate effect.

Task 10 The rewriting challenge

You have 30 minutes in which to rewrite 'Should healthy eating be compulsory at Northfields?' without referring to your earlier version or any of the exemplars.

Use all that you have learned in this section, focusing on the two or three aspects you had most problem with originally, to write a confident article that clearly guides your reader.

The longer writing task

AIMS

- Complete the longer writing task in exam conditions.
- Understand the criteria used to mark it and what the examiner is looking for.
- Set targets to improve your writing for this section of the test.

In this section you will complete a mock longer writing task. You will then use the marking criteria to assess your answer and take part in some writing clinics to work on the areas that need improvement.

Analysing the question

Remember to analyse the writing task set to establish its audience, purpose, form and writer's voice before planning your writing. (Look back at Section 1 if you need reminding how to do this.)

The mock test

Task 11

 Complete the writing task below.

Come and join us

Your school is putting together a new prospectus. You have been asked to write a section of the prospectus as a representative of Years 7–9, in which you:

- *persuade* Year 6 students and their parents that it is a good school to come to, giving your reasons
- *advise* the students as to how to get the most out of the school.

Think about various aspects of school life in your answer, such as the atmosphere, teaching, facilities, buildings, sports and clubs. Remember – you don't have to write about your real school, you can make it as good as you want to!

You have 45 minutes in which to answer this question, including 15 minutes' planning time.

30 marks

Analysing the planning

Two attempts at planning the answer to the longer writing task are given below.

Task 12

Identify what makes the second plan better than the first. You may like to think about these questions when you discuss the plans:

- Has the correct text skeleton been used?
- Are the main points listed on the left and the supporting points (memory joggers) on the right?
- Do the supporting points relate properly to the main points?
- Are the main points in a sensible order?
- Is anything important missed out or included twice?

Planning Exemplar 1

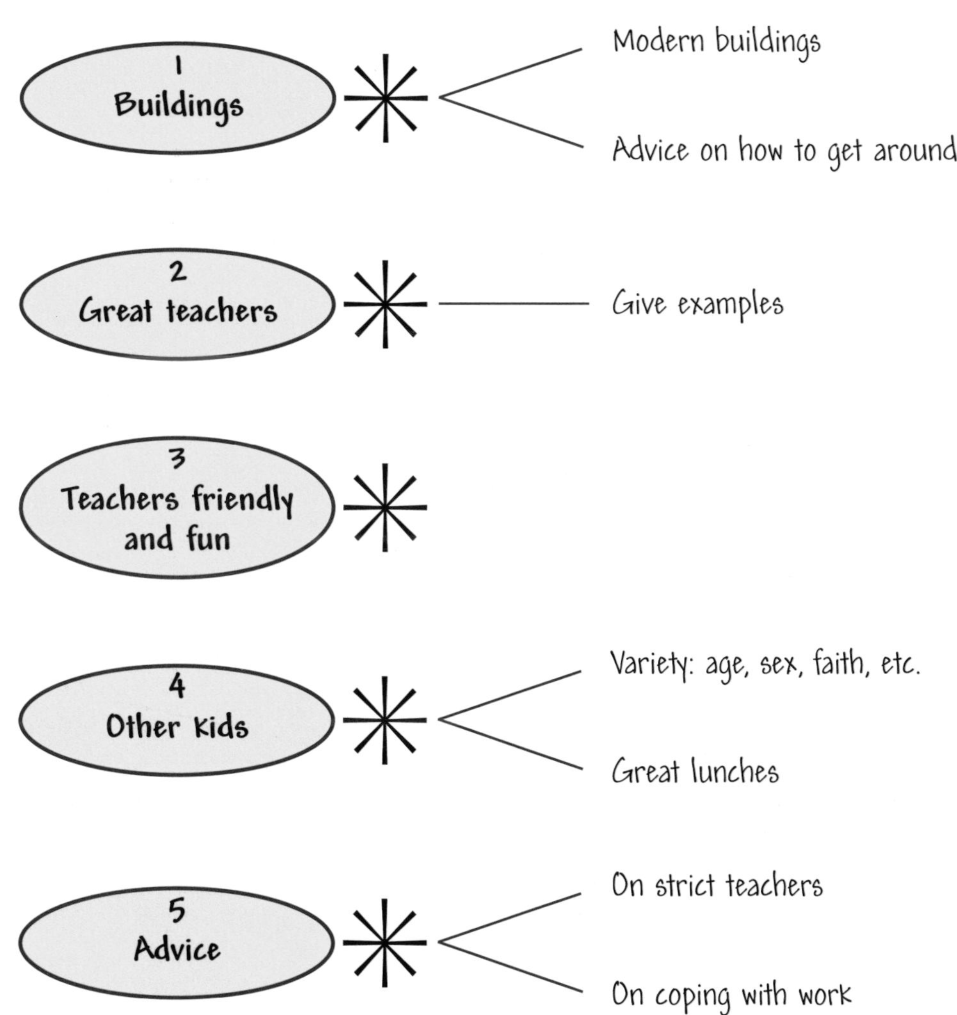

Planning Exemplar 2

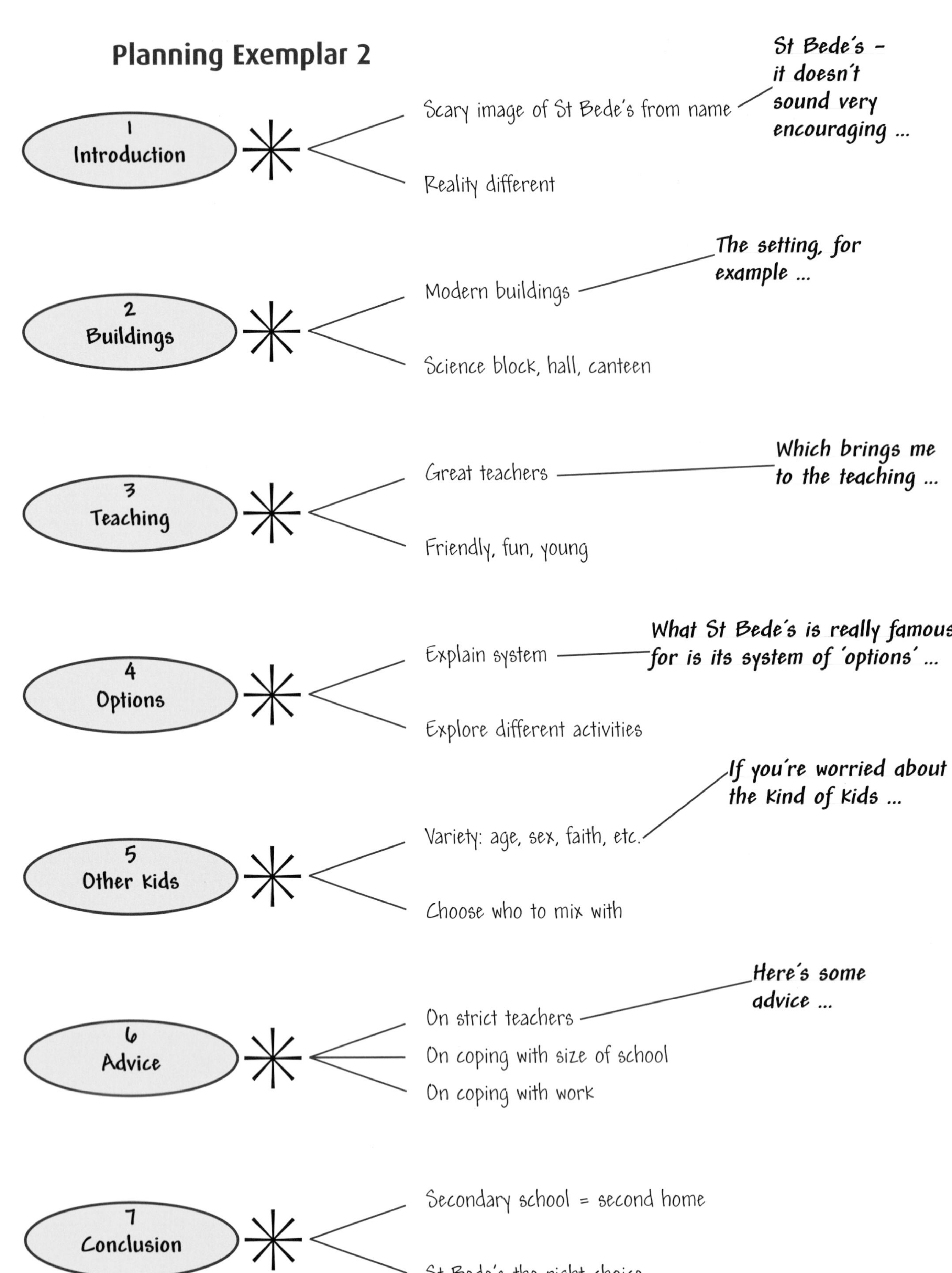
1 Introduction
Scary image of St Bede's from name
St Bede's – it doesn't sound very encouraging ...
Reality different
2 Buildings
Modern buildings
The setting, for example ...
Science block, hall, canteen
3 Teaching
Great teachers
Which brings me to the teaching ...
Friendly, fun, young
4 Options
Explain system
What St Bede's is really famous for is its system of 'options' ...
Explore different activities
5 Other Kids
Variety: age, sex, faith, etc.
If you're worried about the kind of kids ...
Choose who to mix with
6 Advice
On strict teachers
Here's some advice ...
On coping with size of school
On coping with work
7 Conclusion
Secondary school = second home
St Bede's the right choice

REMEMBER

Audience: parents and pupils

Purpose: to persuade parents that your school is the best to send their child to, and to advise students about how to get the most out of school

Form: persuade text type – points with reasons

Writer's voice: write as Year 9 student – formal but friendly, given audience.

- vary sentences – length, type
- coherence and cohesion
- check spelling & punctuation, vary vocabulary

Analysing the writing

Listen to your teacher as he or she reads the two answers to the longer writing task below. These answers will be referred to and discussed in the writing clinics.

Task 13

TR Discuss what makes the second answer better than the first by referring in detail to the marking criteria on page 149.

Exemplar 1

The school is really modern. There are light, airey rooms, a state of the art Science block, a large hall, and a great canteen, its really important for your envirenment to be good. Dont worry about finding your way around the place, you'll soon get used to it.

The teachers are great, too. Mrs Baston makes Maths really cool – you didn't think that was possible did you. Mr Wright is all wright too. Of course you have to work hard, but most teachers manage to make it fun as well.

The students

There is such a wide variety of ages, sexes, faiths and backgrounds, so you have the opportunity to mix with a whole range of people. All of our students are respected, whatever their colour, etc.

If your lucky enough to get accepted by St Bede's here's some advise. Don't worry about the teachers being strict – they are always friendly to Year 7s. Also theres no need to worry about the size of the school (see above). You get used to the work, so no need to worry about that either.

I almost forgot to mention the great lunches. As much food as you can gobble, and really cheap!

Exemplar 2

St Bede's – it doesn't sound very encouraging, does it? When I first heard the name, I thought of dark, draughty corridors and scary teachers swishing their canes. Well, the reality is very different.

The setting, for example. To begin with, it's refreshingly modern. The school has gradually replaced all its old buildings, so you can enjoy light, airy rooms, a state of the art Science block and an impressive modern hall. The canteen makes your mouth water even before you go in. Don't underestimate how important it is to be taught in an attractive environment.

Which brings me to the teaching, and to the teachers. They're great, honest! Of course you have to work hard, but most teachers manage to make it fun as well. Most of the teachers are young and friendly; you'll probably make the same mistake as me and think some of them are sixth-formers.

What St Bede's is really famous for is its system of 'options'. Do you want to play chess or computer games in school time, or go on stage, or row on the river near by? Well you can: each term you choose two options from a long list, and devote two of your lessons a week to them. It's a fantastic way to explore activities you always wanted to do – or that you didn't even know existed!

If you're worried about the kind of people who come to St Bede's, you can relax. There is such a wide variety – different ages (there's a sixth form here, unlike St Brendan's down the road), different sexes, different faiths and different backgrounds. So you have the opportunity to mix with a whole range of people and still enjoy being part of the melting pot.

If you do choose St Bede's – and you're lucky enough to get accepted – here's some advice:

- Don't worry about the teachers being strict – they are particularly friendly to Year 7s as they know what it's like to be new to a big school.
- Don't worry about the size of the school. My year alone was larger than the whole of my primary school, but I soon got used to it.
- Don't worry about the work. You get used to that, too, and there are so many opportunities to shine outside the classroom.

Your secondary school is going to be your second home for the next five (or more) years of your life, so you need to make sure you go to the right one. St Bede's may have a funny name, but it's a cool place to learn and have fun.

Marking criteria for the longer writing task

Composition and effect (14 marks)

- The **form** of the writing. How well does it suit its purpose as part of a school prospectus? Have a series of well-argued points been made?
- The **content** of the writing. Is this relevant to the purpose of the task? Is there a range of well-chosen ideas, both to sell the school and advise the students?
- The **tone** of the writing. Is the tone appropriate to the task and audience? Is it formal but friendly? Is it maintained consistently through the piece?
- The **viewpoint** (writer's voice) of the writing. Has the piece been written from the point of view of a Year 9 pupil, and is this maintained consistently throughout?
- The **style** of the writing. Are the stylistic features appropriate, and is the style lively and interesting? Have rhetorical techniques been used to make the piece as persuasive as possible?

Paragraph organisation and textual cohesion (8 marks)

- The overall structure of the writing (**coherence**). Is it appropriate for the purpose? Is there an introduction and a conclusion? Is the writing organised effectively in paragraphs? Are the paragraphs organised in a logical order?
- The organisation of different sections (**cohesion**). Does each paragraph link clearly with those around it? Are the ideas connected and developed within each paragraph? Is a range of connectives used for clarity and variety?

Sentence structure and punctuation (8 marks)

- The variety of **sentence structure**. Is there a mixture of simple, compound and complex sentences? Have sentences of different lengths been used effectively?
- The **grammatical structures** that have been used. Is there a variety of grammatical structures, e.g. statements, questions, commands, different kinds of subordinate clauses, active/passive, past/present? Are they used accurately, and do they achieve particular effects or emphasis?
- The **punctuation**. Has a wide variety of punctuation been used accurately to vary the pace, clarify the meaning and create deliberate effects?

Assessing what you need to focus on

Task 14

Swap your own answer with a partner's and use the marking criteria on page 149 to assess the effectiveness of your partner's work. Focus on a maximum of four points that you feel need improving and discuss these with your partner.

Listen to what your partner has to suggest about what has worked really well and how you could improve your own answer. Identify the four areas of improvement that you most need to focus on and annotate your essay accordingly.

The writing clinics

Below are five writing clinics related to the key areas identified by the assessment criteria for the longer writing task. Focus on the two or three clinics that will help you most to improve your writing - these will probably be in the areas identified for improvement by you and your partner.

Clinic 1: Planning, coherence and cohesion

Planning

One way of guaranteeing that your essay is coherent and cohesive is to plan it well and refer to that plan when you come to the actual writing.

You may find, of course, that you want to alter your plan when you come to writing your answer, perhaps because the plan is inadequate in some way.

Question 1: Look back at the Exemplar 1 essay and identify where the writer adjusted her plan so that the answer was more coherent.

Top tip

The more effective your plan, the more effective will be your writing. Stick to your plan when you come to write your answer, unless something better occurs to you, or you realise that the plan is faulty in some way.

Coherence

Your writing is coherent if it works well as a whole. Is the format consistent? Is there an introduction at the start and an effective ending to round it off?

Question 2: Discuss in your groups which of the exemplars is more coherent and why.

Cohesion

Cohesion is about linking all the different bits of text in a clear and effective way, so that the reader is guided through the text. That means using connectives and other signposting, and having clear topic sentences.

Question 3: Discuss which of the following sentences makes the best opening to a paragraph on teachers and teaching:

- The teachers are great, too.
- Mrs Baston makes maths really cool.
- Which brings me to the teaching, and to the teachers.
- What about the teaching?

Top tip A clear topic sentence in each paragraph makes your writing cohesive. It makes it even more cohesive if it links the new paragraph in some way with the preceding one.

Clinic 2: Sustaining the writer's voice

Keeping the same tone or 'voice' is an important way of giving your writing a clear sense of purpose and audience. If that voice slips, the reader will know immediately – just as you would notice if James Bond suddenly put on a squeaky voice. The effect is ruined.

The voice can alter in several ways:

- a change in the point of view, e.g. from a student to a teacher
- a change in the formality of the language
- a change in tone, e.g. from light-hearted to serious.

Look at this extract from Exemplar 1, and identify where and how the voice slips. Then redraft to make the voice consistent.

> The teachers are great, too. Mrs Baston makes Maths really cool – you didn't think that was possible did you. Mr Wright is all wright too. Of course you have to work hard, but most teachers manage to make it fun as well.
>
> **The students**
>
> There is such a wide variety of ages, sexes, faiths and backgrounds, so you have the opportunity to mix with a whole range of people. All of our students are respected, whatever their colour, etc.

Top tip Decide on your voice before you start planning or writing, and stick to it throughout. Imagine yourself speaking 'in role' as you write. When you read through your work, keep an eye out for places where the voice slips.

Clinic 3: Varying your sentences

Try to vary the kinds of sentences that you use. Sentences can be varied in a number of ways:

- they can be short, medium length or long
- they can be statements, questions, exclamations or commands
- they can be simple, compound or complex
- complex sentences can have different kinds of subordinate clauses, and the clauses can be in a different order.

Read the fourth paragraph of Exemplar 2 (beginning 'What St Bede's is really famous for') and analyse how the writer has varied the sentences. Compare this with the fourth paragraph of Exemplar 1 (beginning 'If you're lucky enough'). Discuss how this writer could improve their draft by varying the kind of sentences he or she uses. Try out several versions and choose the best. Be prepared to give your reasons.

Deliberate repetition

Sometimes, if you are going for a particular effect, it is better *not* to vary your sentences.

Discuss where the writer has done this in Exemplar 2, and what the effect is. Then use the same method to redraft the third paragraph of Exemplar 1 (on students). You will need an introductory sentence, four bullet points (for age, sex, faith and background) and a closing sentence to round off.

Clinic 4: Punctuating your sentences

Punctuation makes the meaning of your sentences clearer and guides the reader through the text. A variety of punctuation always looks impressive as well. In particular:

- Remember the apostrophes of possession (e.g. *teacher's*) and of omission (e.g. *can't*)
- Remember that *it's* = *it is*, whereas *its* is a possessive, e.g. *its name*
- Beware of the comma splice (see the 'Top tip' below) – take care to show exactly how the clauses relate to each other by rephrasing and/or using different punctuation.

TR

Analyse the punctuation in paragraphs 3 and 4 of Exemplar 2. Why has the writer used each form of punctuation? Where is it effective?

Then analyse the first paragraph of Exemplar 1 and discuss what is wrong with the punctuation there. How could you improve it?

Top tip

Avoid tacking two main clauses together and separating them with a comma (the **comma splice**), for example: '...the sound waves reach the eardrum, this marks the...'. By doing this, you are not making the connection between the clauses clear.

Instead, try:

- a different form of punctuation (e.g. a colon or semicolon), if this fits the meaning
- rephrasing the sentence so that one of the main clauses becomes a coordinate clause (e.g. 'and...') or a subordinate clause (e.g. 'so that...')
- making it into two separate sentences.

Clinic 5: Choosing powerful and effective words and phrases

In a persuade text especially, it is important to make an impact by choosing your words and phrases carefully. This could include using:

- powerful nouns and verbs that make the reader sit up and take notice
- imagery to make a point more vivid in the reader's mind
- just the right word in the context – remember the purpose and audience
- a different word to avoid repetition.

Read the three versions of a paragraph on school buildings below and discuss which one has the most effective words and phrases. Be prepared to give your reasons.

> To begin with, its really modern. There are light, airey rooms, a state of the art science block, a large hall, and a great canteen, its really important for your envirenment to be good. Dont worry about finding your way around the place, you'll soon get used to it.

The setting, for example. To begin with, it's refreshingly modern. The school has gradually replaced all its old buildings, so you can enjoy light, airy rooms, a state of the art science block and an impressive modern hall. The canteen makes your mouth water even before you go in. Don't underestimate how important your environment is for happy learning.

To begin right at the beginning, it's refreshingly modern. The school establishment has refurnished and renovated the majority of its buildings, with the result that the rooms are light and airy, the science block is positively futuristic and the assembly hall is most delightfully attractive. It would be a grave error to underestimate how important it is to be taught in an attractive environment.

Top tip

Don't pile on the adjectives - if the nouns and verbs are powerful and effective, they will often do the job for you.

Make sure the words and phrases that you use are appropriate for the purpose and audience of the writing task.

Now redraft the following paragraph so that the words and phrases have more impact and are less repetitive. Write in continuous prose, not bullet points like Exemplar 2.

If your lucky enough to get accepted by St Bede's here's some advise. Don't worry about the teachers being strict – they are always friendly to Year 7s. Also theres no need to worry about the size of the school (see above). You get used to the work, so no need to worry about that either.

The rewriting challenge

Task 15

You have 30 minutes in which to rewrite 'Come and join us', without referring to your earlier version or any of the exemplars.

Use all that you have learned in this section, focusing on the three or four areas that you identified for improvement, to write a friendly but persuasive piece for the school prospectus.

Exemplars

Key to Colour Coding

Orange	Topic sentences
Mauve	Time connectives
Red	Connectives of opposition
Turquoise	Connectives of addition
Pink	Causal connectives
Yellow	Simple sentences
Green	Compound sentences
Blue	Complex sentences

A Narrative exemplars

Features	Brighton Rock	Stone Cold
Narrative perspective	Third-person omniscient (all-knowing) author: "Hale knew, before he had been..."	First-person dual narrative: "Right now I'm sitting in a doorway watching the passers-by." "Shelter. Yes. I like it."
Writer's voice: – formal or informal	Fairly formal: "They came in by train from Victoria..."	Informal and casual, as if chatting to reader: "I'm invisible, see?"
– personal or distanced	Distant but noticing everything: "With his inky fingers and his bitten nails..."	Personal: "You can call me Link"
– plain or descriptive	Detailed descriptive language, selects powerful words: "bewildered multitudes into the fresh glittering air..."	Simple but powerful everyday language: "It's got a ring to it as I'm sure you'll agree."
Language features: – short sharp sentences – longer complex sentences	Longer complex sentences: "With his inky fingers and his bitten nails, his manner cynical and nervous, anybody could tell he didn't belong – belong to the early summer sun, the cool Whitsun wind off the sea, the holiday crowd."	Short sharp sentences: "It's what they're all seeking. The street people. What they crave."

Task 5

Topic sentence – starting with this orientates the reader

Short sharp sentences build up tension

Formal English used throughout

The light appeared to come from the ceiling. Burden's first thought was that the room was once an immense storage place. High up along the curving walls there seemed to be ventilators but they were far too high for Burden to reach or to see clearly. The light of the room was unvarying and strange. It didn't seem like daylight and yet it did not resemble artificial light. It was a uniform, flat grey. Burden crossed to the opposing wall and, brushing his hand lightly against it, walked back the curving length of the room. It brought him back to the opposite wall. The room was so long and so curved that he could not see from one end to the other. How had he been put in the room? Lowered perhaps from somewhere on the ceiling? There seemed to be no breaks in the ceiling and yet he felt that his eyes probably deceived him.

Objective – calling man by his surname only distances the reader from the victim

Past tense

Straightforward description of features of the room

Unemotional – description focuses on physical surroundings rather than feelings

Task 6

Striking opening line jumps straight into the story

Burden's first awareness was that he was naked and the room was cold. He opened his eyes and saw only the grey light. He thought for an instant that he was lying naked on the floor of the corridor. It was not the corridor, nor his room in the hospital section. It was a bare, enormous room. Perhaps two stories tall. And it was so huge that it curved almost out of sight. There were no windows in it, not a stick of furniture, nothing but the soaring monotony of rough concrete. The floor was smooth and cold to his bare feet. Burden rose and walked slowly. There was enough light for him to see the room in its entirety. It was perhaps twenty feet in width and fifty feet in height and it curved with the building. Cautiously Burden followed the wall, looking for a door, a window, a break in the concrete. But there was none.

Mysterious information makes the reader want to find out more

Narrator seems to be commenting on Burden's every move – increases tension

Task 8

Clues	Questions this raises and effectiveness
He thought for an instant that he was lying naked on the floor of the corridor. It was not the corridor, nor his room in the hospital section.	The reference to 'the' not 'a' corridor suggests Burden is thinking of a particular corridor in a place he has experienced that might link to where he is now. The next sentence places this corridor in 'the hospital section', so he had clearly been in some kind of hospital somewhere for some reason. The word 'section' suggests that it might be attached to a prison.
He began to long for his pyjamas, thin and dirty as they were, for the slippers, cold and sleazy as they were.	This suggests that in the hospital he wore pyjamas and slippers. The fact that the pyjamas were dirty suggests it was not a normal hospital. There is no hint as to why he was being kept in the hospital section.
They would not leave him there to starve. They had to give him food.	'They' would seem to refer to the people who had put him in the hospital, but there is no suggestion of who they are or why they were holding Burden.

Task 9

Unemotional simple description helps reader picture room in a clinical manner.

Blow-by-blow account of Burden's movements make us feel as if *we* are watching him as he tries to establish if he is being watched.

But this was not a dungeon. It was a large room. It was not at all dark, and its shape was more interesting than a box. It suddenly occurred to Burden that someone could enter the other end of the room that curved out of his sight and he would not see him. He rose and walked to a spot he judged to be the exact centre of the arc and sat down again on the floor, able now to see both opposing walls. But he discovered that in that position there were at least two corners of the room he could not see. A sobering thought struck him then. No matter where he sat in the room, there would always be some part of it he could not see. Was that how they intended to get his food to him? To watch him from the ceiling, determine his position, and then allow someone to slip in, leave the food in the blind spot, and then slip out again? Burden rose to his feet. It was a devilishly planned room if that was the plan. It meant that he had to keep walking to be certain he missed no one who entered.

Focus is on Burden analysing his situation logically rather than on becoming emotional.

Blow-by-blow stark account of Burden's attempt to understand nature of room means reader comes to understand things at moment he does.

Task 11

Naked. I was so, so cold. My mind was screaming like a siren as I tried to come to terms with what had happened to me. What was this room where they had placed me? I comforted myself with the thought that this was just the corridor of the hospital section. That would be all right – almost like home compared to this. But no this was a very different place. The room was unbelievably big – so high and long it stretched out of sight. How was I to cope in such a room? Why am I here? Why have they put me here? Why? Why? I heard myself scream.

Task 13

Sentence signpost indicating development of B's thoughts

Topic sentence – starkly sums up B's situation, linking back to previous paragraph which has built up to this point

There was no sound but the steady throbbing of his own blood. The hollow roaring one could hear when cupping a hand over an ear. Burden sighed again – a sick, small. helpless sigh. He sank down to the floor and crossed his legs. It was then that he noticed what seemed to be a stain on the sole of his foot. He took hold of his ankle and turned the sole of his foot towards him. The hair on the nape of his neck rose with terror. Someone had carefully, with ink or iodine, printed in small but clear letters across the sole of his foot.

'You will be alone until you can no longer bear it.'

Repetition of sentence structure keeps focus on each of Burden's actions

Repetition of key words builds up to final crisis

Task 15

Original extract

Mainly simple sentences – first two very short

Unemotional, simple description helps reader picture room in a clinical manner

But how could entry be made? He saw no signs of doors. Perhaps there were ordinary doors behind the concrete, with knobs and locks and wood panelling. Perhaps the walls were not so thick as they seemed. Burden struck the wall with his fist hard enough to hurt himself.

Punctuation – mainly full stops because mostly simple sentences no subordinate clauses. One question mark

Rewritten version

Punctuation – commas to separate off subordinate clauses. In one place uses a dash. Uses colon to link two related clauses

Burden frowned repeatedly: he was asking himself how entry could be made. Regardless of how hard he examined the room, with eagle-like intensity, he was unable to see any sign of any sort of door. Perhaps, behind the endless pall of grey concrete, there were ordinary doors with intricate iron locks, decorative knobs and exquisitely carved wooden panelling. Perhaps, he thought, the very walls were not so alarmingly thick as they seemed to his frightened eyes. Burden suddenly struck the mocking wall with his tightly clenched fist hard – hard enough to cause himself considerable hurt.

Relies on complex sentences, some with several subordinate clauses

Descriptive style including a simile and a metaphor and long noun-phrases

Task 16

She rolled over and was aware of a bright light in the room. How nice, sun at last, she thought. But then she remembered that her room faced East. She sat up with a start. 'Where am I?' she mouthed. She was bewildered by unfamiliar walls and blinded by a light that shone from high up in one corner. She tried to make sense of what had happened. Perhaps I'm still asleep, she thought. But no, she could not be more awake. She stared again. The room was bare except for the light and the bed she slept in. There was a window but very high up – way beyond her reach.

B Recount exemplars

Task 1

Opening line focuses on Paul Gascoigne confirming is biography

Topic sentence – introduces focus of paragraph and introduction

Formal but friendly style – as if talking to reader

Reference to specifics – names, games, places to add detail/signpost events

Imaginative entertaining imagery and phrasing – helps reader picture scene

Gazza Antagonistes

My first sighting of Paul Gascoigne was in 1987, when he was playing for Newcastle. I didn't exactly fall for him that day but I certainly looked twice. There was, as they say, 'something about him'. His giftedness was self-evident: he was a natural. You could tell that from his touch. However the ball came at him, fast, medium or slow, he welcomed it; he took it in his stride.

His appearance was unprepossessing. He was plump, twitchy and pink-faced, and on the small side. And he was cheeky in a puerile sort of way. He was always looking to nutmeg defenders when it would have been easier to pass them by. He wanted the ball *all the time*: for throw-ins, free kicks, corners – goal-kicks, if they had let him. He seemed fragile but he wasn't: there was a mean streak underneath the puppy fat. He was always glancing behind him, or from side to side, even when the ball was nowhere near. He talked a lot, played to the crowd, or tried to. At nineteen, Gascoigne came across as a trainee star, a star whose moment was – well, any second now.

I was intrigued by the way he related to his centre forward, a Brazilian called Mirandinha. Mirandinha had not long before scored for Brazil against England at Wembley, and when Newcastle signed him there had been a small fuss in the press. Wags said that the Newcastle board thought they were signing Maradona. For the most part, though, the appearance of a Brazilian in our English league was a matter for great celebration. We would learn from Mirandinha. He would bring sunshine to our drizzly field of play.

What he actually brought was a repertoire of muttered curses and black looks, and in the game I watched most of them were directed at young Gascoigne.

Opening hook – writer's personal knowledge of Gasgoigne helps reader relate to writer

Past tense

Descriptive language – brings events alive

Effective sentence structure – includes repetition of structure (repeated colons) for effect

Time connective – helps reader understand event happened earlier

Good use of sentence signpost to entertain reader

Task 2

Features	Text 1: Adams	Text 2: Gascoigne
Has the writer used a hook to grab the reader's interest?	Yes: Dives straight into key event	Yes: uses his personal memories of Gascoigne
Is the first person or third person used?	Written in first person – autobiography	Written in third person – biography
Writer's voice: is this a formal but friendly voice as if talking to the reader?	Yes: 'But then, I had been consumed…'	Yes: 'You could tell that from his touch…'
Are topic sentences used to guide the reader through the account?	Yes	Yes
Do time connectives guide the reader through the recount?	Yes: Uses the time connective 'previous year' to signal is referring to an even earlier memory	Yes: Uses the time connective 'not long before' to signal is referring to an earlier event
Is the main tense used the past tense?	Yes: Large variety of past tenses used because reflecting on his thoughts at the time	Yes
Is descriptive, powerful language used to bring the account alive?	Yes: 'Booze acted for me as an anaesthetic'	Yes: 'bring sunshine to our drizzly field of play'

Task 4

Topic sentence – introduces focus of paragraph

Past tense – helps reader follow earlier events

Effective use of repetition

Interesting sentence signpost – compares present and past

The future looks brighter than ever. Hours earlier, Chelsea's interim chief executive, Paul Smith, had warned opponents that the club would not baulk "at spending £50 million" on one player if required. The huge resources in Roman Abramovich's vaults and the human resources in Claudio Ranieri's dressing room signal why Chelsea must be feared in the chase for the championship.

"Our confidence is flying now," observed Terry, echoing the self-belief flooding through Ranieri's players. The view from the vanquished dressing room was inevitably one of defiance. "It is a great result for them but it is too early to say," commented Sir Alex Ferguson on whether this was a decisive moment for Chelsea in the title race. "When you are top in April, you will feel the pressure then."

Time connective – makes reader clear when event happened

Varied choice of words so doesn't have to keep repeating 'Chelsea'

Third-person commentary on events maintained throughout

Powerful language – brings events alive

Task 5

Optimistic statement

The future looks brighter than ever.

"Our confidence is flying now," observed Terry, echoing the self-belief flooding through Ranieri's players.

Short sharp dismissal of Ferguson's complaint

Ferguson was unimpressed with the decision by Alan Wiley, a wholly correct one, to award the first-half penalty that settled this decent but unspectacular game.

Irrelevant.

Strong backing of referee's decision and clear opinion on game

Confident affirmation of both teams' qualities

All of his colleagues were imbued with similar commitment to the cause.

United are not champions by accident and they sought to impose their game on Chelsea.

"The defence were excellent and John Terry is improving every day," Bentley, 79, said.

Statement approving Chelsea's attitude

Only a fool would write off resilient rivals like United and Arsenal but the theme at the Bridge now is 'Going for the Title'.

Task 7

The future looks brighter than ever. Hours earlier, Chelsea's interim chief executive, Paul Smith, had warned opponents that the club would not baulk "at spending £50 million" on one player if required. The huge resources in Roman Abramovich's vaults and the human resources in Claudio Ranieri's dressing room signal why Chelsea must be feared in the chase for the championship.

"Our confidence is flying now," observed Terry, echoing the self-belief flooding through Ranieri's players. The view from the vanquished dressing room was inevitably one of defiance. "It is a great result for them but it is too early to say," commented Sir Alex Ferguson on whether this was a decisive moment for Chelsea in the title race. "When you are top in April, you will feel the pressure then."

Unusual verb

Clever use of repetition

Alliteration makes sentence effective

Powerful choice of words

Alliteration makes powerful adjective more effective

Task 8

"Our confidence is flying now," **mumbled** Terry, **failing to** echo the self-belief **supposedly** flooding through Ranieri's players. The view from the vanquished dressing room was **hardly** one of defiance. "It is a great result for them but it is too early to say," **muttered** Sir Alex Ferguson on whether this was a decisive moment for Chelsea in their **doomed** title race. "When you are top in April, you will feel the pressure then."

Task 9

Introduction: News hook to grab reader's interest

'UNDER THE approving gaze of Roy Bentley, the great centre forward whose goals shot Chelsea to their last title almost a half-century ago, the modern generation yesterday installed themselves as Premiership leaders and bookmakers' favourites with this convincing, thoroughly deserved victory over Manchester United. "They must have a wonderful chance of the title now," smiled Bentley after Frank Lampard's penalty had so embarrassed the champions.

Who? (Roy Bentley) — What? (victory over Manchester United)

Past glories and present strengths rolled into one at the Bridge yesterday. Bentley and Stan Willemse, the left-back from that 1955 trophy-winning side of Ted Drake's, delighted in the marvellous defensive organisation built around the growing colossus that is John Terry, thrilled to the clever forward moves of Lampard and Joe Cole, and warmed to the work ethic that united all the men in blue.

Where? (at the Bridge) — When? (yesterday) — How? (defensive organisation)

Middle paragraph(s): Less important news relating to main topic (including quote about how a key character feels)

The future looks brighter than ever.

"Our confidence is flying now," observed Terry, echoing the self-belief flooding through Ranieri's players.

Ferguson was unimpressed with the decision by Alan Wiley, a wholly correct one, to award the first-half penalty that settled this decent but unspectacular game.

Later paragraph(s): least important news that relates to topic

Irrelevant.

All of his colleagues were imbued with similar commitment to the cause. United are not champions by accident and they sought to impose their game on Chelsea.

Final paragraph: acts as a pointer – hoping to win Premiership plus echo to beginning of article

"The defence were excellent and John Terry is improving every day," Bentley, 79, said.

Only a fool would write off resilient rivals like United and Arsenal but the theme at the Bridge now is 'Going for the Title'.

Task 10

Abrupt single-word topic sentence that comments on previous paragraph and introduces detail of the penalty

Abrupt comment tells you exactly what the writer thinks

Irrelevant. Cole was caught by Keane and the angle simply saved Keane from a red card. Gary Neville and Ryan Giggs led the protests and Tim Howard did the St Vitus' Dance routine on the line, but amid the storm, one man remained calm. Lampard slotted the penalty smoothly to Howard's left before sprinting away and kissing the Chelsea crest on his shirt.

Detail in chronological order helps reader picture exactly what happened

Builds to strong image of Lampard's triumph

Task 11

Planning frame	Plan	Topic sentence
Introduction: news hook to grab reader's interest including Who? What? Where? Why? When? and How? questions	• S scored his first goal for P who are near bottom of Premiership • Schemmel transferred from West Ham to Portsmouth (sometimes known as Pompey) in August 2003 • Has had troubles on and off the pitch in Nov and Dec 2003	Sebastien Schemmel's run of bad luck seems to be over following his new year first goal for struggling Pompey.
Main paragraph: less important news relating to main topic	• P's home ground is known as Fratton Park and the manager is Harry Redknapp • Redknapp refused S permission to train part-time so he could care for his sick mother-in-law in France Redknapp refused S permission to train part-time so he could care for his sick mother-in-law in France • S blamed for Chelsea's first goal in a 3–0 defeat at Chelsea's ground, Stamford Bridge, the previous week	Pompey manager Harry Redknapp refused Schemmel permission to train part-time so he could care for his sick mother-in-law in France.
Final paragraph: should act as a pointer or it may be an idea or image from earlier in the article	• S given a second chance in New Year – scored 35th minute goal	Could this 35th-minute goal signal a second chance for Schemmel and his club?

Task 12

Simple present tense because quotation

Past tense because conversation already taken place

Future because talking about what will happen

"Our confidence is flying now," observed Terry, echoing the self-belief flooding through Ranieri's players. The view from the vanquished dressing room was inevitably one of defiance. "It is a great result for them but it is too early to say," commented Sir Alex Ferguson on whether this was a decisive moment for Chelsea in the title race. "When you are top in April, you will feel the pressure then."

Past because describing past events

Task 13

Quotation from Willemse provides human interest

Reference to Bentley's autobiography builds up to conclusion

"The fans treat us like royalty when we come here," Willemse said, "and none of them could have seen us play. You would have to be 70 to remember us!"

But they have never forgotten around here, some of the more mature fans even arriving with battered copies of *Going for Goal*, Bentley's autobiography, for the great man to sign. Only a fool would write off resilient rivals like United and Arsenal but the theme at the Bridge now is 'Going for the Title'.

Clever play on book title allows article to end on reference to Chelsea's hopes

Task 15

Sebastien Schemmel's run of bad luck seems to be over following his New Year first goal for struggling Portsmouth. Schemmel has had trouble on and off the pitch at the end of 2003, following his transfer to Fratton Park from West Ham in August.

Pompey manager Harry Redknapp refused Schemmel permission to train part-time so he could care for his sick mother-in-law in France. And he was blamed for Chelsea's first goal in a 3–0 defeat at Chelsea's ground, Stamford Bridge, just a week ago. But Saturday's goal has changed all that. "This was a good start for us for 2004," explained Schemmel. "I don't know how the ball went in. It's my first goal for the club. I'm very happy for the team and for my manager and I'm hoping this is a new start for the both of us." And Redknapp seems to agree: "I was pleased for Sebastien," he commented. "We asked him to get forward more and he was there to get on the end of a great cross from Matt Taylor."

Could this 35th-minute goal signal a second chance for Schemmel and his club?

Inform exemplars

Task 2

Features	Text 1	Text 2	Text 3
Writer's voice			
Is it first or third person?	Third person – 'fishes'	Third person – 'Great Whites'	Third person – 'sharks'
Is it formal and distanced?	Yes – 'any of various...'	No – formal but friendly 'it is able to sneak up'	Yes – 'Number of offspring'
Structure			
Is it in logical order?	Yes – moves from definition to features to origin	Yes – moves to general point about colour to more detailed points	Yes – moves from length of life to birth to gestation
Does it include logical connectives?	Yes – 'typically'	Yes – 'When seen from below'	No – note form
Does it use headings?	Yes – 'shark'	Yes – 'White Death'	Yes – 'Shark Life Cycle'

Features	Text 1	Text 2	Text 3
Language features			
Does it include any generalisations?	Yes – 'any of various usually ferocious selachian fishes'	Yes – 'Great Whites often have scratches and scars'	Yes – 'average life span'
Is detail used to illustrate typical features?	Yes – 'long body, two dorsal fins...'	Yes – 'undersides blend in with a bright sky's reflection'	No – all generalisations
Is it in the present tense?	Assumed as in note form – entry not written in sentences as has no verbs	Yes – 'is able'	Yes – 'give birth'
Does it include technical language?	Yes – 'selachian'	Yes – 'bait'	Yes – 'placenta'
Are there any other key language features?	Abbreviations, e.g. 'n.' for 'noun'	Powerful descriptions, e.g. 'streamlined'	Note-form – names aspect, then sums it up

Task 3

3. If I were to be pawed and chewed – and this seemed to me entirely possible, the more I read – it would be by a black bear, *Ursus americanus*.
4. Black bears rarely attack. But here's the thing. Sometimes they do.
5. Herrero is at pains to stress that black bear attacks are infrequent, relative to their numbers.
6. I wanted very much to be calmed by these assurances but could never quite manage the necessary leap of faith.

Task 4

Bear Attacks

Now imagine reading a non-fiction book packed with stories of bear attacks – true tales soberly related – just before setting off alone on a camping trip of your own into the North American wilderness. The book to which I refer is *Bear Attacks: Their Causes and Avoidance* by a Canadian academic named Stephen Herrero...

Now it is important to establish right away that the possibility of a serious bear attack on the Appalachian Trail is remote. To begin with, the really terrifying American bear, the grizzly – *Ursus horribilis* as it is so vividly and correctly labelled – doesn't range east of the Mississippi, which is good news because grizzlies are large, powerful and ferociously bad-tempered. When Lewis and Clark went into the wilderness, they found that nothing unnerved the native Indians more than the grizzly, and not surprisingly since you could riddle a grizzly with arrows – positively porcupine it – and it would still keep coming. Even Lewis and Clerk with their big guns were astounded and unsettled by the ability of the grizzly to absorb volleys of lead with barely a wobble...

Organised in logical order

Present tense

Technical language

Past tense – for examples from past

Powerful language – entertains as well as informs

Topic sentence – introduces focus of paragraph

Generalisation

Mixed levels of formality from formal to chatty reflect difference between information and comment

Task 5

Note: Underlined text is information based on Stephen Herrero's book; plain text is Bryson's comments:

If I were to be pawed and chewed – and this seemed to me entirely possible, the more I read – it would be by a black bear, *Ursus americanus*. There are at least 500,000 black bears in North America, possibly as many as 700,000. They are notably common in the hills along the Appalachian Trail (indeed, they often *use* the trail, for convenience), and their numbers are growing. Grizzlies, by contrast, number no more than 35,000 in the whole of North America, and just 1,000 in the mainland United States principally in and around Yellowstone National Park. Of the two species, black bears are generally smaller (though this is a decidedly relative condition; a black bear can still weigh up to 650 pounds) and unquestionably more retiring.

Black bears rarely attack. But here's the thing. Sometimes they do. All bears are agile, cunning and immensely strong, and they are always hungry. If they want to kill you and eat you, they can, and pretty much whenever they want. That doesn't happen often, but – and here is the absolutely salient point – once would be enough.

Herrero is at pains to stress that black bear attacks are infrequent, relative to their numbers. In the eight decades to 1980 he found just twenty-three confirmed black bear killings of humans (about half the number of killings by grizzlies), and most of these were out west or in Canada. In New Hampshire there has not been an unprovoked fatal attack on a human by a bear since 1794. In Vermont, there has never been one.

I wanted very much to be calmed by these assurances but could never quite manage the necessary leap of faith. After noting that just 500 people were attacked and hurt by black bears between 1960 and 1980 – and twenty-five attacks a year from a resident population of at least half a million bears – Herrero adds that most of these injuries were not severe. 'The typical black bear-inflicted injury', he writes blandly, 'is minor and usually involves only a few scratches and light bites.'

Pardon me, but what exactly is a light bite? Are we talking a playful wrestle and gummy nips? I think not. And is 500 certified attacks really such a modest number, considering how many people go into the North American woods? And how foolish must one be to be reassured by the information that no bear has killed a human in Vermont or New Hampshire in 200 years? That's not because the bears have signed a treaty, you know. There's nothing to say they won't start a modest rampage tomorrow.

Task 6

When Lewis and Clark went into the wilderness, they found that nothing unnerved the native Indians more than the grizzly, and not surprisingly since you could riddle a grizzly with arrows – positively porcupine it – and it would still keep coming. Even Lewis and Clerk with their big guns were astounded and unsettled by the ability of the grizzly to absorb volleys of lead with barely a wobble…

Turns the spiky animal into a verb and uses alliteration to make a powerful image

Very strong phrase to help reader picture the situation

Powerful verbs help you picture men's surprise

Entertaining image because not a word you associate with bears

Task 8

Pardon me, but what exactly is a light bite? Are we talking a playful wrestle and gummy nips? I think not. And is 500 certified attacks really such a modest number, considering how many people go into the North American woods? And how foolish must one be to be reassured by the information that no bear has killed a human in Vermont or New Hampshire in 200 years? That's not because the bears have signed a treaty, you know. There's nothing to say they won't start a modest rampage tomorrow.

Sentence signpost signalling ridicule

Rhetorical question

Mocking suggestions and exaggeration

Deliberately using language to understate the situation

Task 9

Lee was listening hard now. So far Art and Drama had only appeared in option 1. All her hopes of doing both subjects depended on Drama or Art appearing in option 3.

"Now," explained Mr Jones, "in option three you have a choice of six subjects. There's PE (and do remember that PE includes lots of theory as well as practical activity) then Music, History, Geography or IT and, finally, French.

What lunatic thought this lot up? thought Lee in a state of shock – no Art , no Drama. Surely they didn't expect her to choose PE – she 'd always loathed it. No one in their right mind would want her to do French or IT – she was useless at both of them. And Music was a non-starter. So that left History or Geography. How, how could they? It was only Art and Drama that kept her coming to school.

Task 11

Repetition of key words

Beginning clauses with 'but'

Sentence signpost

Of the two species, black bears are generally smaller (though this is a decidedly relative condition; a black bear can still weigh up to 650 pounds) and unquestionably more retiring.

Black bears rarely attack. But here's the thing. Sometimes they do. All bears are agile, cunning and immensely strong, and they are always hungry. If they want to kill you and eat you, they can, and pretty much whenever they want. That doesn't happen often, **but** – and here is the absolutely salient point – once would be enough.

Topic sentence (made up of three very short sentences)

Connective

Authorial comment

Task 12

And what advice does Mr Herrero have to offer us if we're attacked by a black bear? First of all, he suggests we make a lot of noise, for example by banging pots and pans together. An alternative suggestion is to try throwing sticks and rocks. You can't help thinking that this might just turn a somewhat angry bear into a very angry bear indeed. The-all-time great suggestion is to run at the bear. Oh yeah! You can just picture yourself doing that, now can't you? The final icing on the cake is the suggestion that these tactics could provoke the bear. Well, you don't say.

Task 13

'The typical black bear-inflicted injury,' he writes blandly, 'is minor and usually involves only a few scratches and light bites.'

He writes blandly, 'The typical black bear-inflicted injury is minor and usually involves only a few scratches and light bites.'

'The typical black bear-inflicted injury is minor and usually,' he writes blandly, 'involves only a few scratches and light bites.'

Task 14

The brackets mark off the additional information clearly and make it very clear where it begins and ends

If I were to be pawed and chewed – and this seemed to me entirely possible, the more I read – it would be by a black bear, *Ursus americanus*. There are at least 500,000 black bears in North America, possibly as many as 700,000. They are notably common in the hills along the Appalachian Trail (indeed, they often *use* the trail, for convenience), and their numbers are growing. Grizzlies, by contrast, number no more than 35,000 in the whole of North America, and just 1,000 in the mainland United States principally in and around Yellowstone National Park. Of the two species, black bears are generally smaller (though this is a decidedly relative condition; a black bear can still weigh up to 650 pounds) and unquestionably more retiring.

The dashes separate the additional clause from the main information in the sentence making it clear that it's an aside

If commas had been used here, the sentence would be rather hard to follow. The brackets make the additional information clear

Task 15

Their numbers are growing and, in the hills along the Appalachian Trail, they are notably common – indeed, they often use the trail for convenience. By contrast, in the whole of North America grizzlies number no more than 35,000 and (principally in and around Yellowstone) just 1000 in the mainland United States National Park. Black bears are, of the two species, unquestionably more retiring and generally smaller – though this is a decidedly relative condition; a black bear can still weigh up to 650 pounds.

Main Task

The Smokies are the home of ...

It's surprising how stupid people can be ...

The all-time award for stupidity ...

A staggering 9 million people visit ...

But the animal that makes the Smokies famous ...

HOW TOURISM CHANGING LIFE OF BEARS

1. Animal and plant life of Smoky Mountains
   - North America, home to 67 varieties of mammal, 200 types of bird and of 80 reptile – all larger numbers than found in comparable-sized areas almost anywhere else in temperate world

2. Info about bears – for which the Smokies are famous
   - Smoky Mountains most famous for bears – estimated 400–600
   - About a dozen people a year are injured by bears in Smoky Mountains
   - The bears have lost their fear of people

3. Why bears have lost fear of people
   - Around 9 million people visit Smokey Mountains a year – many to picnic
   - Bears associate people with food
   - People like taking pictures of bears
   - Bears don't seem to mind being photographed

4. Examples of stupid human behaviour around bears
   - Sometimes people try to stroke bears or feed them from their hands
   - One woman smeared honey on toddler's fingers for bear to lick off for video – bear ate hand

D Explanation exemplars

Task 1

Text 2

Why Anthony was always late

Anthony found it impossible to keep to deadlines. As a consequence, he was always late for school. The reasons varied from his faulty alarm, to the hours spent by his sister in the bathroom, and the fact that he liked chatting to people on his way to school. In addition, he couldn't get homework done on time. His favourite excuse was that this was because of football training or even because 'The dog ate it'. As a result, he often had several detentions a week.

Topic sentence – introduces focus of paragraph

Generalisation – helps reader categorise information

Sentence signpost – helps reader understand what is being explained

Structure – a series of logical steps building up explanation

Causal language – helps reader understand how one thing leads to another

Text 3

How polluting are aircraft?

Jetliners may be getting less noisy and more fuel efficient, but they are undoubtedly the fastest growing source of $C0_2$ greenhouse gas emissions. Because they are injected straight into the upper atmosphere, $C0_2$ emissions from aircraft are three times more damaging in their 'warming' effect than those from cars, homes and industries. And because of the huge growth in passenger air traffic from the UK, such emissions are likely to be more than double by 2030, rising from 5% to 30% of the UK's total contribution to global warming.

Structure – a series of logical steps building up explanation

Sentence signpost – helps reader understand what is being explained

Topic sentence – introduces focus of paragraph and directs reader

Powerful language – helps reader picture what is being explained

Causal language – helps reader understand how one thing leads to another

Technical vocabulary – explained as it is introduced

Text 4

How does sand and shingle get onto a beach?

Sand and shingle are washed on to beaches by waves. When a wave breaks, it surges up the beach carrying particles of sediment with it – this is called swash. When the wave draws back toward the sea, the particles are also dragged back towards the sea. This is called backwash.

Waves often approach beaches at an angle. When this happens, swash and backwash cause pebbles to move in a zigzag course along the beach. This is called longshore drift.

Formal impersonal language including passive

Generalisation – helps reader categorise information

Structure – series of logical steps building up explanation

Powerful language – helps reader picture what is being explained

Connective – helps reader understand what is being explained

Topic sentence – introduces focus of paragraph and directs reader

Technical vocabulary – explained as it is introduced

Causal language – helps reader understand how one thing leads to another

Task 3

	Text 2: Anthony	Text 3: Aircraft	Text 4: Sand
What shape does the explanation take?	Multicausal, leading to particular outcomes	Linear explanation	Reversible
Do sentence signposts and causal connectives guide the reader through the explanation?	Yes – "Anthony found it impossible to ..."	Yes – "Jetliners are undoubtedly the fastest growing ..."	"When a wave breaks..." This shows the reader ...
Is the writer's voice formal and distant, with some technical terms being used?	No – formal but friendly	No – formal but lively	Yes
Audience	Probably readers of story/novel	People interested in causes of pollution – probably in an article	People interested in geographical occurrences – probably in a text book
Purpose	To explain aspect of character	To explain airliners' contribution to pollution	To explain about how beaches are formed

Task 6

Lions are nowhere near as fast as the cheetah. Their top speed is about 80 kph. A wildebeest can do about the same and keep it up for much longer. So lions have had to develop more complicated tactics. Sometimes they rely on stealth, creeping towards their victims, their bodies close to the ground, utilising every bit of cover. Sometimes an individual works by itself. But on occasion, members of a pride will hunt as a team – and they are the only cats that do so. They set off in line abreast. As they approach a group of their prey – antelope, zebra or wildebeest – those lions at the ends of the line move a little quicker so that they encircle the herd. Finally, these break cover, driving the prey towards the lions in the centre of the line. Such tactics often result in several of the team making kills and a hunt has been watched in which seven wildebeest were brought down.

Topic sentence – introduces focus of paragraph which directs reader and helps establish writer's voice

Sentence signpost – helps reader understand what is being explained

Technical language

Structure – a series of logical steps building up explanation

Causal language – helps reader understand how one thing leads to another

Powerful language and imagery – helps reader picture what is being explained

Generalisation – helps reader categorise information – present tense helps expresses this

Task 7

Powerful choice of language – helps reader picture the scene

In gesture, their tails are particularly eloquent. Normally they are carried pointing downward. An erect tail indicates aggression; pointed forward over the back, social excitement; held between the legs tight under the belly, fear. By hunting in well-co-ordinated teams, they have become so successful that in parts of the African plains, they make the majority of kills and the lions merely use their bigger size to bully their way onto a carcass, the reverse of the popular conception of the relationship between these two species.

Range of precise descriptive terms – help reader picture situation

Powerful verbs and nouns – help reader picture the scene

Task 8

Casual chatty language – suggests might be commentary for children's television

Giving the Cheetah a name makes it seem more like a pet or a friend

Version 1

Hey, just look at Cheeky the cheetah go go go! Dream on, Olympic gold medal winners, because he's the all-time winner at 110 kilometres an hour. And, man, that's fast!

Matey, very friendly tone

Very formal impersonal tone

Version 2

The cheetah (whose name derives from the Sanskrit term for speckled – *citra*) is a large feline frequenting Africa and SW Asia. It has an elongated body and is the swiftest known mammal, with the potential to achieve a velocity of over 110kph for curtailed periods of time.

Highly technical language – suggests written for academic specialist audience

Task 11

HOW CAN PREDATORS CATCH FAST-MOVING GRAZERS?

Rejected moving on tips of toes – need toes (claws) as offensive weapons

Solution – lengthened limbs by making spine flexible – at full-stretch, hind and front legs overlap like galloping antelope

a) Cheetahs – fastest – 110 kph but v. energy-consuming – keep up speed for only 1 min: either – succeeds quickly / retires exhausted – antelope gallops off

b) Lions – much slower – 80 kph – Wildebeest can keep up same speed for longer So developed tactics – stealth (on own or as team – only cats to do this) Encircle herd then front breaks cover – drive prey towards lions behind

c) Hyenas even slower – 65 kph tactics more subtle and greater teamwork – whole pack works together Use sound and gesture to communicate Very successful hunters – in some parts of Africa they make the majority of kills and lions bully way in

Task 12

Causal connective introducing lions' solution

'they'/'their' only used to refer to lions throughout to help reader follow explanation

But on occasion, members of a pride will hunt as a team – and they are the only cats that do so. They set off in line abreast. As they approach a group of their prey – antelope, zebra or wildebeest – those lions at the ends of the line move a little quicker so that they encircle the herd. Finally, these break cover, driving the prey towards the lions in the centre of the line. Such tactics often result in several of the team making kills and a hunt has been watched in which seven wildebeest were brought down.

Aside to bring out unusual feature

Sentence signpost introducing explanation

Connective indicating end of explanation

Sentence signpost summing up significance and consequences

Task 15

Lions are nowhere near as fast as the cheetah. Their top speed is about 80 kph. A wildebeest can do about the same and keep it up for much longer. So lions have had to develop more complicated tactics. Sometimes they rely on stealth, creeping towards their victims, their bodies close to the ground, utilising every bit of cover. Sometimes an individual works by itself. But on occasion, members of a pride will hunt as a team – and they are the only cats that do so. They set off in line abreast. As they approach a group of their prey – antelope, zebra or wildebeest – those lions at the ends of the line move a little quicker so that they encircle the herd. Finally, these break cover, driving the prey towards the lions in the centre of the line. Such tactics often result in several of the team making kills and a hunt has been watched in which seven wildebeest were brought down.

Hyenas are even slower than lions. The best they can manage is about 65 kph and in consequence their hunting methods have to be even more subtle and dependent on teamwork. The females have separate dens where they rear their pups, but the pack as a whole works together and holds and defends territory. They have a rich vocabulary of sound and gesture with which they communicate among themselves. They growl and whoop, grunt, yelp and whine and at times produce a most terrifying chorus of orgiastic laughs. In gesture, their tails are particularly eloquent. Normally they are carried pointing downward. An erect tail indicates aggression; pointed forward over the back, social excitement; held between the legs tight under the belly, fear. By hunting in well-co-ordinated teams, they have become so successful that in parts of the African plains, they make the majority of kills and the lions merely use their bigger size to bully their way on to a carcass, the reverse of the popular conception of the relationship between these two species.

Commas – used to separate actions in a list

Dash – used to separate off additional information in the middle of sentence (embedded clause)

Full stop – indicates end of sentence

Semicolons – used to separate clauses in a list

Comma – to separate off subordinate clause at beginning of sentence

Task 16

The reasons for train delays are many and varied. Regular train travellers have even been known to wonder if there is a handbook of excuses which, at moments of significant delay can be flicked through by train managers in a desperate search for a good excuse. Reasons seem to fall into three categories: human and mechanical error, the wrong sort of weather and vandalism.

Engine failure is a front runner in the error category, and at least it is something we can all understand. Slightly more befuddling is the excuse that the carriages are in the wrong place. This is often announced as if carriages had a mind of their own and had wilfully set off in the middle of the night to the wrong place just to be awkward. Another firm favourite – shortage of drivers – raises the question of are they being paid enough, while the one guaranteed to maximise anger is the announcement that the guard has not turned up for work.

The wrong sort of weather is another an all-too-frequent reason given for delays. Sometimes it is understandable, especially in the case of flooding, which is highly visible. The autumnal favourite 'leaves on the line' tends to raise eyebrows but then who would want the trees next to the lines to be cut down? 'Ice on the rails' is also a good excuse but the would-be traveller is left wondering how colder countries cope.

By far the most worrying are the all too frequent announcements about vandalism ranging from the standard 'children throwing things on to the line' to the much more disconcerting 'someone is shooting at trains'. At least that one is worth retelling when you finally reach home.

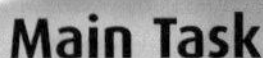
Main Task

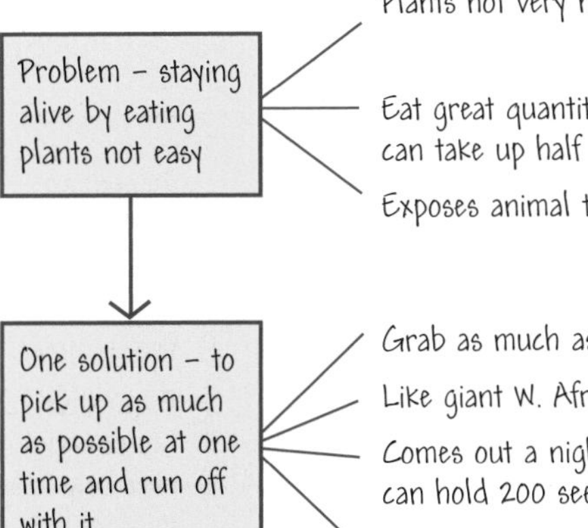
Problem – staying alive by eating plants not easy
Plants not very nutritious
Eat great quantities to survive can take up half a day
Exposes animal to attack
One solution – to pick up as much as possible at one time and run off with it
Grab as much as poss and run off
Like giant W. African rat
Comes out a night & loads pouches – can hold 200 seeds/roots
Returns to borrow and sorts & eats food

Eating plants to stay alive is no easy business ...

One way for an animal to minimise this risk ...

E

Persuasion exemplars

Task 1

"What should we do?" The question should be: "What have we done?" The US and the UK couldn't care less about the Iraqi people. We've been killing them for years, through sustained bombing and the brutal sanctions which have deprived hundreds of thousands of children of essential medicines. Many of them are dying and are dead from the effects of depleted uranium, used in the Gulf war. The west has shown total indifference to these facts.

What is now on the cards is further mass murder. To say we will rescue the Iraqi people from their dictator by killing them and by destroying the threadbare infrastructure of their country is an insult to the intelligent. We have no moral position in this matter whatsoever.

Strong opening, quoting a question and rewording it

Emotive language – appealing to picture of children

Short punchy sentence to end paragraph effectively: reference to facts to back up argument

Contractions for impact: as if writer is speaking directly to reader

Powerful adjectives and verbs to persuade reader to point of view

Clear sentence signpost to show what the topic of the second paragraph is: the proposed invasion of Iraq

Criticising opponents' argument as a method of promoting his own argument

Careful organisation of points: paragraph 1 = the past/present, paragraph 2 = the future

Rhetorical effect – rhythm of sentences in second paragraph (short, long, short)

Task 2

Key Features of Persuade Texts:

1. Use of rhetorical techniques to persuade audience of point of view, or to buy/believe something.
2. Clear structure, often a series of points in logical order.
3. Direct reference to the audience, e.g. use of second person ('you').
4. Attractive visual presentation to win audience over.
5. Powerful and/or emotive language to grab audience's attention.

Task 4

1. I have a dream of freedom and justice.
2. I have a dream.
3. I have a dream of universal brotherhood.
4. I have a dream.
5. I have a dream that God's plan will come true.
6. With this hope and faith we can do anything.
7. When we are free, we will be able to sing 'My country, 'tis of thee' with new meaning.
8. The people of America must be free if she is to be a great nation.
9. Call people to be free across America.
10. This will bring freedom to all people at last.

Task 6

Repetition – opening phrase is repeated, but in a short sentence on its own for rhetorical effect

Quotations from the Bible – these give religious force to the speaker's message

Personal pronouns – first person pronouns 'I,' 'our' and 'we' put speaker and audience on same side

Cohesion – opening phrase of this paragraph picks up final phrase of last paragraph, and begins a new point with it

I have a dream today.

I have a dream that one day every valley shall be exalted, every hill and mountain shall be made low, the rough places will be made plain, and the crooked places will be made straight, and the glory of the Lord shall be revealed, and all flesh shall see it together.

This is our hope. This is the faith with which I return to the South. With this faith we will be able to hew out of the mountain of despair a stone of hope. With this faith we will be able to transform the jangling discords of our nation into a beautiful symphony of brotherhood. With this faith we will be able to work together, to pray together, to struggle together, to go to jail together, to stand up for freedom together, knowing that we will be free one day.

This will be the day when all of God's children will be able to sing with a new meaning, "My country, 'tis of thee, sweet land of liberty, of thee I sing. Land where my fathers died, land of the pilgrim's pride, from every mountainside, let freedom ring."

Formal language – adds to the seriousness of the message

Sentence structure – repetition of 'and' at the start of each clause for rhetorical effect

Repetition – 'with this faith' begins three sentences. Infinitive used to begin four clauses in final sentence

Figurative language – two powerful images here help to get the message across

Emotive language – this paragraph refers to children, freedom, patriotism and religion – all emotive issues to inspire audience

Task 9

Are the students of Challington School meekly going to accept this decision to close their school? Certainly not! We will fight for our right to be taught in an excellent school. We will fight for our right to be taught in a happy school. And we will fight for our right to be taught in a local school. Closing the school is ridiculous – comic, almost. But this is no comedy: it's a tragedy, and we will not let it happen.

Task 10

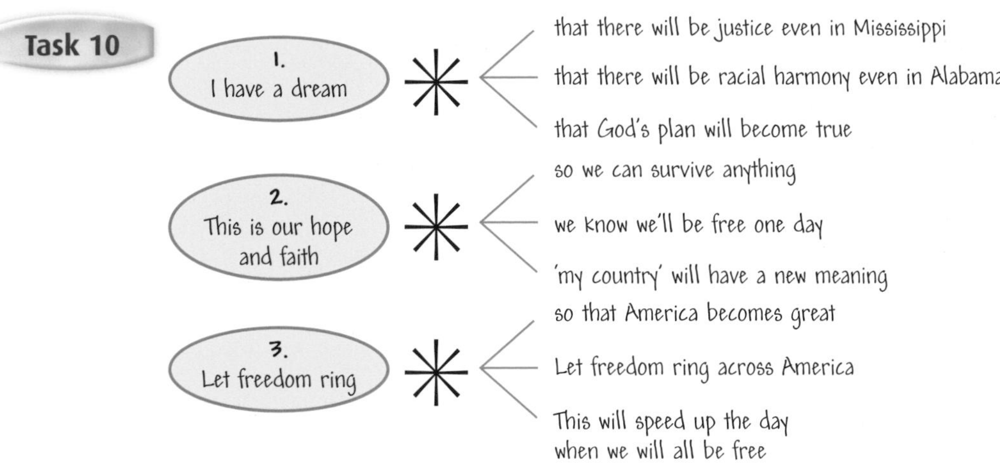
1.
I have a dream
that there will be justice even in Mississippi
that there will be racial harmony even in Alabama
that God's plan will become true
2.
This is our hope and faith
so we can survive anything
we know we'll be free one day
'my country' will have a new meaning
3.
Let freedom ring
so that America becomes great
Let freedom ring across America
This will speed up the day when we will all be free

Task 12

2 We promise to lower the voting age to sixteen. We promise to to lower the voting age.

3 Trust in our strength and courage, and we will not fail. Use our skill and determination and we will gain a great victory.

4 Are more mothers going to lose their sons in this war? Are more children going to lose their fathers?

Task 13

Britain's youth are being ignored/But the young are Britain's future

My vision for Britain's youth/More money for youth issues/More choice in what we learn at school/More skateboarding parks

Why I'm the right candidate/I'm energetic/ I'm imaginative and hard-working/I know what you want

Other candidates are useless/Dave is out of touch/Marilyn only cares about sports issues

My slogan: A vote for me is a vote for you

Task 15

1. It is a matter of honour to defend our title.
2. This is a team exhausted after Wednesday's game.
3. With courage and determination, we will win this game.
4. This is the day when we will show them why we are top of the league.

Argue exemplars

Task 1

My second reason has been mentioned, the medical reason. There is now strong scientific evidence and medical proof that heavy blows to the human head – whether to a heavyweight boxer like Muhammad Ali whose head suffered through his contests, or a middleweight, or any boxer – can destroy some of the brain cells.

Sentence signpost – marks second point

Appeal to evidence to give argument authority

Reasonable and restrained tone

Evidence – to back up second main point

Alliteration of 'h' as rhetorical technique to give argument force

List of three – another rhetorical technique

Task 2

Key Features of Argument Texts:

1 Clear structure, usually a series of points in logical order

2 Generally third person used, though direct reference to the audience can be made, e.g. use of first person to get on audience's side

3 Reasons given for the main points

4 Formal language used, but depends on purpose and audience

5 Restrained tone or emotive language with rhetorical techniques, depending on purpose and audience

Task 5

First person – to get audience on side

Emotive language – to move audience

Short sentence surrounded by longer ones – to break rhythm and keep reader interested

Reasonable tone – implies others are the unreasonable ones (insane)

Our love affair with the motor car blinds us to logic and common sense. We strain every sinew to protect children from paedophile murderers. Yet the number of child pedestrians killed on the roads annually is ten times greater than the number killed by perverted strangers. It is also higher than in France or Germany. The yearly toll of death on the roads exceeds that exacted by Osama Bin Laden's madmen in New York in 2001, and is vastly higher than the number of Britons killed in all recent terrorist attacks. On any sane risk assessment, speed cameras on roads, which have been shown to cut deaths and serious injuries by 35 per cent, are more necessary than armed marshals on aeroplanes.

Clear topic sentence

Logical connective – shows this sentence opposes previous one

Final sentence sums up argument on basis of evidence given (note statistic)

Task 7

Who could live further away than your uncle Andrew in Australia? Yet what could be easier than to email them a quick message, and attach a photo? Whether it's Australia, America or Algeria, we are all just as close when we're communicating over the Net.

The Internet is a vast shopping centre full of wonderful gifts and unbeatable bargains. Why worry about the crowds of shoppers on a Saturday afternoon? Online shopping can save us hundreds of pounds and countless hours wasted traipsing round the high street.

Task 9

Opponents criticise the quality of the information on the Internet, as if cyberspace is the only place where you have to sift through mountains of rubbish to find what you want. As for those who prefer writing and phoning to email – they must have more money and time than sense. And the claim that it is dangerous to shop on the Internet is simply untrue nowadays.

Task 11

2. We are illogical

- More children killed on roads than by perverts
- More people killed on roads than by terrorists
- Cameras more important than marshals on planes

Final sentence of paragraph gives the verdict after the evidence presented = effective way to end para. A connective like 'So' would make this clearer

Another clear topic sentence to show new point, though this isn't linked by a connective to previous para

3. Bad motorists shouldn't get special treatment

- Cars can cause death, injury, theft of space
- Cameras deter shoplifters/ survey airports
- Why shouldn't cameras survey cars?

Another series of examples backing up main point, but no connectives used to make this clear

Rhetorical question comments on last example only, but acts as effective end for this section

Advice exemplars

Task 1

12 things you can do about violence

1. **SAY NO!**
If someone tries to hurt you or forces you to do something you know is wrong, say NO! Say it loudly, clearly and repeatedly.

2. **BREAK THE SILENCE**
If you are being hurt or know that someone else is being hurt by someone, tell an adult you can trust. Make it clear to people who ask you to keep secrets about violence that you won't.

3. **DEMAND A BULLYING POLICY**
Find out if your school has a policy about bullying. If it doesn't, get together with your classmates and teachers, talk to your head teacher or write to the board of governors at your school and demand a bullying policy.

Layout – series of points in a logical order. The numbered list makes structure clear. Repetitive structure for clarity: command in capitals, then two sentences developing point

Clear title – states what advice is about and acts as hook for reader

Direct address – lots of commands, makes it clear and urgent

Language – clear and direct. Some contractions, otherwise formal tone to suit serious topic

Task 2

Key Features of Advice Texts:

1 Clear structure, often a series of points in logical order
2 Presentational devices to make structure clear
3 Direct reference to the audience, e.g. use of second person; use of commands
4 Reasons sometimes given for the advice
5 Either a conversational, informal tone or a clear formal tone, depending on purpose and audience
6 Straightforward language – avoids too many rhetorical or 'selling' techniques

Task 5

'If you're going to squabble, go outside'
Bickering and squabbling often bothers the listener more than the antagonists. Faced with low-level warfare of the most irritating kind, try moving the battlefield to somewhere where you can't hear them. As long as you're sure that no one will get hurt, this could solve your problem.

Separate them
If the bickering starts again, separate them. If they can't play together, they'll have to play alone. Each will claim to be delighted at this prospect, but playing alone is seldom as much fun as playing with someone else. They now have an incentive to sort things out between themselves.

Let them solve their own problems
If you want them to sort out the cause of the problem, different tactics are required. Tell them they have a certain amount of time to get the matter sorted, after which you'll take away the toy, turn off the television or remove whatever is causing the disagreement. The best long-term solution to squabbling and bickering is to help your children develop their own ways of settling their differences. Reaching a compromise provides excellent lessons in negotiating and problem solving. When the agreement breaks down – as it undoubtedly will – make them go back and work things out again.

Life skills
Conflict and disagreements are facts of life. When peace finally breaks out between brothers and sisters, it's because they have used problem solving and negotiation skills instead of fighting. These will be very useful when they have to deal with other children at school and in the peer group.

Subheading marks the second piece of advice

Conversational tone – note contractions

Subheading marks the next piece of advice

Causal connective – signposts reason for advice

Subheading – to make structure clear

Contraction – gives conversational tone

Subheading – to make structure clear

Softened form of command – to make a suggestion rather than instruct

Direct address – to engage reader

Clear explanation – takes reader through the advice, step by step

Reason given for advice

Direct address

Softened form of command – to make a suggestion rather than instruct

Second person – to engage reader

Direct address

Reasons given for advice

Task 8

Let's face it, if you've got a brother or sister you're going to get into a fight with them sometime or other. But you're only going to work things out properly between you if you quit fighting and start talking. 'Negotiating' and 'problem solving' are fancy names for some really useful skills that you'll need at school too.

Task 9

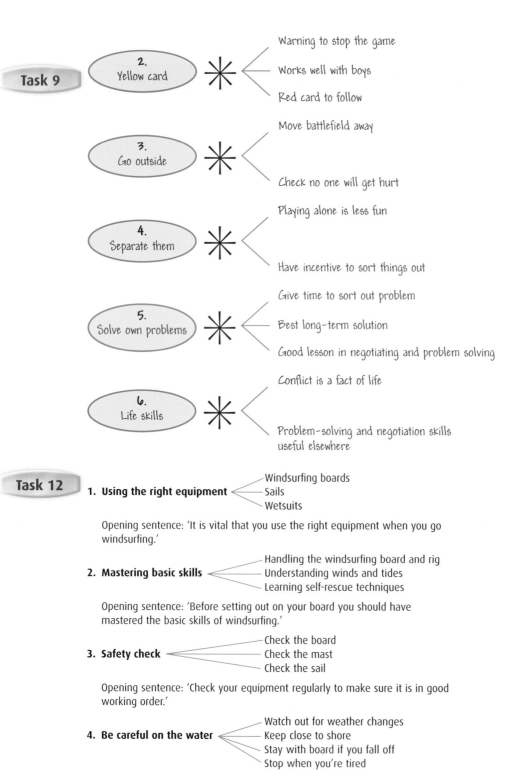

2. Yellow card
- Warning to stop the game
- Works well with boys
- Red card to follow

3. Go outside
- Move battlefield away
- Check no one will get hurt

4. Separate them
- Playing alone is less fun
- Have incentive to sort things out

5. Solve own problems
- Give time to sort out problem
- Best long-term solution
- Good lesson in negotiating and problem solving

6. Life skills
- Conflict is a fact of life
- Problem-solving and negotiation skills useful elsewhere

Task 12

1. **Using the right equipment**
   - Windsurfing boards
   - Sails
   - Wetsuits

   Opening sentence: 'It is vital that you use the right equipment when you go windsurfing.'

2. **Mastering basic skills**
   - Handling the windsurfing board and rig
   - Understanding winds and tides
   - Learning self-rescue techniques

   Opening sentence: 'Before setting out on your board you should have mastered the basic skills of windsurfing.'

3. **Safety check**
   - Check the board
   - Check the mast
   - Check the sail

   Opening sentence: 'Check your equipment regularly to make sure it is in good working order.'

4. **Be careful on the water**
   - Watch out for weather changes
   - Keep close to shore
   - Stay with board if you fall off
   - Stop when you're tired

   Opening sentence: 'If you follow these few bits of advice, you'll be safe on the water and get the most out of your trip.'

5. **Emergency procedures**
   - Spotting a windsurfer in trouble
   - Calling for help
   - Giving first aid
   - Self-rescue

   Opening sentence: 'If you do get into trouble, or spot a windsurfer in trouble, there are some important procedures to follow.'

Task 15

Everyone has special qualities and talents, and each of your children has qualities that are different from their siblings'. Is he or she artistic, practical, a good cook, a natural comic, a great socialiser or sporty? Help competitive children by identifying their strengths and developing their confidence in their own unique abilities. Make sure they understand that their talents, though different, are equally valued by you.

Discursive exemplars

Task 1

Introduction – in the form of a definition

Sentence signpost – shows which point of view is being put

Logical connective – shows this statement puts the opposing case

Present tense and third person used throughout

Structure – paragraphs organised as a series of points/topics, not by view

Euthanasia – for and against

Euthanasia (literally, 'a good death') means a death brought about by a doctor providing drugs or an injection to bring a peaceful end to someone who is terminally ill or in great pain.

Some people believe that only God can give and take away life. Many religious people, therefore, do not agree with suicide and assisted dying. However, there are many religious people who do support voluntary euthanasia. In the Netherlands, Catholic or Dutch reformed clergymen may be present at assisted deaths.

Opponents of euthanasia believe that it is the slippery slope to involuntary euthanasia – that soon we will be killing the sick or elderly against their will. Supporters of euthanasia assert that voluntary euthanasia is based on the right to choose for yourself, which is totally different from murder.

Those who disagree with euthanasia also believe that it would damage society if it were legalised, as it would remove the traditional principle that man should not kill. Supporters of euthanasia, however, point out that we already let people die when they refuse treatment which could save their life.

Title – makes it clear that text is to set out arguments on both sides

Causal connective – shows this statement follows from previous one

Evidence given – backs up claim

Formal and impersonal language – note passive

Restrained tone and language throughout

Task 2

Key Features of Discursive Texts

1 A series of paragraphs presenting two views or passages, organised either by topic or by view/passage
2 Sentence signposts and connectives used to show whose point of view is being discussed, and what stage we are in the argument
3 May include an introduction presenting the debate/question, and a conclusion giving a verdict/personal view
4 Language is formal and often impersonal, with a restrained tone
5 Present tense used to make general points.

Task 5

Sentence signpost – shows both texts are being described

Clear signposts – each author begins his clause

Connectives – lead reader through the sentence

Formal language – long, carefully controlled, complex sentence

Both writers begin their books by plunging us into the middle of the action. Adams describes – or rather hints at, and later describes – the famous penalty shoot-out with Germany in Euro '96, and Hamilton takes us onto the pitch with Gazza on a particular day in 1987. This method is direct and effective. The structure of the passage from *Addicted* is particularly interesting and complex. We begin with a key moment of anticipation – Adams is expecting disaster both on the football field and in the bar afterwards – then, in the second paragraph, look back over several years to give this moment real meaning and context, and finally, in the third paragraph, return to the detail of the shoot-out. Hamilton's structure is remarkably similar: he begins with a key moment (emphasised by the single-sentence paragraph), fills that out in the second paragraph and gives some context in the third.

Vivid language at times to engage the reader

Varied sentence structure/length to engage reader

First person used here for variety – generally third person used

Evidence – not quoted directly but referred to, to back up claim at start of sentence

Task 10

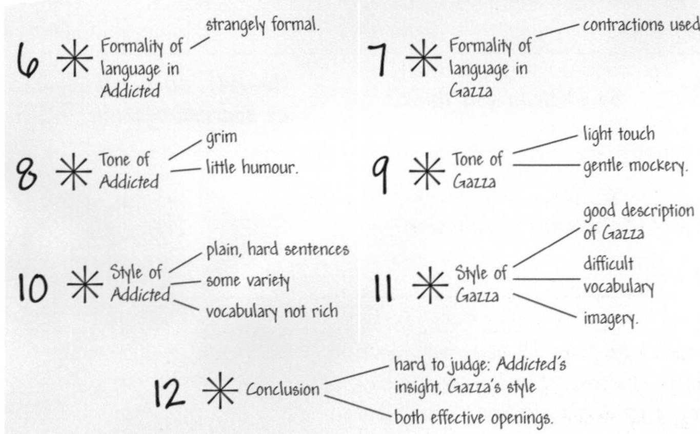

6 * Formality of language in Addicted
strangely formal.
7 * Formality of language in Gazza
contractions used.
8 * Tone of Addicted
grim
little humour.
9 * Tone of Gazza
light touch
gentle mockery.
10 * Style of Addicted
plain, hard sentences
some variety
vocabulary not rich
11 * Style of Gazza
good description of Gazza
difficult vocabulary
imagery.
12 * Conclusion
hard to judge: Addicted's insight, Gazza's style
both effective openings.

Task 13

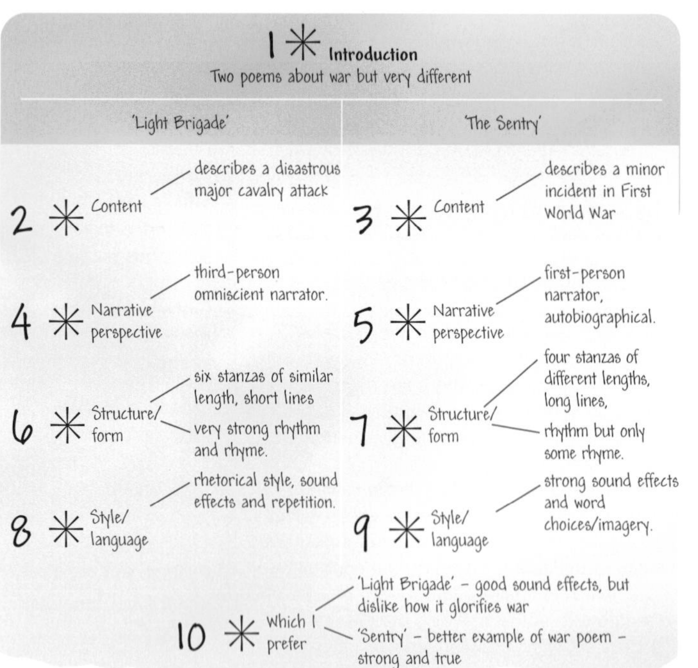
1 * Introduction
Two poems about war but very different
'Light Brigade'
'The Sentry'
2 * Content
describes a disastrous major cavalry attack
3 * Content
describes a minor incident in First World War
4 * Narrative perspective
third-person omniscient narrator.
5 * Narrative perspective
first-person narrator, autobiographical.
6 * Structure/form
six stanzas of similar length, short lines
very strong rhythm and rhyme.
7 * Structure/form
four stanzas of different lengths, long lines,
rhythm but only some rhyme.
8 * Style/language
rhetorical style, sound effects and repetition.
9 * Style/language
strong sound effects and word choices/imagery.
10 * Which I prefer
'Light Brigade' – good sound effects, but dislike how it glorifies war
'Sentry' – better example of war poem – strong and true

Task 14

1 According to their opponents, however, euthanasia is the slippery slope to involuntary euthanasia...

2 Euthanasia, they believe, would damage society if it were legalised...

Task 16

Westall uses rhythm and repetition to good effect when he writes, 'Everything was just the same: same whistling milkman, same cart-horse.' The repetition of 'same' and of the shape of the two noun phrases emphasises the point he is making. Similarly, the rhythmic, repetitive 'bit by bit, day by day' in *The Sorrow of War* reinforces the slow natural growth of the jungle.

I Writing for the Test exemplars

Task 7

No reminder of audience, purpose, form or writer's voice or style reminders

No attempt at sentence signposts/topic sentences to get writing going in right direction

Planning Exemplar 1

Introduction – lots of different views on issue

Facts

For	Against
Banning only way of changing children's diets	Won't work – don't like veg – Lee
Have to do something – Yasmin	Exaggerated – anyway what about anorexia

Conclusion – not going to be able to make kids eat what don't like – tell us what you think.

Reminder of audience, purpose, form or writer's voice to help planning go in right direction

Planning Exemplar 2

Composition and effect

A: pupils, parents, staff

P: to get people thinking about whether healthy eating should be compulsory in schools

F: Discursive essay – points for both sides

WV: write as Year 9 student – formal but friendly given audience.

Sentence signposts establish appropriate WV and help provide frame that will guide writer and reader

Those arguing for compulsion believe that...

Introduction as hook & outline problem – facts — ***This is because...***

For	Against
Compulsion only way of changing children's diets	Won't work – pupils will opt out of school dinners L quote
Have to do something – obesity is growing problem – Y quote	Scaremongering – latest fad – increase in anorexia as well

Whereas, those arguing against compulsion point out...

The compulsion lobby point out that time is not on our side

However, such talk is dismissed as scaremongering...

Email your views — ***So what do you think?***

Brief style reminders to help composition develop appropriately

REMEMBER
- Vary sentences
- C&C — ***Coherence & cohesion***
- Check spelling & punctuation, vary vocabulary

Clinic 3

"I won't bother having any lunch if I can't have chips. I'll be straight down the local chippie." Responses like Lee Wilson's sum up the feelings of many students. Attitudes like this have encouraged many people to argue against the ban pointing out that many of the pupils just don't like so-called healthy food like green vegetables.

Task 12 Planning Exemplar 1

No introduction included in plan – straight into first main point

No reminder of audience, purpose, form or writer's voice or style reminders

Persuade text skeleton used for plan, i.e. main points on left and supporting points on right. Some lapses (see below)

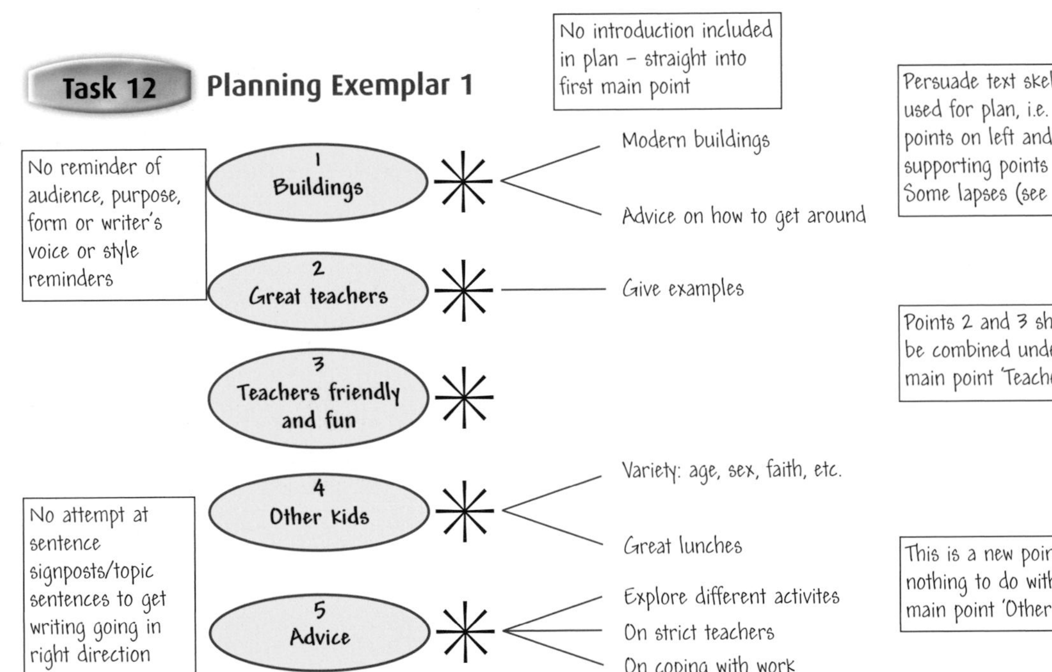

Points 2 and 3 should be combined under a main point 'Teachers'

No attempt at sentence signposts/topic sentences to get writing going in right direction

This is a new point – nothing to do with the main point 'Other kids'

Planning Exemplar 2

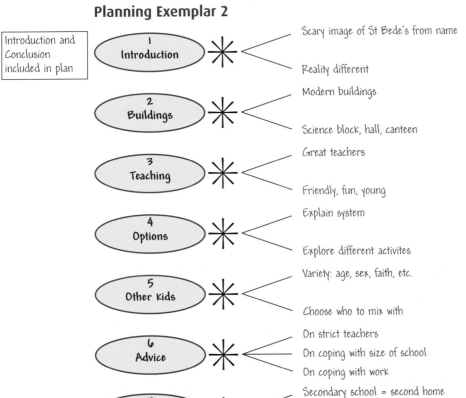

Introduction and Conclusion included in plan

Persuade text skeleton correctly used as main planning tool

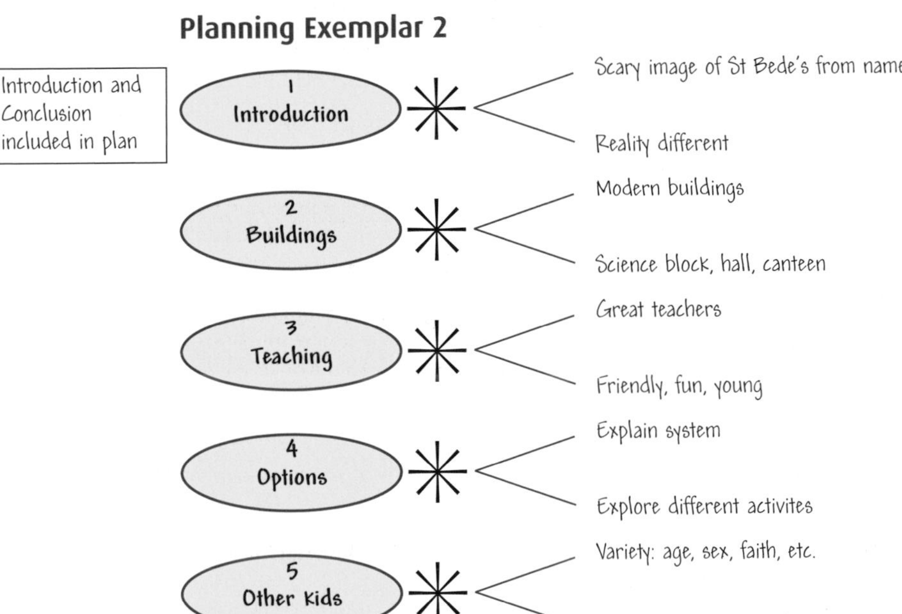

Sentence signposts establish appropriate WV and help provide frame that will guide writer and reader

6 Advice
- On strict teachers
- On coping with size of school
- On coping with work

7 Conclusion
- Secondary school = second home
- St Bede's the right choice

REMEMBER

Audience: parents and pupils

Purpose: to persuade parents that your school is the best to send their child to, and to advise students about how to get the most out of school

Form: persuade text type – points with reasons

Writer's voice: write as Year 9 student – formal but friendly, given audience.

- vary sentences – length, type
- coherence and cohesion
- check spelling & punctuation, vary vocabulary

Reminder of audience, purpose, form and writer's voice to help planning go in right direction

Brief style reminders to help composition develop appropriately

Published by HarperCollins*Publishers* Limited
77-85 Fulham Palace Road
Hammersmith
London
W6 8JB

Browse the complete Collins catalogue at:
www.collinseducation.com

10 9 8 7 6 5 4 3 2 1

ISBN 0-00-717760-7

British Library Cataloguing in Publication Data

A Catalogue record for this publication is available from the British Library.

Acknowledgements

The following permissions to reproduce material are gratefully acknowledged:

Text: Extract from *Metamorphosis*, from *Metamorphosis and Other Stories: Works Published in Kafka's Lifetime* by Franz Kafka, translated by Malcolm Pasley (Penguin Classics, 2000), translation copyright © Malcolm Pasley, 1992, reproduced by permission of Penguin Books Ltd., pp7, 131; extract from *Brighton Rock* by Graham Greene (Heinemann, 1938), p7; extract from *David Copperfield* by Charles Dickens, p7; extract from *Anita and Me*, reprinted by permission of HarperCollins Publishers Ltd., © Meera Syal, 1996, p8; extract from *Stone Cold* by Robert Swindells (Hamish Hamilton, 1993), Copyright © Robert Swindells, 1993 p8; extract from *Love That Dog* by Sharon Creech, 2001, reproduced by permission of Bloomsbury Publishing, p8; *The Room* by David Karp, pp10, 11, 12, 14, 15, 17, 19, 155, 156; extract from *Addicted*, reprinted by permission of HarperCollins Publishers Ltd., © Tony Adams, 1998, pp24, 131; extract from *Gazza Agonistes* by Ian Hamilton, 1998, reproduced by permission of Bloomsbury Publishing, pp24, 25, 157; *Chelsea United in Blue* by Henry Winter © Telegraph Group Limited, 2003, pp26, 27, 28, 29, 30, 32, 33, 34, 157, 158, 159, 160; *White Death* from *Eyewitness: Shark* by Miranda MacQuitty (1992), reproduced by permission of Dorling Kindersley Ltd., p40, 131; *Shark Life Cycle* adapted from Nova Online website, www.pbs.org/wgbh/nova, p40; *Bear Attacks* © Bill Bryson, extracted from *A Walk in the Woods* by Bill Bryson, published by Black Swan, a division of Transworld Publishers. All rights reserved, pp42, 43, 44, 45, 46, 48, 50, 162, 163, 164; extracts from *Geography 21: The United Kingdom*, reprinted by permission of HarperCollins Publishers Ltd., © Simon Ross, 1999, pp54, 55, 131, 165; *How Polluting are Aircraft* from the article *The Battle for Britain's Runways* appearing in The Week, 7 February 2004, pp55, 165; extract from *Life on Earth* by David Attenborough (Collins, 1979), pp57, 58, 59, 60, 62, 63, 166, 167; *Fears Grow* adapted from www.chemical-biological-attack-survival-guide.com, p68; *What Should We Do?* by Harold Pinter, taken from *The Guardian*, pp69, 168; *What to Do After the Attack* from *Protect and Survive*, 1980. Parliamentary copyright material from *Protect and Survive* is reproduced with permission of the Controller of Her Majesty's Stationery Office on behalf of Parliament, p70; extract from speech by Martin Luther King, copyright 1963 Martin Luther King Jr., copyright renewed 1991 Coretta Scott King, pp71, 72, 79, 81, 131, 169; parliamentary material from Hansard is reproduced with permission of the Controller of Her Majesty's Stationery Office on behalf of Parliament, pp84, 85, 170; 'In Defence of Speed Cameras' by Peter Wilby, taken from an article which first appeared in *The New Statesman*, 12 January 2004, pp86, 87, 94, 170; extract adapted from Relate website, www.relate.org.uk, p99; *12 Things You Can Do About Violence* from *What's at Issue? Violence & You* by Bridget Lawless, reprinted by permission of Harcourt Education, pp100, 171, 172; *Beat the Bickering Between Siblings* from www.raisingkids.co.uk, pp101, 102, 107; extract from *Your Life 2*, reprinted by permission of HarperCollins Publishers Ltd., © John Foster, 2000, p110; Sony Walkman review adapted from www.21st-century-home.co.uk, p112; excerpt from *Charge of the Light* Brigade by Alfred Lord Tennyson, p122; excerpt from 'The Sentry' by Wilfred Owen from *Wilfred Owen: The Complete Poems and Fragments*, edited by John Stallworthy, © The Executors of Harold Owen's Estate 1963 and 1983 published by Chatto and Windus, p122; extracts from *The Machine Gunners* by Robert Westall (Macmillan Children's Books, UK, 1975), pp125, 127; extracts from *The Sorrow of War* by Bao Ninh published by Secker & Warburg. Used by kind permission of the Random House Group, pp125, 127.

Images: Giant Pouched Rat by Alan Weaving/ardea.com, p65; Royal Marines Commando advertisement image courtesy of the Advertising Archives, p69.

Whilst every effort has been made both to contact the copyright holders and to give exact credit lines, this has not proved possible in every case.

Project management by Lucy Hobbs
Edited by Nancy Candlin
Cover design by ABA Design Ltd
Internal design by Ken Vail Graphic Design
Printed and bound by Printing Express Ltd., Hong Kong